understanding **environmental philosophy**

Understanding Movements in Modern Thought
Series Editor: Jack Reynolds

This series provides short, accessible and lively introductions to the major schools, movements and traditions in philosophy and the history of ideas since the beginning of the Enlightenment. All books in the series are written for undergraduates meeting the subject for the first time.

understanding **environmental philosophy**

Andrew Brennan & Y. S. Lo

ACUMEN

We dedicate this book to the memories of Lucky and Jeff.

First published in 2010 by Acumen

Acumen Publishing Limited
4 Saddler Street
Durham
DH1 3NP
www.acumenpublishing.co.uk

ISBN: 978-1-84465-200-6 (hardcover)
ISBN: 978-1-84465-201-3 (paperback)

British Library Cataloguing-in-Publication Data
A catalogue record for this book is available from the British Library.

Typeset in Minion Pro.
Printed in the UK by the MPG Books Group.

Contents

Acknowledgements

Y. S. Lo gratefully acknowledges support for her research on environmental philosophy from a Stephen Leung (梁鶴年) scholarship from the Chinese University of Hong Kong as well as a postdoctoral scholarship at La Trobe University, Melbourne. We both are grateful for financial support and leave from La Trobe University that helped to bring the book to completion. Special thanks for support and facilities to John Haldane and the Centre for Ethics, Philosophy and Public Affairs, University of St Andrews, where both authors were fellows during the final preparation of the book. We also want to express heartfelt thanks to Acumen's prepress manager, Kate Williams, for forbearance and professionalism, as well as to our respective spouses for supporting our collaboration and showing tolerance significantly above and beyond all reasonable limits.

one

Introduction: the place of environmental philosophy and its basic concepts

Overview

Most people now under twenty-five have a high probability of being around in fifty years' time. What will the world be like then? At current consumption rates, oil is due to run out in just over forty years, and people then will be living in societies that derive much of the energy for transport from other sources. No one has worked out a viable alternative aviation fuel, so there may be less international air travel, and it may cost much more than at present. Since increasing atmospheric carbon dioxide levels profoundly influence climate change, there will be a drive to reduce reliance on coal as a source of energy, even though there is enough coal on earth to last for another four centuries or so (at present rates of use). Within half a century, the switch to cleaner forms of energy, and the resulting reduction in air pollution, could be one of the major differences from the present. In most of the world's major cities there should be many days where breathing is comfortable and visibility is sparklingly clear, in stark contrast to the situation at present.

Even if the air gets cleaner over the next half century, this will not make much difference to climate changes that – having already started – cannot be stopped. For some time, climate modellers have been warning of the problem of tipping points. These are thresholds for the world's climate, ocean and ecological systems, at which they experience massive discontinuities. Tipping points occur when a system begins to undergo a rapid irreversible change from one state to a quite different one. After the tipping point is reached, the change is impossible to stop, even though it may take some time for the system to reach its new state. Such tipping points might include the sudden collapse of a major ocean current, the failure of seasonal monsoon rains, the sharp intensification of severe-weather events, or a sudden and unexpected increase in the rate of melting of snowfields or ice sheets (Lenton *et al.* 2008). There is the (we hope remote) possibility of a domino effect. This happens when a tipping point in one system is reached, and that change then triggers a further system to tip, which in turn triggers a further system to tip and so on.

The Greenland ice sheet holds nearly 6 per cent of the planet's fresh water. When it tips into an irreversible thaw this would steadily release water into the North Atlantic with economic, social and environmental consequences. To protect against a one-metre rise in sea level, the United States would need to spend $156 billion. The island nations of the Maldives and the Marshall Islands would disappear under the waves, much of Bangladesh would be uninhabitable and other countries would lose vital agricultural land. Encroaching salt water would reduce the availability of fresh water, leading to widespread death of plants and animals and reduction in agricultural production. Another part of the planet on the verge of tipping into an irreversible change is the enormous West Antarctic ice sheet. If both the Greenland ice sheet and West Antarctic ice sheet melt faster than expected, there would be a six-metre rise in sea level, dramatically changing the shape of the world map. In less than 300 years, New York, London and Bangkok would be flooded, agriculture and fisheries would collapse, and there would be mass human starvation, while wars, disease, enormous population displacement, poverty and massive loss of life would occur. While we do not yet know whether we are at – or have passed – tipping points for these parts of the climate system, it is pretty certain that within fifty years that knowledge will be available.

One other system at risk of tipping is the Indian summer monsoon. In May each year, heating of the Indian land mass draws moisture-laden air in from the surrounding oceans. As the air strikes the Himalayas it is deflected upwards, creating powerful low-pressure systems generating massive downpours and flooding to which local populations and agriculture were adapted. Land clearing, agriculture and air pollution make an impact on the planetary albedo (reflectance) over the Indian subcontinent, hence affecting the basic mechanism driving the monsoon. Some models predict worsening of the monsoon, others a weakening of it. Either result could wreak vast damage on agricultural production. In the light of concerns about these – and several other – tipping points, it is small wonder that people worry about whether the next century will see the beginnings of environmental catastrophe, with increasing floods, rapid rises in sea levels, droughts, famine, massive increases in environmental refugees, and wars breaking out as populations are displaced and fresh water becomes ever more scarce. In fifty years' time, it should be possible to identify which tipping points have been triggered, even though we will then be unable to do anything to reverse the changes taking place.

One prominent environmental pessimist, Clive Hamilton, gave a lecture to the Royal Society of Arts in Sydney in 2009, where he stated:

> It now seems almost certain that, if it has not occurred already, within the next several years enough warming will be locked in to the system to set in train feedback processes that will overwhelm any attempts we make to cut back on our carbon emissions. We will be powerless to stop the jump to a new climate on Earth, one much less sympathetic to life.
>
> (Hamilton 2009)

Who stands to lose most from the new climate that is "less sympathetic to life"? The picture for the future is quite mixed. Bangladesh, the Marshall Islands and other low-lying countries are already feeling the effect of rising sea levels, and parts or all of these countries will probably disappear before too long, rendering their inhabitants not so much homeless as landless. On the other hand, income-rich industrial cities and countries are planning already to improve their coastal defences to protect cities, suburbs and agricultural land. London may have to bring forward the date on which it replaces its existing flood barriers on the Thames, and Venice may have to rethink its current strategies on preventing major flood destruction. Further south, India and Pakistan face severe losses in agricultural production, but predictions for prosperous northern countries are better. The United States and Canada may benefit from increasing crop production and more harvests in a carbon-enriched and warmer atmosphere. In Europe, the rich countries of the north may do quite well under a changed climate, while agriculture in Spain, Italy and Greece will come under pressure.

In fact, while the effects of climate change will be felt all over the world, the human impact of climate change will be strongest in the income-poor countries of the world, and will be felt most sharply by the poorest people in these countries. So why care about it? If you, reader of this book, are already living in one of the income-rich industrial countries, you have little to fear for your own prosperity or that of your children. Or if you are prosperous and have the means to move, you are unlikely to suffer much from climate change even if you live in an income-poor country. It is the poorest and most vulnerable people who generally suffer most from storms, droughts, floods and other disasters. The so-called "natural" disasters are – in common with war, disease and other afflictions – not democratic in the way they strike groups of people. There is much uncertainty about the future. But one thing is certain: climate change will certainly not affect all people equally. So, in the light of scary predictions about the future, what would be the most rational thing to do? Maybe to try to get as rich as possible, so as to look after ourselves and our families?

This book is about philosophy and ethics, not about making money. Ethics goes beyond self-interest. The possibility of ethics in practice relies on the very fact that people (or most of them anyway) are open to considerations other than self-interest. Ethics assumes we are moved by consideration of other people's interests and suffering. So, if you are not capable of being motivated by the plight of other people, and if you only do things that you think will advance your self-interest, then you may as well stop reading this book now. The arguments we discuss will have no relevance for you unless you are capable of – or at least willing to be open to – being moved by considering the well-being of others.

If you do care about such issues you are not alone. In a review published by the UK Treasury in 2006, Nicholas Stern commented that under modest assumptions about climate change over the next fifty years:

> generally, poor countries, and poor people in any given country, suffer the most, notwithstanding that the rich countries are responsible for the bulk of past emissions. These features of climate change, together with the fact that they have an impact on many dimensions of human well-being, force us to look carefully at the underlying ethical judgements and presumptions which underpin, often implicitly, the standard framework of policy analysis. (Stern 2007: §2.3)

We are going to assume that you – like Stern – do care about others. Since ethics goes beyond considerations of narrow self-interest, environmental ethics will raise questions that go beyond purely human interests. This is a book about environmental philosophy, so we also assume that the reader is interested in questions about non-human living things, and about environmental systems and the planet as a whole. The Stern review suggests that up to 40 per cent of species could face extinction due to climate change, and many people have found this a matter of moral or ethical concern also. We turn to species later in the book. At first, we look at ways of going beyond the here-and-now (Chapter 2) by thinking about the interests of future people, and our duties – if any – to them. Questions about future people take us outside the circle of our immediate cares for ourselves, our loved ones and the people we know, and make us consider our responsibilities to those who are distant from us, those who belong to different racial, ethnic and religious groups, and so on. This is the first stage of expanding the circle of our moral concern and starts the journey of exploring how our moral concerns, sentiments and motivations can be extended beyond human beings, to animals, their lives and interests and then outward to other living things and to nature in general.

After future people, we turn to animals. Newspapers the world over feature stories about cats rescued from trees, sewers, washing machines and other less likely predicaments, and volunteers spend days trying to save beached whales. The lives and behaviour of animals – especially mammals – can readily catch our imagination and trigger thoughts about whether we owe them responsibilities or duties of any kind. Chapter 3 asks about the moral status and value of animals, seeing how far beyond self-interest our moral capacities will take us. Despite our love of some animals, others are often treated as nothing more than mere resources for human use and consumption. Is there something morally problematic with a purely instrumental attitude towards our co-inhabitants of the earth? Some philosophers have argued that animals, living things and natural things in general all have a value in their own right, which they possess independent of their use to humans, and they therefore call for restraint from humans in using them. We begin to examine these arguments in Chapters 3 and 4, seeing whether they stand up to rational scrutiny. By then, we will find that philosophy seems able to take us a long way beyond self-interest, and we start to face interesting questions about the limits of our capacity for ethics and morality. Are there any things that we cannot come to see in a moral light and consider as having actual or potential moral value?

It is not uncommon in environmental management to cull feral animals or some individual members of overpopulated indigenous species for the protection of the integrity of the ecosystems of which they are parts. We ask in Chapter 5 whether these actions – harmful to many individuals but beneficial to the environment as a whole – are morally permissible. For some commentators, the culling of overabundant species is not just permissible, but actually mandatory for the greater good. We examine this logic to see if it is ever acceptable to sacrifice individuals for the sake of the good of the larger system to which they belong. One big problem is whether individuals are just instruments for promoting the larger good of the system in which they are placed. Is this a way of applying to nature a philosophy that, when applied to human affairs and communities, would be a kind of fascism or totalitarianism? We explore whether some ideas about environmental management amount to a kind of "eco-fascism" that fails to show the proper respect due to individual animals and living things.

Environmental philosophy over the past forty years has often argued for recognizing the value of things that are natural, wild and free. In Chapter 6 we turn to the examination of the idea of nature. Do natural things have a certain value that manufactured things – artefacts – necessarily lack? Some writers have argued that domestic animals – because they are bred, designed and created by humans – are nothing more than artefacts, and that their value is thereby reduced. According to this view, a wolf is much more valuable than a dog. Likewise, an old-growth forest devoid of human interference is seen as more valuable than a botanic garden. Consider a mining company that had performed open-pit mining in some previously unspoiled area, and then subsequently restored the land form and surface ecology of the area. What is the value of the restored environment? Might it be just as valuable as the original unspoiled, untouched, environment, or does it lack the authentic value of the original?

Human beings themselves – never far from the focus of all philosophical enquiries – have a puzzling status and Chapter 6 also explores this topic. We ask whether everything with which human beings interfere thereby becomes unnatural, and whether humans themselves can be in nature while still having culture. What is it for something to be natural? We explore different senses of the word "natural" and examine the way naturalness has been thought to be morally relevant in a variety of environmental philosophies. Some philosophers have claimed that all natural things are beautiful, but are they beautiful simply because they are natural? Alternatively, is there something else about natural things that makes them beautiful? These provocative questions take us into the consideration of topics that span environmental philosophy and other areas of aesthetics and ethical theory.

By this stage in the book, environmental philosophy has taken us beyond self-interest in many ways, but in a surprising way it has also brought us back to questions about ourselves. We have examined a range of theories, and certain shared features have now emerged. The common underlying strategy in many attempts to extend our ethics involves a logic that forces us to confront a question about ourselves rather than about others. Here is the reason why. Many theories of environmental philosophy take humans as their starting-point, and share a basic commitment to the inherent worth humans possess. That shared commitment is the common basis for extending the scope of ethics beyond the human world and out to include animals, plants, ecosystems, and even rivers, mountains and glaciers. So the extension of value to natural things is nearly always based on the assumption that human beings themselves are valuable. But this value is itself mysterious. What is the source of universal and equal human dignity and worth? One important source of this idea is a religious framework in which the Creator loves all that he has made, especially humans – the jewel of creation – fashioned in his own image. God's love for the whole of nature, what he sees to be good, gives a coherent metaphysical foundation for the existence of value that is spread widely throughout nature and not located just within one species. Chapter 7 explores this idea and then subjects it to investigation. Some analysts have pointed out that a huge problem faces us in a world without faith: the ethics by which people live only appear to make sense within the very framework that secularism rejects. As Ivan Karamazov famously contended, if there is no God then everything is permitted. For those who do not want to found a theory of ethics and value on religion, the puzzle is to find a new structure within which notions of value, dignity and equality can make sense. The chapter explores the possibility of basing value and ethics on a purely secular foundation. If this is not possible, then neither environmental, nor human, ethics will be credible in the absence of a religious framework.

At a time of continuing and deepening environmental anxiety, we naturally wonder if people in some societies and cultures behave better toward the environment than people in others. If that is the case, we need to find out which societies and cultures are more environmentally friendly and which ones are not so. We also need an explanation as to why that is the case. If successful, we can perhaps gain insight into how we should reorganize our way of being in the world in order to better relate to the larger environment. A great deal of work has theorized the pathology of contemporary environmental crises, suggesting that some of our underlying cultural, religious and political beliefs and attitudes are responsible for our behaving badly toward the environment. In other words, our religious worldviews, our basic political and social ideas, are not environmentally innocent. Human-centredness – *anthropocen-*

trism – is the number one suspect. The anthropocentric perspective is that by and large human beings are the only intrinsically worthwhile things on earth, and that everything else exists to service our wants and needs. As we show in Chapter 8, many theorists in the field blame this perspective for our environmental problems. This is why so much effort in environmental philosophy has been expended trying to refute anthropocentrism. We examine a number of theories in which anthropocentrism plays a key role as the guilty party. But we also show that the case against anthropocentrism has not yet been clearly proved.

In our final chapter, we turn to some underexamined parts of environmental philosophy, asking to what extent our troubles are related to the consumer society and the pressures it generates. We also consider whether environmental care is an individual responsibility. What about the great corporations, whose financial and economic activities have impacts on culture, economy and environment alike? Are they the hidden destroyers of nature and do the people who work for them have any chance of holding them in check? What role can governments play in controlling the greedy hunt for growth at all cost, and can science and research play a part in finding ways for us to manage ourselves and the natural world better than we presently do?

Environmental philosophers have often seemed to think that if people no longer believe that they are the most important things in the world, they will start to behave in more respectful ways towards non-human things and the environment at large. Much of the advocacy within the environmental movement has been criticized for its quasi-religious fervour, and for spreading high hopes of green salvation. Underlying the attempt to convert sceptics to the environmental cause is a simple, but overoptimistic hope: that our beliefs and values will themselves be reflected in our behaviour and everyday action. The last two chapters raise doubts about this hope. If the world is to be liveable in fifty years' time, then many things about our current policies and beliefs will have to change. A change in outlook, in our beliefs about human beings and in our understanding of values – these will perhaps be part of the solution; but changes in individuals' beliefs and values will not be sufficient to solve the environmental issue. The problems we face result from a mass of complex interrelated factors, vested interests, economic structures and corporate actors. To solve these problems, we will need to tackle matters of governance that extend beyond questions of individual morality (Norton 2005).

While this book covers most of the main debates in environmental philosophy, it has been our intention in writing it to provide a more general introduction to philosophy. All the way through, we show how to lay out arguments and chains of reasoning in a clear way, one that allows the skeleton of the argument to be seen clearly so that elementary lapses in logic can be easily detected. As a result we not only lay bare some of the mistakes that writers have made, but are able to show how some well-known ideas lack any very firm foundation. The skills you learn from studying this book can be transferred to other areas of philosophy, politics and policy studies too: in fact, to any field where conclusions are defended by arguments that are meant to be systematic and convincing. We have always looked to find the most cogent way of making sense of an idea, a political or ethical position, or an argument. In any argument, the reasons that support the conclusion are called the premises. When an argument is cogent, then the truth of its premises makes the conclusion more likely to be true than false. Arguments that fail to be cogent in this way may still be interesting, and their conclusions may be true, but it would not be rational to accept the conclusions of such arguments purely on the basis of their premises.

Working through environmental philosophy, we inevitably encounter some of the most fascinating and puzzling questions of philosophy itself. As well as looking at the theories of many contemporary thinkers, we introduce the work of some classic figures in moral theory, particularly David Hume and Immanuel Kant. We also introduce some of the central problems of ethics: problems about value, dignity and respect that have not been successfully answered by philosophers so far. As you work through the book, the level of difficulty of the topics increases, and the last three chapters make tougher demands on the reader than the first six. The final chapter goes beyond philosophy itself and looks at the structure of the larger systems that simultaneously shape our lives and give rise to some of our environmental problems. While much of ethical theory focuses on individual people and their personal moral responsibilities, we turn attention in the last chapter to larger actors – such as governments and businesses – to see what roles they have played in causing social and environmental problems. The ways in which these larger factors shape the lives of individuals, their role in causing climate change, dispossession and exploitation of poor people, and their contribution to many of the global problems we now face: these all deserve, we think, some attention, even though philosophy itself has for the most part ignored such influences on our lives.

Basic concepts

In tackling the key questions outlined above, we use some basic tools, described in this section. Many people believe that it is morally wrong for human beings to pollute and destroy parts of the natural environment and to consume a huge proportion of the planet's natural resources. If that is wrong, is it simply because a sustainable environment is essential to human well-being? Or is such behaviour also wrong because the natural environment and its denizens have certain values in their own right, which ought to be respected and protected?

The distinction between instrumental value and intrinsic value is of central importance in answering these questions. *Instrumental* value is the value that things have in virtue of being a *means* or instrument to service some other ends. *Intrinsic* value, in the sense of *non-instrumental* value is the value that things have as *ends in themselves*, that is, in their own right and completely regardless of whether they are useful as means to other ends. Fruit bats, as their name implies, eat fruit. The trees and fruits they depend on are thus of instrumental value to the bats. It is not widely thought that fruits have value as ends in themselves. On the other hand, a piano teacher has, in more than one sense, instrumental value for those who want to learn to play the piano. Over and above this, most people think that a person, as a person, has intrinsic value (sometimes also called "inherent worth"): a value in their own right independently of their prospects for serving the ends of others. The value of the piano teacher, in other words, is both instrumental (as teacher) and intrinsic (as human person).

Rousseau

Jean-Jacques Rousseau was the pre-eminent nature philosopher of the eighteenth century. In his last work, *Reveries of the Solitary Walker*, he wrote:

> No one imagines that the structure of plants could deserve any attention in its own right ... Linger in some meadow studying one by one all the flowers that adorn it, and people will take you for a herbalist and ask you for something to cure the itch in children, scab in men, or glanders in horses ... These medicinal associations ... tarnish the colour of the meadows and the brilliance of the flowers, they drain the woods of all freshness and make the green leaves and shade seem dull and disagreeable. ... It is no use seeking garlands for shepherdesses among the ingredients of an enema. (Rousseau 1979: 110)

For another example, a certain herb may have instrumental value because it provides the ingredients for some medicine or is an aesthetic object for human observers. But if the plant also has some value in itself independently of its prospects for furthering some other ends such as human health, or the pleasure from aesthetic experience, then the plant also has intrinsic value. Because the intrinsically valuable is good as an end in itself, it is commonly agreed that something's possession of intrinsic value generates a moral duty on the part of moral agents to protect it, or at least to refrain from damaging it (O'Neill 1992; Jamieson 2002).

When talking about duties, we need to separate out direct and indirect ones. If all people have intrinsic value, we owe them respect, and this is owed *directly* to them. It is sometimes said that from respect for persons there follow other duties, for example not to mislead them, to tell them the truth, to avoid doing them harm, and so on. But the scope of respect is limited. Once, on a tram in Melbourne, we heard the driver use the public address system to rebuke a passenger who had put his feet up on one of the seats. The driver announced, "Show respect for the tram, and take your feet off the seat." What did the driver mean? Trams are not typical of the things that have value in their own right. On the contrary, they are typical of things with purely instrumental value. So the driver may have meant that passengers have direct duties to other passengers, and that keeping the tram seats clean is one of these duties. In philosophical parlance, we could say that the passenger has a *direct* duty to other passengers in respect of keeping the tram clean. Any duty to the tram is indirect. Damaging a tram seat, or making it dirty, does not wrong the tram: it wrongs other passengers who will be using the tram. The driver may have meant this. There is another interpretation; namely, that the driver thought the tram was a special or sacred place, and felt that the passenger was directly harming the tram or breaking the rules about special places. According to this interpretation, it would seem that some people regard trams as intrinsically valuable and worthy of direct respect.

Many traditional Western ethical perspectives are anthropocentric or human-centred in that either they assign intrinsic value only to human beings alone (*strong* anthropocentrism) or they assign a significantly greater amount of intrinsic value to human beings than to any non-human things. We can call the second view *weak* anthropocentrism. The weak anthropocentrist holds that the protection or promotion of human interests or well-being at the expense of non-human things turns out to be nearly always justified. For example, Aristotle (*Politics* 1256b) stated that "nature has made all things specifically for the sake of man" and that the value of non-human things in nature is merely instrumental. Generally, anthropocentric positions find it problematic to articulate what is wrong with the cruel treatment of non-human animals, except to the extent that such treatment may lead to bad consequences for human beings. If we are cruel to animals, it may – for example – harden our hearts to humans. Anthropocentrism often recognizes some wrongness in anthropogenic (i.e. human-caused) environmental devastation. As you might expect, such destruction is wrong according to the anthropocentric outlook only when it threatens human well-being either now or in the future.

In this book, we will not make a distinction between *ethics* and *morality*, although sometimes these terms are used for different purposes. In contemporary ethical and moral theories, human beings have always been taken as the *paradigm case* of intrinsically or inherently valuable objects. If anything at all in the universe is intrinsically valuable, then a person is. One central question in environmental philosophy is whether it is possible for things other than human beings to have intrinsic value and, if so, what these things might be. Trams may be an extreme case, but we shall be examining arguments that depict animals, living things more generally and a range of other natural things as candidates for having intrinsic value.

If animals have value in their own right, this does not mean that they lack instrumental value too. Consider the red fox, for example. In parts of the world it is disliked by farmers because of its tendency to kill beyond need. Other farmers, in different parts of the world, like it because it eats the rodents who destroy grain. In the latter case the fox has positive instrumental value, while in the former case it has negative value (what is sometimes called "disvalue"). Foxes may also have instrumental value (or disvalue) in other ways. Where fox fur is prized they may be valued for their pelts, and where nature films are popular they may be valued for the pleasure given by documentaries about them. The very same animal may thus be valued in very different ways. If the red fox also has a value in itself independently of its usefulness to humans, then we will say that it has intrinsic value as well.

It is not only in the case of abundant animals, like foxes, that the very same species can be a source of value and disvalue at the same time. While foxes thrive, many of their carnivorous cousins are endangered, including many of the big cats such as Bengal tigers, cheetahs, leopards and the Florida panther. One puzzling question is whether we have more of a duty to preserve endangered animals than abundant ones. Suppose individual animals are intrinsically valuable, something we shall be discussing in detail in Chapter 3. One fox, one koala, one pine marten or

> **The fox**
>
> The red fox (*Vulpes vulpes*) is the world's most widespread and successful carnivorous mammal. As well as hunting and killing small animals, it will eat carrion, worms and lizards, and is a commonly seen scavenger in urban areas. It is depicted in conflicting ways in literature, folk tales and children's stories. The wily fox is sometimes the heroic underdog, or the clever trickster. In China, Japan and Korea, the fox is regarded not only as cunning but also as having magical powers. Poultry farmers in Europe often regard the fox as a cold-blooded killer because foxes will kill in excess of what they can eat (in order to bury small caches of food for future provision). In most countries, foxes are not a particular problem for agriculture, and often control rabbits and rodents in ways that benefit farmers. This may be one reason why in Japan foxes are regarded as messengers of the farming gods.

one badger would seem to be no more or less valuable than another. Conservation efforts are often directed to saving a species in danger of extinction, while overabundance is seen as a problem. Populations of the very same species may be threatened in one place and overabundant in another. For example, koala bears are the target of conservation efforts in the southeast of the state of Queensland, Australia, where their management and conservation is mandated by legislation. By contrast, in another part of Australia – on the tiny Kangaroo Island – they are currently threatening to eat themselves and other species out of house and home and are likely to be culled in the near future. So even if each koala, considered in itself, has the same intrinsic value as any other koala, there seem to be places where they are a nuisance – hence not of value – and other places where they are of high value and in need of protection.

This is a bit puzzling. If a koala is more valuable in one place than in another, then does this mean it has the same intrinsic value in both places, but that it has some additional value in the places where it is rare or the population is in decline? And does it lose some value in places where it is overabundant? Is rarity, or being under threat, itself something of value? One reason this is a puzzling question is that rarity cannot be a value in its own right. Industrial accidents are far too common in many workplaces, and many safety regimes exist with a view to reducing the number of accidents in businesses and factories. If these campaigns are successful and the rate of industrial accidents decline, no one will be campaigning to stop them going extinct. So if rarity in itself is not a reason for valuing something, we need to explore more deeply to understand why so much care and attention is given to threatened and endangered populations.

One common argument for focusing on endangered species is that we may lose something useful if we let an endangered species decline into extinction. Who knows whether one day a little-known plant species may yield chemical substances or genes of tremendous medical significance? As we have seen, foxes can be problematic for free-range poultry farming, yet can be valued by crop farmers because they control the rodents that damage harvests and eat much needed grain. Children in temperate agricultural communities are often reminded that a rose is a weed when it grows in a cornfield, a remark that is meant to draw attention to the fact that a rose is of no benefit to the crop farmer. A clump of wheat, likewise, is a weed when it grows in a flower farm. As we find, in Chapters 4 and 5 there is a serious problem posed by these cases. This is because different theorists give different roles to the surrounding context in determining our responsibilities to individual living things (and to populations of them).

The key puzzle

In a well-known passage, the linguist Benjamin Lee Whorf commented that one benefit of studying a very different language is that it helps us see our native tongue in a fresh light: "we find that the exotic language," he wrote, "is a mirror held up to our own" (Whorf 1956: 138). What may come as a surprise is that something similar happens in environmental philosophy. Nearly all the main theories of environmental philosophy begin from the assumption that human beings are of value for themselves. Now why should this be so? Taking a secular outlook, they are unable to give the traditional reply that our inherent value is due to the fact that the Creator loves us all equally. Instead, theorists look for some other property, one that will be plausible as a foundation for the claim that we have value in our own right. For example, suppose that humans are conscious beings with some freedom of choice. The theorist then speculates that perhaps things that are conscious and have freedom of choice are precisely the things with value in their own right, that is, they are the intrinsically valuable things in the world.

Once this step is made, the extension of value beyond the realm of human beings becomes a real possibility. After all, it seems likely that there are some animals that have consciousness and that also have some freedom of choice (the great apes, the more intelligent breeds of dog, and so on). Since the feature that was identified as explaining the fact that humans are intrinsically valuable is also found in certain non-humans, it seems to follow that these non-humans will also possess value in their own right. This form of argument has high pay-offs. First, a feature has been found that supposedly explains the intrinsic value of human beings within a secular framework. Next, the existence of that feature confirms the principle that all the things with the feature in questions have intrinsic value. Finally, the recognition that things other than humans have the feature, and hence have the same kind of value that humans have, has enabled us to identify the presence of intrinsic value outside the human realm. We are therefore not worried about being thought narrow-minded, elitist or prejudiced in the theory of value that we adopt. For our theory of value is not completely human-centred.

In this way the question of human beings and their value cannot really be separated from the question of non-human things and their value. Once we start with a feature or property that seems to explain why humans are intrinsically valuable, that feature leads us to recognize inherent value elsewhere in the world. The kind of reasoning involved here is often called *abduction*, or *argument to the best explanation*. It is an important form of argument throughout the entire field of philosophy, and so it is not surprising to find it widely used in environmental philosophy. We shall show how one major theory after another uses argument to the best explanation in order to make plausible the idea that properties such as *being a subject of a life, being a self-maintaining living organism,* or *being self-choosing and self regulating* are the best explanation of the fact that human beings are the paradigm case of intrinsically valuable things. But these properties always apply not only to humans but also to things other than humans as well. Since in each case the properties define different classes of things, the result is that the major theories disagree with each other over the range and scope of intrinsic value. In other words, the major theories all disagree about what things in nature are, or are not, inherently valuable.

Whorf found that by studying an exotic language, he was forced back to think in new terms about his own familiar one. In the same way, our exploration of alternative theories in environmental philosophy pushes us back up against the great mystery of our own value. As the various theories extend the range of valuable things from animals to living things, then on to communities, species and ecosystems, we have to face uncomfortable questions. For example, are all the things that are intrinsically valuable equally valuable, or are some more valuable than others? If some things are more valuable than others, then does that mean that – say – humans, as a species, are possibly more valuable than foxes or pandas, and does it also mean that some humans have more intrinsic value than others? These are difficult questions to confront, especially given the political and ethical commitments to egalitarianism built into major policy declarations. For example, Article 1 of the United Nations Universal Declaration of Human Rights states: "All human beings are born free and equal in dignity and rights. They are endowed with reason and conscience and should act towards one another in a spirit of brotherhood." The claim of universal equality here is inconsistent with the meritocratic idea that some human beings may have more dignity, or higher value, than others ("dignity", let us suppose, can be read to mean the same as "intrinsic value").

Article 1 also hints that being "endowed with reason and conscience" may be the feature that explains the universality of human dignity. But are humans the only beings so endowed? Dogs give the impression of having some kind of conscience, given their guilty looks when caught in the act of doing something forbidden. Even in the eighteenth century, writers were prepared to accept that dogs have reason and intelligence. Using the form of argument to the best explanation, we could ask whether being endowed with reason and conscience is the best explanation of human value. But then, if dogs, bears, foxes and primates are also similarly endowed, could we not use Article 1 as a basis for arguing that at least some non-human animals should also be able to claim the same rights as humans?

The expansion of rights motivated by such an argument will not take us very far beyond humans, but it would still be a significant expansion, and of great importance to the species identified as holders of rights. They would now be entitled to a high degree of protection. As we show

---

Expanding circles

P1. It is an indisputable fact that human beings are intrinsically valuable. [paradigm case of intrinsic value]

P2. The moral principle that things that are endowed with reason and conscience are intrinsically valuable, together with the fact that human beings are so endowed, provides the best explanation for the undisputable fact stated by P1. [claim about best explanation]

P3. The moral principle, that all things that are endowed with reason and conscience are intrinsically valuable, is true or acceptable. [confirmation of the moral principle, from P1 and P2, by *argument to the best explanation*]

P4. At least some dogs are endowed with reason and conscience – to a higher/lower/equal extent. [empirical claim]

C. At least some dogs are – more/less/equally – intrinsically valuable. [from P3 and P4, by *consistent application* of the confirmed moral principle]

---

later, environmental thinkers have not hesitated to argue for much wider expansion of intrinsic value, with some of them arguing that there is no difference in inherent value between a human, a dog and a cabbage. Since that seems a difficult idea to accept, we have to consider whether there may be something wrong with the general form of argument leading to such a conclusion. Doing that, however, brings us again back to confront puzzles about human dignity and value. Three ideas in particular have to be examined. The first is whether humans have a special value simply through being human (this is an idea that Peter Singer and others have derided as "speciesism": a prejudice of the same sort as racism and sexism). The second is the idea we have already discussed, namely anthropocentrism in both its strong and weaker forms. Third is the idea of equality. We show how the value egalitarianism built into Article 1 has played a part in developing a wider form of egalitarianism about values in the natural world as these have been explored by environmental philosophers.

Throughout the book, it is the same key puzzle that continually reappears: are human beings especially valuable, and, if so, in what does that special value consist? Environmental philosophy, as we present it, faces an endlessly recurring problem. We start with assumptions about ourselves: the specialness of being human demands that we respect people and act appropriately towards them. Arguments are then put forward to show that there are other things that share the special value, previously thought to be uniquely human. The wider the class of especially valuable things becomes, the less special humans themselves seem to be. But this now makes the starting-point of the whole enterprise seem doubtful, since it looks as if human beings are not especially valuable at all. But can we live with the consequences of this reasoning? To spell these out, the consequences are that we either give more protection to animals, plants, and other living things than we currently do, or that we reconsider whether human beings themselves really deserve the kinds of protection built into the Universal Declaration of Human Rights. Each alternative seems to ask more of us than we can manage. Particularly in the income-rich countries, there is a real problem of finding ways to halt the large-scale destruction of animals, plants and natural systems on which much economic wealth is based. On the other hand, treating people as being of no more moral importance than dogs or monkeys would be regarded as an outrageous insult to human dignity. In this way, environmental philosophers always seem to be in danger of sawing off the branch on which they are sitting, a predicament that makes the subject one of the more exciting and interesting branches of contemporary philosophy.

two

Future generations: what consideration do we owe them?

Sudden and slow disasters

What humans do at one time affects humans living at other times. Sudden and shocking disasters can wake us up to the realization that things are wrong. In 1952, a dense sulphurous and smoky fog enveloped much of London for several days. Twelve thousand people died either during the smog incident, or within a few months of it. As a result, air pollution measures, including controls on the burning of coal, have cleaned up the air in British cities and avoided a repetition of the "big smoke".

Other human actions bring a continuing legacy of woe. A massive industrial tragedy in 1984 killed thousands of people and left hundreds

---

London smog

In London, Friday 5 December 1952 started clear and cold, but during the day a smoky inversion fog formed. By evening it had become thick and sulphurous (people burned poor quality, high-sulphur coal in those days). Transport, theatres, cinemas and the rest of city life ground to a halt over the weekend and for the first few days of the following week. Visibility was so bad that schools had to close, and cars were abandoned in the street. Barry Linton describes a trip to school: "I was 7 – we lived in Hackney and although my school was only 100 yards away, my Dad had to hold on to me and grope along walls and fences to find the school door, only for me to be sent home because nobody else made it in" (http://news.bbc.co.uk/2/hi/uk_news/2542315.stm). It is estimated that around 12,000 people died directly as a result of the toxic, and highly acidic, smog (Davis 2003).

---

of thousands chronically ill when a cloud of dense and lethal gases was released from the Union Carbide chemical plant at Bhopal in India. People are still dying in Bhopal today, as the toxic legacy of the leak brings kidney disease, cancers and horrific birth defects to those living

Union Carbide

"It felt like somebody had filled our bodies up with red chillies, our eyes tears coming out, noses were watering, we had froth in our mouths. The coughing was so bad that people were writhing in pain. Some people just got up and ran in whatever they were wearing or even if they were wearing nothing at all. Those who fell were not picked up by anybody, they just kept falling, and were trampled on by other people. People climbed and scrambled over each other to save their lives – even cows were running and trying to save their lives and crushing people as they ran." These are the words of a survivor describing the night of 2–3 December 1984 when the decommissioned Union Carbide chemical plant in Bhopal, capital city of the Indian province of Madhya Pradesh, emitted a cloud of poisonous gas. More than three thousand people died that night, either from the toxic chemicals themselves, or trampled underfoot in the panic that engulfed the neighbourhoods close to the Union Carbide plant. Around eight thousand were dead within a week. Half a million people were exposed to the gas and twenty thousand have died to date as a result of their exposure.

After the disaster, there was no proper clean up and the plant still leaks chemicals, which contaminate local wells and water supplies today. As a result more than 120,000 people still suffer from ailments caused by the accident and the subsequent pollution. Monstrous birth deformities, miscarriages and high rates of cancer and other diseases continue to this day. The company blamed sabotage for the gas cloud – consisting of methyl isocyanate (MIC) and a number of other toxic ingredients. Poor safety standards, untrained workers, and inappropriate storage of MIC have also been blamed for what was the worst industrial accident of the twentieth century. The company reached an out-of-court settlement with the Indian government, but much of the money did not reach the victims. In 1991, the local government in Bhopal charged Warren Anderson, Union Carbide's chief executive at the time of the disaster, with manslaughter. If tried in India and convicted, he faces a maximum of ten years in prison. He has successfully evaded an international arrest warrant and a summons to appear before a United States court. It has been alleged that the Indian government has not wanted to take firm action against Union Carbide, or its parent company Dow Chemicals, on behalf of the people of Bhopal because the government is keen to attract more investment to India from giant transnational corporations.

The people carrying the toxic legacy are poor, relatively uneducated and without influence.

Source: Bhopal Medical Appeal,
http://bhopal.org/index.php?id=11&L=kpdknsklefd (accessed July 2010)

near the abandoned pesticide factory: a form of slow disaster triggered by the earlier incident. Things we sometimes regard as "natural" disasters are also due to human action, or made worse by human action. Every day, there is news of environmental disasters: some sudden such as floods, tsunamis, and fires, while others are slow, taking the form of droughts, the melting of ice caps, the spread of deserts, or the steady loss of topsoil. Like the great smog of London, or the industrial disaster in Bhopal, these environmental disasters are not the result purely of nature's forces, for there is increasing evidence that our practices of land clearing and fossil fuel burning are causing large disruptions to the planet's climate. As we bring about changes in the climate, both sudden and slow disasters can be blamed on us: not on us as individuals, but on what we have done collectively in building cities, developing farming systems and establishing industries.

If the theories of human-induced climate change are right, then children who have not yet been born will bear the legacy of what we are doing nowadays. The sudden and slow effects of climate change will take their toll on the health, welfare and life quality of tomorrow's children, just as children in Bhopal today are still suffering from the effects of the 1984 disaster. How can there be any philosophical puzzle lurking here? If we can make sense of the toxic legacy of Bhopal, then it seems obvious that we should also be concerned about not leaving a similar legacy to the future. Nothing may seem more simple than the commitment to leave the planet in good shape for future generations, making sure that our industries are safe and clean and that our effects on the climate reduce the chances of more disasters, whether sudden or slow.

Where common sense finds no problem, philosophers have found things to worry about, and in this chapter we shall look at some of these. As you will see, we think that some of the philosophical worries are the result of simple confusions. To start getting into the puzzles, suppose someone argues like this: "If we have duties to future people, this will give us a reason to care about the environment now, and will give us a reason to change our behaviour if by doing so we can make the lives of future people better." The assumption in this statement is clear: that we have duties to future people. But who exactly are these people? And do we really have duties to them? These will be the questions for this chapter, and we shall look at three ways of answering them.

Utilitarianism

It seems obvious that there are at least some future people to whom we have duties. Normally, parents hope their children will live better lives than they themselves have, and parents are generally thought to have duties to their children. So as the natural resources on earth become increasingly limited and the planet increasingly unliveable, parents, at least, are likely to worry that their children (and their children's children, and so on) will probably live worse lives than they do. So parents at least would feel a duty to some future people, namely their own children, and their descendants. And to talk of a more general duty to future generations would just generalize that everyday notion. Where, then, is the problem?

We start by exploring the utilitarian answer to the question: do we have moral duties to future generations? Utilitarianism is an ethical theory (in short, an *ethic*) that links the concepts of right and good in the following way: an action is right only when its consequences are good. For example, if you think that what makes an action right is that it brings more happiness all around than any alternative available to you, then you are thinking like a utilitarian, and your standard of utility is happiness. For Jeremy Bentham, one of the founders of contemporary utilitarian ethics, we should always act in order to bring about as much utility as possible:

> By utility is meant that property in any object whereby it tends to produce benefit, advantage, pleasure, good, or happiness (all this in the present case comes to the same thing) or (what comes again to the same thing) to prevent the happening of mischief, pain, evil or unhappiness.　　　　([1789] 1970: 12)

Bentham's form of utilitarianism emphasizes pleasure or happiness as the most important consequence for actions to aim at (and pain or sadness as the things to avoid). His theory is usually called hedonic utilitarianism (after the Greek word for pleasure, *hēdonē*). There can be different measures of utility: say, welfare, or the satisfaction of people's considered preferences. So there are forms of utilitarianism that argue that it is right to increase, maintain or at least not diminish people's welfare. This kind of welfare utilitarianism will also be problematic in light of the arguments we are about to mention. And the same will be true of preference utilitarianism, the theory that demands we aim at the satisfaction of people's considered preferences as our target for action.

P1. The higher the balance of people's happiness over suffering (call this balance "utility"), the better the world is. [1st utilitarian principle]

P2. We have a moral duty not to make the world worse, but to make it better or even the best that we can. [2nd utilitarian principle]

P3. We have a moral duty not to reduce utility, but to increase or even maximize it. [from P1 & P2]

P4. The fewer environmental resources people have, the less effectively they can satisfy their needs and desires.

P5. The less effectively people can satisfy their needs and desires, the lower the utility.

P6. We have a moral duty not to reduce people's environmental resources. [from P3, P4 & P5]

P7. The interests of future people matter just as much as the interests of existing people.

P8. We have a moral duty not to reduce future people's environmental resources. [from P6 & P7]

C. We have a moral duty not to over-consume environmental resources – that is, not to consume them at a rate higher than their recovery rate. [from P8]

But this theory will also face similar objections to the ones we raise. So, for simplicity, the argument we will study (utility) is put in terms of hedonic utilitarianism.

The duties to future people may not be to make sure they have better lives than we do, but simply be to make sure their lives are no worse than ours, or perhaps that their lives are at least no worse than some minimally acceptable level. The core utilitarian argument is written in the box, with premises labelled with a "P" and the final conclusion marked "C". (Notice that some of the premises will also be intermediate conclusions.) The first two premises simply state the core understanding of a utilitarian ethic, where happiness is the measure of utility. Since the consequences of our actions, in terms of pain and pleasure, sadness and happiness, are the measure of what is good, then a world where people have the highest amount of pleasure and happiness in relation to pain and unhappiness will be the best of all. Imagine two different ways the world might be. In one scenario, a large number of people are very happy, and only a small number of people are unhappy for some of the time. In a different scenario, many of the world's people are unhappy to a significant degree, and only a small number of people are very happy. Premise P1 implies that the second scenario is worse than the first one. The best of all possible worlds would be one in which happiness is maximized and sadness minimized. Our moral duty, then, is to avoid increasing worldly unhappiness and, if possible, find ways of raising the amount of happiness in the world, which is what premise P3 states. Premises P4 and P5 then link utility, understood in terms of happiness and unhappiness, with environmental resources. But if premises P4 and P5 are true, it follows that we have a duty not to reduce environmental resources and opportunities for people. For it appears that possibilities of happiness and pleasure will be linked to the availability of environmental goods and services of all kinds (not just the resources for industry and manufacturing, but the pleasures of fresh air, beautiful scenery, studying the lives of animals and plants, and so on).

At this point, someone may be tempted to argue that we only need to care about the environmental resources and services that are available to people who exist: real people. Since those who are still to be born are not yet here, then maybe they have no weight in our current decisions. Although this is an objection that has interested some philosophers, we will take it as obvious that future people will have interests, and that these interests can be helped or harmed by what we do now. So although future people are not around at the moment (and so not able to enter the discussion or make complaints), their interests are something we can consider. They will have an interest in avoiding suffering and pain, just as all of those who presently exist have such interests. And they will have interests in being happy and securing some pleasure, just as currently existing people have such interests. Utilitarians normally accept a principle of equality: that equal consideration should be given to equal interests. But if that principle is accepted, then premise P7 would have to be accepted too: that the interests of future people should be given the same weight as the interests of present people. With all these premises in place, the conclusion seems to follow that we have a moral duty not to reduce the environmental goods and services available to future people, lest we damage their interests. And so we have a moral duty not to overconsume environmental resources.

Two problems

There are two important problems with the utilitarian argument as outlined here. The first is factual, or empirical, while the second is philosophical, or conceptual. The factual problem is that premise P4 is debatable, and may even be false. One common response to the idea that contemporary people are eating the future at an unsustainable rate, and that they are destroying the means by which future people can survive, is to claim that technology will fix the problem. This argument is not just about whether technology can fix problems of climate change by finding ways to pull carbon out of the atmosphere, or develop non-polluting energy sources. It can also be about how well technology can compensate for loss of various natural goods and services by supplying alternative, artificial replacements. So, even if climate change cannot be fixed by technology, the hope of optimists is that technology will provide ways for people to adapt and flourish in the new climate regime that has resulted from land clearing, urbanization and industrialization.

While this is a really important question of fact, the question of whether technological optimism is true or false is not the main philosophical issue. The important point – from the philosopher's point of view – is that the optimists just possibly might be right, and if they are right, then the reduction in environmental goods and services is not going to lead to an inevitable reduction in the capacity of future people to satisfy their needs and desires. In other words, if the optimists are right, then future people's interests will not be harmed by our present activities. Indeed, it may be that the stresses we are placing on planetary ecosystems are just of the right kind to drive major technological innovations that will bring untold happiness to future human beings. Implausible as that may seem to many people at the moment, we cannot rule out the possibility of such a future.

Generally, if we find one of the premises or assumptions of an argument to be false, then the argument loses much of its conviction. Even if an argument is valid, falsity of one of the premises undermines the cogency of the argument. For example, if we assume that all dogs are cats, and that all cats are frogs, then we can validly conclude that all dogs are frogs. How so? Well, for an argument to be valid, it simply needs to satisfy the following condition: if all the premises were to be true, then the conclusion would be true as well. Now in the silly argument about dogs, cats and frogs, this condition is satisfied. If it were true that all dogs were cats, and that all cats were frogs, then it would be true that all dogs are frogs. So this silly argument is formally valid. But it lacks any power of conviction, because both of its premises are in fact false. That is why the argument is not sound, for a sound argument is one that is valid, and where the premises are also true.

So, going back to the utilitarian argument in the box, what are we to say? If premise P4 is false, then the argument fails to convince, because it is not sound. But notice that we are not able to say with certainty whether P4 is true or false, for P4 is debatable. So we can take account of this uncertainty by weakening the final conclusion. For example, we may have a duty that is divided: either we should not reduce the environmental goods and services available to future people, or, if we do, then we should aim to provide them with better technologies to compensate them. Because of this uncertainty over premise P4, many governments and organizations may be doing two different things at present; namely, trying to limit the amount of environmental damage being done (in case P4 is true), while at the same time exploring technologies for the future that will have a beneficial effect on the interests of people not yet alive (thereby trying to bring it about that P4 is false).

Let us now turn to the problem that raises ethical or moral issues, rather than questions about facts. This is the problem of premise P3, which is ambiguous. When we talk about happiness, pleasure, welfare or any other measure of utility, are we thinking about the *total* amount of it that is distributed over a group of people, or simply about the *average*? Think of 100 people, and suppose we measure their happiness in units called "hedons". Suppose everyone is more or less equally happy and scores 50 hedons of happiness each week. So the total happiness in the group each week is 50×100, or 5000 hedons, divided equally across all. But now suppose we add 100 people who are not so happy – say, 100 people whose average happiness is only 25 hedons a week. The combined group contains 100 people who score 50 hedons each week, plus 100 who score only 25 hedons each week. So the 200 people in the combined group have a total happiness of 7500 hedons. This means that adding another 100 people to the group has increased *total* happiness, even though the *average* happiness of the whole group has now declined. Obviously, the average happiness of the group of 200 is now only 37.5 hedons each week (namely, 7500 divided by 200).

Utilitarian philosophers famously disagree on whether total or average happiness in a group is what matters. But this disagreement does not matter. For a second problem with the utilitarian premise arises whichever measure we select! Here is premise P3 again:

P3. We have a moral duty not to reduce utility, but to increase or even maximize it.

Suppose, to start with, that "utility" here refers to *total* happiness. Then the premise implies that we have a moral duty to increase the number of human lives on earth so long as that will increase the total utility in the world. What does that mean? Well, suppose we have a world population of seven billion people, and the addition of each extra person adds a life that is worth living, hence increases total utility. Then premise P3 implies that we have a moral duty to add that extra life. Yet suppose that as the planet becomes more and more crowded, and resources become ever more scarce, the addition of extra people brings down the general level of happiness until each new child that is added to the total can look forward to a life that is barely worth living. Premise P3 seems to recommend we do keep going, even though the final result is itself morally horrific: bringing children into the world in order to experience lives that are hardly worth living. This "repugnant conclusion" (a phrase coined by the philosopher Derek Parfit) looks like one we should try to avoid (Parfit 1984: ch. 17).

Can the average utilitarian do better? If "utility" in premise P3 refers to average utility, another kind of repugnant conclusion is forced on us. For P3 would then imply that we have a moral duty not to increase the number of human lives on earth if that will reduce the average utility in the world – that is, if the utility of each new person's life is lower than the average prior to the addition of the new person. But wait a moment. If we are very-very-happy people who can produce very-happy children, P3 implies that we still should not produce them, simply because the addition of very-happy people will lower the average! This looks like a kind of hedonic elitism. If happy lives are good enough, then why should we not be willing to bring into existence children who will lead happy lives, even if their lives will not be quite as happy as their parents' lives are?

Either way, it seems that premise P3 puts the utilitarian into a quandary. If total happiness is what counts, P3 encourages us to produce children even if we expect their lives to be miserable, so long as those lives are barely worth living. If average happiness is what counts, then P3 would forbid us from bringing into being children whose lives might involve a small reduction in happiness compared to our own lives. Without further argument, then, we can put utilitarianism aside, not simply because P4 is factually debatable, but also because P3 leads to morally debatable conclusions.

Disappearing beneficiaries

While the utilitarian argument was meant to convince us that we have duties to future generations, the "disappearing beneficiaries" argument points in the opposite direction and suggests that we have no duties at all to the future. Consider any transport infrastructure policy. When a decision was made in the nineteenth century to build rail networks linking towns and cities all over Europe, the result was that travel became easier, people who would never otherwise have met actually got together, and as a result marriages took place and children were born who would not otherwise have been conceived. Call those who are born as a result of a transport infrastructure policy the "Xs" and those different people who will be born otherwise in the same places, if no such policy is adopted, the "Ys" (see premise P1 in the two boxes below). Suppose the policy is a beneficial one that will improve the living standards of people in the future. The Xs will be the beneficiaries of the policy. Can we therefore say that the Xs will be worse off if the policy is dropped? No, for if the policy is dropped and the transport infrastructure is not built, then the Xs will not exist at all, and so there is no question of complaints on their behalf. Nor can the Ys legitimately complain that they have missed the benefit of the policy. For if the policy is indeed implemented, the Ys will not be born at all. Either way, no legitimate complaint about the policy can be made on behalf of anyone.

Policies on climate change, water usage, farm subsidies, energy choices and so on will all make a difference to who meets whom, and as a result make a difference to who is, or is not, born. Those who exhort us to work for the benefit of future generations need to address the counter-intuitive conclusion of the "disappearing beneficiaries" argument. Suppose, for example, we follow a policy that suits those now alive, and might be thought to harm those not yet born. For example, suppose we continue business as usual, clearing more land and basing our economies on fossil fuels as our major source of energy. This behaviour leads very quickly – let us further suppose – to activation of the tipping elements described in Chapter 1 and to massive destruction of agriculture all over the world, and other dire consequences. As a result of not adopting any mitigating policies – ones that would benefit the future inhabitants of the planet – there is an impact on who is born. Those who would have been born only if climate-mitigating policies are implemented, the Xs, will not be born at all now, precisely because we are not implementing those policies. Those who will not exist cannot be made worse off, as premise P3 below makes clear. Therefore, we are not making any of the Xs worse off, and so do not owe them any duties.

As we have seen, the argument also suggests that the future people who will actually be born as a result of our not adopting climate-mitigating policies, the Ys, cannot themselves make legitimate com-

Disappearing beneficiaries I

For any future-benefiting policy:

P1. Those who will be born as a result of our adopting the policy (call them the "Xs") will be different people from those who will be born as a result of our not adopting the policy (call them the "Ys").

P2. If we do not adopt the policy, then the Xs will not exist. [from P1]

P3. If one will not exist, then one will not be worse off.

P4. If we do not adopt the policy, then the Xs will not be worse off. [from P2 & P3]

P5. Our not adopting the policy will not make the Xs worse off. [from P4]

P6. We owe people a moral duty to adopt a certain policy only if our not adopting the policy will make them worse off.

C1. We do not owe the Xs (those who will be born as a result of our adopting the policy) any moral duty to adopt the policy. [from P5 & P6]

Disappearing beneficiaries II

For any future-benefiting policy:

P1. Those who will be born as a result of our adopting the policy (call them the "Xs") will be different people from those who will be born as a result of our not adopting the policy (call them the "Ys").

P7. If we do not adopt the policy, then (i) the Ys will exist but not benefit. But if we do adopt the future-benefiting policy, then (ii) the Ys will not exist at all. [from P1]

P8. Option (i), existing and not benefiting, is NOT worse for the Ys than option (ii), not existing at all.

P9. Our not adopting the policy will not make the Ys worse off. [from P7 & P8]

P6. We owe people a duty to adopt a certain policy only if our not adopting the policy will make them worse off.

C2. We do not owe the Ys (those who will be born as a result of our not adopting the policy) any duty to adopt the policy. [from P6 & P9]

Joining together the conclusions in the two arguments, we finally get:

C. We do not owe any future people any duty to adopt any future-benefiting policy. [from C1 & C2]

---

plaints against us for failing to adopt those policies. For if we had adopted those policies, they would not have existed at all, as premise P7 below spells out. The next crucial premise is P8, which states that existing but not benefiting from climate-mitigating strategies is no worse than not existing at all. Therefore, we have not made the Ys worse off by failing to adopt the future-benefting climate-mitigating policies, and so do not owe them any duties. Putting together the conclusions regarding the Xs and the Ys, the result is the ultimate conclusion C: that we do not owe any future people any duty to adopt any future-benefiting policy – be they the ones who would be born as a result of the policy being adopted (i.e. the Xs) or the ones who would be born as a result of the policy not being adopted (i.e. the Ys).

This may seem like a weird conclusion until we think through the implications of the idea that the identities of those who exist in future depend very much on the policies we choose to pursue now. Those who do not exist in future because of our present policies have no claim on us, unless we can make sense of the nonexistent having a claim on the existent. But that notion just does not seem to make sense. Moreover, those who will exist only because of our present policies – even when these policies do not benefit the future – will have no basis for complaining to us either. Why not? The Ys are those who will come into being as a result of our not adopting future-benefiting policies. It is exactly our non-adoption of those policies that has brought the Ys into existence. So, unless – what seems unlikely – their lives are not worth living (that is, it would have been better for them not to exist at all), they have no grounds for complaint against us for our non-adoption of those policies.

A simple mistake?

The details of the "disappearing beneficiaries" argument may seem technical and complicated. The bare bones are given in the above two boxes summarizing the two parts of the argument. When combined, the resulting argument shows how philosophical problems can arise quite unexpectedly over something that might seem to be too obvious to worry about; namely, that we should simply try to leave the planet in as good a state as possible to future generations. We shall now argue that much of the cleverness of the argument is misdirected, for it is based on a simple mistake.

There are two objections to the complete argument. The first is that premise P8 may actually be false. Many scientists are already predicting that large-scale ecological disasters will happen as a result of human-caused climate change. These will include an increasing displacement of people, crop failures, and huge population movements inside and between countries as changing weather patterns and rising sea levels make previously inhabitable and productive areas no longer habitable. Ecological refugees appear in increasing numbers, warfare breaks out, perhaps triggering large-scale nuclear exchanges and the planet is plunged into chaos. If anything like that actually happened then, owing to the failure of present and previous human generations to take preventive measures on climate change, it might actually be better for those future people not to be born. In such a scenario premise P8 would not be true.

Here is an analogy. Imagine that you are a parent thinking of sending your children to a new school. You have a choice over which school to use. The one that is nearby is dirty, decrepit and full of bullying, abuse and violence. You learn that more than 70 per cent of the children going to that school will suffer physical abuse at some point. Would good parents inflict such schooling on their children? If the children do go to that school and suffer bullying, persecution and low standards of education, they would be justified in complaining that their parents failed to look after them properly. Likewise, if the earth becomes – in a relatively short time – a decrepit junkyard where people experience horrific suffering, war, environmental disasters, disease and poverty, then the people living then would have grounds for complaint against the present generation for putting them in that situation. The analogy suggests that we do have a duty not to deprive future people of an environment and minimum living standard in which their dignity can be respected. Recall that the Ys are the people who do not exist if we adopt certain climate-mitigating policies. So if we do not adopt these policies, and the Ys do come into being (and have to suffer horribly) then they will be justified in complaining that we have wronged them by bringing them into a world where human life is not worth living.

The second criticism is more significant, because it does not depend on thinking about possible scenarios. There seems to be a simple point the "disappearing beneficiaries" argument has overlooked. There is a significant group of future people, namely those who will be born anyway (call them the "Zs") regardless of whether or not we adopt certain policies. In terms of numbers, the Zs are a significantly large group of people, just like the Xs and the Ys. The crucial difference is that unlike the Xs and the Ys, the Zs are not "disappearing beneficiaries". The Zs are those future people who will be born anyway regardless of what environmental policies this generation adopts. And the Zs will also be affected by the consequences of this generation's policies. So, it is clear that the Zs will be made worse off by us not adopting environmental policies that will benefit them. Thus, it is clear that we owe the Zs a duty of care, minimally a duty not to make the environment that they will be living in unliveable. The "disappearing beneficiaries" argument is a fraud. For it makes the illegitimate jump to the final conclusion C, claiming that we do not owe any duties to future people. This mistake is the result of strangely overlooking the Zs, an important group of future people, the existence of whom is sufficient to impose on this generation a responsibility to take good care of the earth's environment for their sake.

Like the utilitarian argument discussed earlier, the "disappearing beneficiaries" argument is a sneaky one. By careful scrutiny of the logic of the argument, we have seen through its rhetorical veneer. Under the surface, the skeleton of the argument has revealed serious deficiencies in it. Once we see what is wrong with the argument, then there is nothing in it that should distract us from a perfectly sound moral concern for the large number of future people whose welfare will be very much influenced by what we do now.

Younger generations

We now introduce an argument inspired by Avner de Shalit's (1994) claim that future generations of people are not radically separated from present generations. After all, what do we mean by a "future generation"? Many people regard their children as representing the future, and when they grow old enough to become grandparents they can think of the situation that their children, and their children's children, face. The older people in a community do not just have theoretical obligations to yet unborn future generations. Instead, they have obligations to real people: their children, their grandchildren, and their great-grandchildren. It is on this network of obligations among real people

---

Younger generation argument
P1. People owe a moral duty to younger (but current) generations not to reduce their capacity to satisfy their needs and desires.
P2. The younger generations' capacity to satisfy their needs and desires positively depends on (i) how many environmental resources are available to them and (ii) how good their technologies are.
P3. We owe a moral duty to our younger generations not to overconsume environmental resources without compensating them with sufficiently better technologies. [from P1 & P2]
P4. Our younger generations owe their younger generations the same moral duty. [from P1 & P2]
P5. Our younger generations' younger generations owe their younger generations the same moral duty. [from P1 & P2]
and so on …

of different ages that the younger generation argument is based.

Unlike the earlier arguments, this one is really short and easy to follow. Let us think of the children and grandchildren of people now alive as forming a current younger generation. The older people owe some responsibilities to them, including responsibilities not to reduce the younger generation's capacity for satisfying its needs and desires. Now, as we saw in the case of the utilitarian argument, we have to either pass on good technology to the younger generation or ensure that any reduction in environmental resources is compensated for by developing new technologies that can compensate for reduced resources. Putting all that together, leads simply to an argument that is more convincing than the ones already assessed.

Some people might want to query the idea that we owe duties of any kind to our children and grandchildren. But luckily the view that parents owe their children a duty of care is widely accepted. Further, our love, care and concern for our children and grandchildren is not morally problematic. On the contrary, it is one of the most fundamental features of human life all over the world, independent of religious and cultural frameworks. So if once this set of cares, obligations and duties is acknowledged, then there is a reason to care about the future of the planet. For future generations are already sharing the planet with us, and we have duties to them, just as they have duties to their children and grandchildren and so on.

One final point about the future needs to be considered in the context of developing an environmental ethic. So far, we have only thought about future generations of humans. But what about the animals, plants, land forms, rivers and mountains? Do they have any part to play in our thinking about the future? Might we have duties to some of them, as well as to the coming generations of human beings? As we saw in Chapter 1, an ethic that focuses purely on human beings as the sole objects of value in the world is anthropocentric. While it is perfectly all right to think about the future in anthropocentric terms, and while human interests now and in the future may inspire us to work hard to conserve plants, animals and natural environments, many philosophers have argued for favourable moral consideration to be given to non-human nature. We finish the chapter by looking at just one argument that suggests there are valuable things on earth besides human beings, and – if that argument has force – it raises the big question: to what non-human things do we have moral responsibilities?

The last people argument

Suppose a huge pandemic has wiped out nearly all the people on the planet. By a weird quirk of fate, the infection has left the survivors in poor health and completely unable to reproduce. As the human species dwindles in numbers desperate attempts are made to use existing stores of eggs and healthy sperm and the technology for assisting infertile people in order to produce new children. But it is all to no avail. In fact, it becomes increasingly clear that humans are going to disappear from the face of the earth. The last people still have access to high technology, the legacy of civilizations and science that will never be seen on earth again. Some of them, depressed and bitter, wonder if there is any point at all in leaving anything alive at all after the end of humanity. One of them reflects ruefully on the closing lines of T. S. Eliot's poem, "The Hollow Men": "This is the way the world ends / Not with a bang but a whimper".

They wonder if it might be better just to end the whole thing with a bang: a bang big enough to completely destroy all remaining life on earth. Others, less depressed, are horrified at the prospect of such vandalism. How can their fellow human beings even contemplate such a horrific act, they wonder. The "big bang" advocates point out that they are not advocating the death or killing of any human beings. They will arrange things so the destruction of all other life on the planet only happens after the last human being has died. What, they say, can be wrong with that? With no humans left to taste the food, savour the beauty, and enjoy the sights and sounds of nature, what does it matter if all other species are wiped out?

Big issues are at stake here. To what do we owe moral duties or moral consideration? If our only duties are to other people, then what would be wrong with the last people destroying all other life on earth, so long as in doing so they destroy no people? If we owe no duties to non-people, then there is no obligation on the last people to leave animals, trees, flowers, fish, flies or any other living things behind them. In the story we have just told, both groups of people probably agree that there is lots of value in plant and animal life. Vegetarians and vegans eat various plants with pleasure; meat eaters delight in consuming parts of some animals; people enjoy spending time with companion animals; others love the sights and sounds of nature; scientists study living things, painters are inspired by them; and so on. All these ways of being valuable are ways of being valuable with reference to human interests and purposes. If we value things for their beauty, their taste, for the pleasure we get from observing their behaviour, then these are all ways of valuing things as a means to our ends. Such instrumental value will disappear when people die. So, if instrumental value to people is all the value that non-human things have, then why would it be wrong to destroy them after all humans have gone?

The problem about the last people raises very neatly the question of whether things that are not human have only instrumental value. We already introduced in the opening chapter the distinction between intrinsic and instrumental value, noting that it is not an exclusive one. While Kant thought we had to show moral consideration towards humans and all rational beings in general, he thought there was no question about whether we had duties towards dogs or other animals. In his *Lectures on Ethics*, he insisted that shooting a dog that was no longer of service was not a failure of duty to the dog "for the dog cannot judge," but was instead a failure in our duties towards other human beings. Kindness to animals encourages us to be kinder in our behaviour towards other people. Kant's view on the moral status of animals strikes many people as plainly wrong. Even though dogs cannot judge, cannot verbally complain about their treatment and cannot argue with people, there are still better and worse ways to treat them. If you think in this way about dogs, then you will think that it is wrong to say that only humans are ends in themselves. Perhaps dogs too are non-instrumentally valuable. That is, they are valuable even if they are of no use to anyone else, and so deserve respect, care and protection from harm even if no one finds them useful.

Since human beings are usually seen as the paradigm case of things that are intrinsically valuable, the intrinsic value, or inherent worth, or dignity of a human being is the foundation of the idea of universal human rights. Each person, it is believed, is born with an inherent worth, or value, which should be respected and protected from harm,

---

Last people argument
P1. We ought to be morally outraged by the suggestion of destroying all non-human things and beings on earth after the demise of the last people.
P2. The best explanation for our warranted moral outrage is that at least some of the non-human things and beings on earth have a value in their own right, independently of their use for human beings.
C. At least some of the non-human things and beings on earth have a value in their own right, independently of their use for human beings. [argument to the best explanation, from P1 & P2]

regardless of whether the person is useful to others or not. The important question in the last people argument is whether any non-human things and beings on earth likewise have intrinsic value. If so, then the last people would be acting wrongly if they set out to destroy all the non-human life on earth. For in setting out to do this, they would be setting out to destroy things of value in themselves, values independent of their usefulness to human beings.

In some ancient cultures, very rich and powerful people (lords, princes or emperors) sometimes arranged for their concubines and servants to be killed and buried with them after their own demise. There was no point for their concubines and servants to go on living, for they were not seen to have any value or status in their own right. Rather, they existed simply for the use and service to the rich and powerful. Nowadays, we would be outraged by such ideas. For each human being, we have accepted, is intrinsically valuable. Each human being deserves to live and be let live simply for his or her own sake. The story of the last people's plan to destroy all the non-human things and beings on earth after their own demise can be seen as an intuition test, designed to provoke a similar feeling of outrage from the reader. Like the rich and powerful of ancient times, the last people would plan to destroy every non-human thing on earth that will no longer be useful to them. If the story of the last people elicits a repulsed response from you, if you feel a sense of outrage towards the last people's plan, then, arguably, your outrage is evidence showing that the non-human things and beings on earth do have a certain value in themselves, which should be respected, treasured and protected, regardless of whether they would be useful to any future people.

Putting this another way: we are only outraged by the idea of the last people planning to destroy all the non-humans on earth if we think those non-human beings are to some extent valuable in themselves and should be protected from harm independently of their service to the last people. So, the story of the last people provides premises for an argument to the best explanation, pointing to the conclusion that at least some non-humans beings on earth have intrinsic value. Postulating that non-human things on earth have intrinsic value is the best explanation for our feeling moral outrage towards the last people's plan for global destruction. As we already saw in Chapter 1, this form of argument is quite compelling and is used in many areas of the sciences and also in detective work. No other equally simple explanation seems to fit the fact of the moral outrage felt towards the global destruction plan. Provided the story of the last people evokes moral outrage in the readers, then the best hypothesis to explain this outrage is that things other than people have intrinsic value. Humans, in other words, are not the sole possessors of intrinsic value.

The last people argument was originally put forward as a purely science-fiction example (Routley & Routley 1980), for it was doubtful whether even massive nuclear explosions or release of chemical weapons could actually bring about the destruction of all life on earth. In the past thirty years, the situation has changed. There are now a number of scientists who have expressed concerns about a runaway greenhouse effect, one in which increasing and irreversible changes brought about by the continued injection of carbon into the atmosphere ultimately lead to the demise of all life on earth and the irreversible heating of the planet to the point at which the seas boil away. Warnings about such a scenario have been issued by senior scientists, including James Hansen, Director of NASA's Goddard Institute, and therefore provide the basis for a more realistic last people scenario. As Hansen has emphasized, given the sophistication of our contemporary knowledge and model-ling skills, we cannot claim ignorance about the risks associated with continuing "business as usual" in the high-carbon economy. What is different from the Routleys' original scenario is that the destruction of life on earth would not occur rapidly: the unfolding disaster of runa-way climate change would seem relatively slow by reference to human timescales – unfolding over centuries (Hansen *et al.* 2007). This new scenario poses an even grimmer moral choice than the original. By knowing what we know and continuing business as usual, our present form of life is threatening both human and non-human life alike. We would be like parents with a brood of young children who are gambling away the family fortune while another baby is on the way. Humans have in the past turned fertile lands into barren wastes by forest clearing and agriculture. Runaway climate change would extend such destruction to the entire globe.

There is much more to be said about value, responsibility and the duties of human beings towards future people, nature and non-human things and beings on earth. These ideas will feature again in the follow-ing chapters. For now, we simply note that in considering our duties to the future, it is not just future generations of humans that count. The last people argument has shown that there may well be other values at stake apart from the values of human life and human experience. In the fol-lowing chapters we consider extending the scope of intrinsic value first to animals, then to living things in general. But even this broader scope may not be wide enough to capture our sense of what we owe to nature and its denizens. Could there also be intrinsic value in landscapes, forests, rivers, lakes, mountains and ecosystems themselves? Whether value can be found in such things, or even whether the attribution of value to them makes sense, will be explored in Chapters 5 and 6. Expanding the scope of intrinsic value also means expanding the scope of human care and responsibility. Things that are of intrinsic value make a claim on us – they are the things we are obliged to care about, show moral respect for and treat in an appropriate way. Just what the scope of such responsibilities is will now be explored in more detail.

three

Animals: are they as morally valuable as human beings?

Animals and human beings

Philosophers and scientists in the past were often inspired by the examples of sympathy, intelligence and nobility in animals to draw comparisons between them and us. The use of animals in experiments is criticized by a character in Shakespeare's play *Cymbeline*. When the queen declares she will test some poisonous compounds on animals – "such creatures as / We count not worth the hanging" as she puts it – Cornelius, a physician, protests: "Your highness / Shall from this practice but make hard your heart" (*Cymbeline* I.v), the same worry expressed by Kant two hundred years later. The Renaissance essayist and philosopher Michel de Montaigne wondered whether when he played with his cat she was actually playing with him, and was often unable to resist his dog's demands for attention.

Montaigne

[T]here is a kind of respect and a duty in man as a genus which link us not merely to the beasts, which have life and feelings, but even to trees and plants. We owe justice to men: and to the other creatures who are able to receive them, we owe gentleness and kindness. Between them and us there is some sort of intercourse and a degree of mutual obligation. I am not afraid to admit that my nature is so childishly affectionate that I cannot easily refuse an untimely gambol to my dog wherever it begs one.   ("On Cruelty" [1588], in Montaigne 1991: bk II, essay 11)

In his "Apology for Raymond Sebond", Montaigne lists examples – many of them clearly fictitious – of the nobility of animals, and their similarities to humans (we weep when we lose animals we love, he states, and then asks "do they not do the same when they lose us?" [1991: bk II, essay 12]). Even before Montaigne, the witty "Disputation of the Donkey" (1417) showed that some writers, like its author Anselm Turmeda, strongly disapproved of cruelty towards animals and believed it not at all obvious that humans were superior in dignity or merit to animals. In the disputation, the animals and the humans debate over whether humans are really more noble than the animals. In a brilliant rhetorical move, the disputation depicts the animals as picking the most miserable of their kind – a mangy donkey without a tail – to present the case for the nobility of animals against Friar Anselm. The poor friar goes on to lose eighteen of the nineteen arguments, only winning the debate by a final appeal to the claim that God appeared on earth in human form, thereby establishing the "true" superiority of humans over the animals.

David Hume, the great Scottish Enlightenment thinker, devoted a whole section of *An Enquiry Concerning Human Understanding* to the question of whether animals are rational. In *A Treatise of Human Nature*, he wrote: "Next to the ridicule of denying an evident truth, is that of taking much pains to defend it; and no truth appears to me more evident, than that beasts are endow'd with thought and reason as well as men. The arguments are in this case so obvious, that they never escape the most stupid and ignorant" (2001: I, iii, 16). For Hume, as for many

---

Similarities
- Basic emotions and dispositions – fear, frustration, disappointment, content, satisfaction, suspicion, trust – seem to be much the same in humans and animals.
- Sociability is a feature of many animal species, which live in communities, with rules, hierarchical structures.
- Some animals seem to possess what were once thought to be purely human abilities. For example: the magpie's aesthetic judgements in nest building; the canine's loyalty to his family; the killer ape cruelty that chimpanzees are capable of in territorial disputes.
- Companion animals share communities with human beings.
- Work animals contribute to human communities.
- Some wild animals also accept human beings as companions and friends.
- Some animals seem to have the ability to enjoy a good animal life in the way that human beings can enjoy a good human life.

Sources: Morris (1967, 1994), Russell (2002)

contemporary writers, the similarities between humans and animals did not involve just reason and emotion, but also basic anatomical and physiological processes, as well as the capacity for aesthetic judgement, the ability to live in social groups and the intelligence to integrate into human social structures.

Human treatment of animals

For the rest of this chapter, we shall take animal similarity to human beings as an established fact. The history of physiology since the nineteenth century supports the idea that there are enormous commonalities between human and animal physiology and body chemistry, to such an extent that animal models are now indispensable in the understanding and treatment of human disease. The studies of twentieth-century ethologists such as Niko Tinbergen, Konrad Lorenz, Robert Ardrey and Desmond Morris show that animals are subjects of centred social and emotional lives that are similar to human ones. A problem immediately arises. If animals are so close to us physiologically that we can study human health and disease using animal experiments, and if they are so like us that we can learn from their behaviour facts about the emotional and psychological importance of family and maternal support, the way to build functioning communities and the destructive effects of anxiety and stress – if these similarities are real – then are we not obliged to give animals the same moral consideration we give to human beings?

People generally condemn practices that involve the systematic killing of human beings, those that cause large-scale human suffering, and those that deprive humans of liberty by confinement or slavery. Yet many people find it quite acceptable for animals to be subjected to apparently very similar kinds of treatment. This is a difference that has prompted thinkers to explore the idea that animals deserve moral protection and consideration to the same degree that humans do. If this idea is accepted then it has important consequences, for it will show the possibility of extending the circle of moral care and concern beyond the world of human beings. To extend the circle of concern in this way would be significant for two reasons. First, it would change dramatically the way we think about acting towards animals and using products derived from them – whether in food, clothing or medicine. Second, it would open the possibility of further extensions of ethical concern – to other parts of nature, to a variety of living things apart from animals – and this has been a question for recent environmental philosophy.

> *Exploitation*
> What humans regularly do to animals:
> - Kill them for food, textiles, furs, ivory, medicinal products, and so on.
> - Breed, intensively confine and manipulate them for milk products, pâtés, eggs, cheap meat, and so on.
> - Subject them to prolonged immobilization or other deprivation for special meat products or for metabolic studies.
> - Kill and harm them in scientific research in education, medicine, drug testing, weapons testing, and so on.
> - Kill (cull, eradicate) unwanted animals in pounds, and by shooting, trapping, coursing, and so on.
> - Kill (hunt, collect) for recreational purposes, sport, "connecting with nature", and so on.
> - Confine in zoos, wildlife parks, homes (as companions, pets, or display items).
> - Exploit their labour in agriculture, recreation, transport, policing, warfare, and so on.
> - Kill, injure and displace them through destruction of natural habitats.
> - Injure and kill them by driving vehicles on roads that do not exclude animals.
> - Breed experimental crosses (show dogs, tumbler pigeons) for a variety of human interests.
> - Produce experimental clones and breed transgenic animals with abnormalities for medical, agricultural and military research

Think how different the word would be if animals were given the same protection that human beings enjoy. At present, if certain non-human things are obstacles to human progress, development or profit, then they are removed for the sake of human interests. As we saw in Chapter 1, plenty of people accept the practice of culling so-called "pest" animals that threaten human safety, damage agricultural resources (hence farming profits) or threaten indigenous species. The killing of introduced or "feral" animals would have to be rethought entirely if animals enjoyed higher protection. At the same time, many governments and voters in democratic countries support the clearance of forests and natural landscapes for new farmlands, mining, and the building of new roads, new cities and suburbs. Such developments create jobs and wealth, and improve the living conditions of many people, but at the expense of the lives and well-being of many animals, as well as contributing to pollution, climate change and species loss. In this case, too, serious protection for animals would diminish the impact of some of these behaviours and have huge economic implications.

It is important not to overestimate the benefits that would come to animals were they better protected. Given that the world is unjust, many groups of people suffer discrimination and displacement and fail to have their human rights respected. So even if animals were given more protection, it would not mean heaven for them. As we shall show in the final chapter, the clearing of land, building of dams and pursuit of development are often carried out at the expense of human life and freedom and the destruction of functional human communities, all despite the fact that there are international agreements about respect for human rights.

In reply, it can be admitted that some groups of human beings (slaves, prisoners, poor people, refugees, people from certain racial, ethnic or religious backgrounds) have been – and still are – treated in ways very similar to how animals have always been treated by human beings. But this situation has now become a real concern to advocacy and human rights groups and to many ordinary people as well. Although slavery still exists, there is near universal condemnation of it, and serious attempts are being made to eliminate it along with the evils of traffic in human beings. The enslavement – or worse – of animals is, by contrast, something that the majority of people are comfortable with, and they also appear to be quite comfortable using the animal products generated by the use and abuse of animals. If the closeness in physiology and behaviour between humans and animals were to become a ground for treating animals more like humans and for reducing the unthinking imposition of pain, injury and a range of other harms on them, this would probably mean a major change in the way the world is organized, and a major reduction in the amount of frustration, suffering and pain endured by animals because of human action.

Questioning human treatment of animals

Since the animals that we kill or otherwise exploit are very similar to us in some fundamental ways, there is a major puzzle to be solved. We seem much more ready to extend our sympathy to another human than towards an animal. Animals have been used by humans for thousands of years, and it may be that our emotions reflect the way animals have served our material interests. If the cost of giving up the practices that harm animals is very high, then – for the sake of our own peace of mind – we may choose to curb our sympathy for the animals, instead of changing our exploitative practices. This limiting of our sympathy may make sense of why animals seem to get such a bad deal. If sympathy is at the heart of our ethical responses to people, then it seems unlikely that we are incapable of feeling sympathy for animals. Instead, it may be that most people divert their attention away from questions of animal suffering and pain. By focusing on the material benefits derived from the uses of animals, we can overlook many of the harms that would otherwise prompt our compassion and fellow-feeling. If we start paying attention to animals, there may be the prospect of compassion and sympathy (see "The flea", page 103).

On the other hand, some writers have queried the idea of whether what is "natural" to us matters at all. Singer has drawn comparisons between the attitude most people take towards animals, and the attitude that some people take towards those of other races. For Singer, our discrimination against animals is just like the discrimination that some people show towards those of other races, and both kinds of discrimination may be "natural". Suppose, then, that people are naturally inclined to be less sympathetic towards those in other racial or ethnic groups. In addition, suppose that it is also natural for us to feel even less sympathy for animals. Singer's question is whether such supposedly natural human inclinations are morally appropriate or inappropriate. If they are appropriate, then there must be something else apart from "naturalness" that makes them appropriate. What, then, are the objective grounds that justify people's preferential inclinations and feelings towards their own kind? On the other hand, if racial and species preferences are not morally appropriate, then what ground is there for determining that, and what kind of education and legislation is called for as a way of counteracting our natural inclinations?

These questions raise an issue for the whole philosophical tradition of the West, which has been undeniably anthropocentric. The tradition has either assigned intrinsic value to human beings alone or has assigned significantly greater intrinsic value to human beings than to anything non-human. By "intrinsic value" we refer here to the value something has independent of its usefulness, that is, regardless of whether it is a means to (instrumental to) some other end. Human beings are the prime example of things of non-instrumental value. On the other hand, dairy cattle clearly have instrumental value in providing milk and cheese for human consumption. In the traditional Western view of animals, dairy cattle either have no intrinsic value, or have very much less than humans have.

What might be the reasons for thinking that human beings are more intrinsically valuable than animals and all the other non-human things on earth? The usual answer is that humans possess certain special qualities such as self-awareness, intelligence, free will, a moral sense: things that non-human beings either lack or have in only negligible degrees. Supposedly, it is only in virtue of these special qualities that something can be intrinsically valuable, and only intrinsically valuable beings and things deserve respect, love, care and protection from harm. In addition, many traditional ethical perspectives are meritocratic, in that they believe that those who are significantly higher up on the scale of intrinsic value are entitled to dominate and benefit from those who are significantly lower down or at the bottom of the scale.

These traditional anthropocentric and meritocratic ways of thinking structure much of our thinking about matters of right and wrong, and how to prioritize conflicting interests. The interests of those who are lower down on the intrinsic value scale are often sacrificed for the sake for the interests of those who are higher up on the scale. Intrinsic value is a measure of someone's status and bargaining power in the evaluative and moral discourse of right and wrong. Consider, for example, the sacrifice of animals in scientific research into new and better ways of treating and preventing human diseases. Why is that morally defensible? When confronted with this challenge, most people will reply that it is because the life of a human being is much more intrinsically valuable than the life of an animal. When human lives are at stake, human interests nearly always outweigh those of non-human things and beings. Similarly, the use of animals and animal products in agriculture, the food industry, the textile industry, zoos, circuses and recreational hunting can all be defended in the same way by combining anthropocentrism and meritocracy. If human beings are indeed vastly more intrinsically valuable than all the non-human beings on earth, and if those who are vastly less intrinsically valuable or not at all intrinsically valuable are nothing more than instruments and resources to be used for the benefits of those who are highly intrinsically valuable, then it will follow that human beings are indeed morally permitted to exploit all the non-human things and beings on earth in any way they like – so long as human interests are promoted.

Anthropocentric meritocratic positions will for ease of reference be called "anthropocentrism" in what follows. Such positions usually recognize that people can behave wrongly regarding non-human things and beings. I can behave wrongly towards you regarding the cake on the table if I take the slice that was meant for you. The cake itself has no interests that I harm by taking it. But if you were looking forward to eating your slice of cake, then I harm your interests by taking it. My behaviour regarding the cake was wrong, but the wrong I did was a wrong to you. For anthropocentrism, many of our acts can be wrong regarding animals, although the wrongness involved is never seen as a direct wrong done to the non-human. Rather, any wrongness involved in an act towards a non-human being is ultimately derived from and explained in terms of its harms (or potential harms) towards the human. As already noted, Kant thought that cruelty towards animals is wrong only to the extent that it might desensitize people to cruelty towards humans. For Kant, only humans count in morality. Our duty not to be cruel to animals is owed directly to humans and not to the animals themselves. Likewise, anthropocentrists will only admit indirect (or non-intrinsic) wrongness in human-caused environmental devastation. For such destruction is wrong only to the extent that it can damage human interests and well-being, which is materially dependent on a sustainable environment.

The "Merit" argument contains three premises and two conclusions. The first premise claims that human beings have certain qualities and abilities that animals lack or barely have. Premise P2 claims that those qualities and abilities are morally so special that their possession completely determines a being's intrinsic moral worth and status. The core idea of P2 is that the more a being possesses those special qualities and abilities, the more intrinsically valuable it is. So, if one being has more of those qualities and abilities than another, then the first is more intrinsi-

---

Merit

The anthropocentric/meritocratic argument

P1. Human beings possess certain qualities (e.g. self-awareness, intelligence, free will, moral sense) that animals and non-humans in general lack or barely have. [empirical premise]

P2. Those who possess the qualities in question to a greater extent are more intrinsically valuable, whereas those who possess the qualities to a lesser degree are less intrinsically valuable. [evaluative premise]

C1. Human beings are much more intrinsically valuable than animals and non-humans in general, whose intrinsic value, if any, is merely negligible. [human superiority over non-humans, from P1 and P2]

P3. It is morally justified to treat those who are not intrinsically valuable, or are negligibly so, as nothing but instruments or resources to be used for the benefit of those who are highly intrinsically valuable. [evaluative premise]

C2. It is morally justifiable to treat animals and non-humans in general as nothing but instruments or resources to be used for the benefit of human beings. [human exploitation of non-humans, from C1 and P3]

cally valuable than that other. If something completely lacks those qualities and abilities, then it is not intrinsically valuable at all. Together with P1, P2 logically entails the intermediate conclusion C1, the claim that human beings are significantly more intrinsically valuable than animals.

The next step of the anthropocentric argument, when laid out formally and strictly as in the box "Merit", is to employ an additional moral premise P3. This claims that whoever is significantly more intrinsically valuable is morally justified in using and exploiting those who are significantly less so. The idea of this premise is a bit like saying that the biggest guy in town should be allowed to extort from those who are weaker, only in this case what is being compared is not who is the most powerful in term of physical force, but instead who is the most intelligent, self-aware, free and moral. The last of these properties is a bit odd. Suppose for the moment that it is all right to take the superiority of human intelligence as a justification for using and killing animals to serve human ends and interests. Does the appeal to a sense of right and wrong work in the same way? Instead of thinking about humans versus animals, think of this idea in relation to two groups of humans. Suppose one group claims to be the moral superiors of the other. Can they then argue that because they are morally better than the other group then they should be allowed to use and even kill people from the other group?

Such an appeal to moral superiority looks very weird. The very idea of using others to serve one's own ends seems inherently at odds with the idea of being a moral person. The only case where a moral person would be able to use others in any way at all would be where the "others" in question have no moral worth or status whatsoever. In that case, damage to their well-being will not pose any moral problem at all. It is exactly this way of thinking that the anthropocentric argument aims to justify. Conclusion C1 concludes that the moral worth and status of animals, if any, is completely negligible compared to that of human beings. Premise P3 then adds to the argument a further idea: the thought that things with negligible intrinsic value can justifiably be sacrificed for the sake of those who possess significantly higher intrinsic value. As a result, animals, given their negligible worth, do not really count in the moral calculus of right and wrong. Hence, the argument ends with the final conclusion C2, claiming that whatever human beings do to animals, the humans can do nothing wrong, given their superiority over the animals.

As we shall see later, the argument just analysed is only one particular version of a more general argument for anthropocentrism, which takes human beings as having superiority over everything else on earth, not just over animals.

Critical discussion

Premise P1 is arguably a factual claim. Given that there are p
cal tests for qualities such as self-awareness and intelligence, its claim
can be empirically verified to some extent. To be credible, the defender
of P1 needs to give clear and objective criteria and procedures for measuring each of the qualities mentioned. To be unbiased, the defender
of P1 must also be willing for those standards to be applied to human
beings. This would mean allowing the possibility that not all human
beings are the same in the degree to which they possess those qualities
and abilities. Given the varied circumstances under which people are
born, raised, educated and treated in life, there is no reason to think that
all human beings will be exactly the same in self-awareness, intelligence,
free will and moral sense.

Seen as a factual claim, defence of P1 is problematic. The anthropocentrist will have a hard time dealing with the many studies that
seem to show that higher mammals do display some significant levels of
self-awareness and intelligence of different kinds. Even non-mammals
such as pigeons can carry out simple reasoning tasks, and an octopus
can solve a maze problem in order to find food. The self-awareness and
kinds of intelligence displayed by some mammals seem no less than that
displayed by a young human child or a human adult with some kinds
of brain damage. So, the fact that an individual is a member of the species *Homo sapiens* (i.e. biologically human) is by itself no guarantee of
superior mental powers. Many human beings are born with deficits that
impede the development of mental qualities and abilities any greater
than those of dogs or cats, and many other will lose those qualities
and abilities either through accident or misfortune, or in the natural
course of aging. It does seem directly contradictory to experimental and
factual evidence to claim that all human beings (including the severely
mentally handicapped, the irrecoverably demented, the highly dependent addicts, the brain-damaged and the psychopathic serial rapists and
killers) are more self-aware, more intelligent, more free and are more
morally conscientious than all animals. Such a sweeping claim, which
puts all human beings on a par with each other and all of them above all
of the non-human animals, appears to be simply false as a matter of fact.

By contrast, premise P2 is a moral claim that links something's intrinsic value directly and solely to its possession of the special qualities
and abilities identified in P1. Intrinsic value, according to P2, should
be assigned to things solely according to the degree to which they possess the special qualities and abilities in question. If a being possesses

those qualities and abilities to a high degree, then it is highly intrinsically valuable. If a being possesses those qualities and abilities only to a negligible degree compared to others, then the being's intrinsic value is also negligible compared to that of others. If a being completely lacks those qualities and abilities, then it is not intrinsically valuable at all.

Here is a surprising feature of the argument. If premise P2 is true, then given that not all human beings have those special qualities to the same degree, it will follow from P2 that not all human beings have equal intrinsic moral value, worth and status. Those human beings who are less self-aware, less intelligent, and have less free will and little moral sense will be inferior in their intrinsic value, worth and status to other humans. In addition, if P3 is also true, then it will follow that people who possess more of the special qualities and abilities to a greater extent will be justified in using and exploiting people who possess those qualities and abilities to a lesser extent. Premises P2 and P3 can be used to construct an argument for one group of human beings legitimately having dominion over another group and that argument is structurally exactly the same as the argument for human dominance over animals.

In the parallel argument, premise P1* points to the factual (empirical) observation that human beings do not all share equally the special qualities in question. For example, people with brain damage or serious mental deficits often have less self-awareness and lower intelligence than other people. Irrecoverable drug addicts and those suffering from

---

Human inequality

P1*. Some human beings possess certain qualities (e.g. self-awareness, intelligence, free will, moral sense) that some other human beings lack or barely have. [empirical premise]

P2. Those who possess the qualities in question to a greater extent are more intrinsically valuable, whereas those who possess the qualities to a lesser degree are less intrinsically valuable. [evaluative premise]

C1*. Some human beings are much more intrinsically valuable than some other human beings, whose intrinsic value, if any, is merely negligible. [human inequality, from P1* and P2]

P3. It is morally justified to treat those who are not intrinsically valuable, or are negligibly so, as nothing but instruments or resources to be used for the benefit of those who are highly intrinsically valuable. [evaluative premise]

C2*. It is morally justifiable to treat some human beings as nothing but instruments or resources to be used for the benefit of some other human beings. [human exploitation of humans, from C1* and P3]

obsessive compulsive disorders have less free will than others. Psycho-pathic serial rapists and killers lack the moral sense that other people have. Some human beings (perhaps Aristotle, Einstein, Gandhi) have some of the desirable qualities to a high degree, while most people have a mixture of those qualities in varied amounts. There is no guarantee that any such quality or ability will be equally, uniformly and uniquely shared by all and only human beings.

Given premise P1*, the empirical facts of human diversity in qualities and abilities, the moral principle P2 will inevitably produce the result, C1*, which directly contradicts a general and deeply held conviction. This is the idea that all human beings are equal in their intrinsic value, worth and moral status, simply because they are human beings and regardless of whatever qualities and abilities they happened to have or lost. The conclusion of studying this parallel argument is significant. Anthropocentrism cannot consistently endorse the moral principle P2 in the argument for the superiority of humans over animals, without at the same time allowing the very same principle to be used to argue that some human beings are superior to others. Likewise, the anthropo-centrist employs the additional moral principle P3 to justify the second anthropocentric conclusion C2, that humans should be allowed to use and exploit animals. To be consistent, the anthropocentrism would apparently have to allow the same principle to be used to argue for the meritocratic oppressive view that some human beings should be allowed to use and exploit some other human beings.

A tragic aspect of human history is that something like the argument for human inequality lay behind attempts to justify slavery and – up to the middle of the twentieth century – also underpinned attempts to validate the supposed superiority of white Europeans over the rest of the world. After the horrors of the Holocaust became well known, the United Nations published a series of declarations on race. The first of these, published in 1950, was composed by the anthropologist Ashley Montagu, and declared that "scientists have reached general agreement in recognizing that mankind is one: that all men belong to the same spe-cies, Homo Sapiens" (Montagu 1950). The need for these declarations was not just a reaction to the repellent actions of anti-Semitic regimes. It was also driven by the recognition that a programme aimed at scien-tifically justifying white superiority had been systematically conducted over the past three-quarters of a century. This supposedly "scientific racism" had been searching for a measurable physical feature or ratio on the basis of which a further set of characteristics – social, political, linguistic and so on – could be ascribed. These latter characteristics were precisely those that had been deemed capable of setting up an order of different groups of human beings in relation to a supreme ideal: the white European.

The basis of scientific racism was a combination of factual and theoretical ideas on the one hand and ethical counterparts of these on the other. The basic motive was to classify *Homo sapiens* into subspecies or varieties. The scholars who worked on race were convinced that some test or measure must be available by which it would be possible to identify those races of humans that had degenerated to a stage where their entitlement to self-determination was questionable (see Malik 1996). Colonization could then be regarded as a civilizing influence on people who were not really capable of managing their own affairs. The very same degeneration was also supposed to be present in European society itself: the Irish, the poor and the working classes were themselves regarded as subvarieties of privileged white races. In fact, race, class and nation were not clearly distinguished in late-nineteenth-century Britain. Texts at the turn of the nineteenth and twentieth centuries often called the distinctions between the Irish, Welsh, Scots and English "racial".

Some historians have suggested that, for the British, racial purity was already compromised, given the wide intermarriage among various ethnic groups and between different social classes. In the eighteenth century, Hume pointed out in his essay "Of National Characters" (published some time between 1741 and 1747) that the English were so mixed as a people that their national identity seemed to consist in having no national identity. While Hume is now venerated as one of the great Enlightenment philosophers, it is interesting to read in the same essay how, despite his detestation for slavery, Hume reveals his conviction that Africans lacked the ingenuity, intelligence and civilization that even the "lower" races in Europe possessed. In this way, Hume was no different from most Enlightenment and nineteenth-century thinkers, who largely agreed in thinking that "natives", as they were often called, were vastly inferior to the races of Europe (Barkan 1992). The underlying structure of this view of the world is given in the box above, "Human inequality", a view that has led some people to think our attitude to animals is like a kind of racism (as we see in the following section).

What would a diehard defender of anthropocentrism do in the face of this situation? Some would want to defend P1 (the key premise in the traditional argument for anthropocentrism) and its correlate P1*. A diehard might then simply embrace the consequences. Such people would be forced to argue that doing experiments on very young children or adults with severe learning difficulties or mental impairment may be morally acceptable. For consistency they should also bemoan the end of imperialism and colonialism. This, however, would be a morally indefensible line to take in the contemporary world, where there is widespread agreement about equal human dignity and universal rights for all human beings. From this examination, we see that the moral principles of anthropocentrism are highly doubtful. The strategy of constructing a parallel argument has proved very powerful in revealing a deficiency in traditional ways of thinking, one that may well lead to a reconsideration of how we should relate to animals. It has also used an interesting technique of reducing an argument to absurdity.

We are left in a difficult situation given our traditional beliefs and values. Is it possible to consistently defend anthropocentrism without ending up occupying a morally indefensible position, or without being forced into the repugnant position in which some people claim the right to be masters over the others? Are there better reasons for privileging humans over non-humans, which will not lead to the consequence of permitting objectionable treatment of people who are less intelligent, less self-aware, have less free will, or are less morally conscientious?

Is anthropocentrism speciesism?

The strength of the above objection to anthropocentrism relies crucially on the fact that not all human beings equally possess the qualities that anthropocentrism takes as special. A possible reply from the anthropocentrist is that perhaps there is indeed a certain quality that all human beings, *qua* human being, share equally, and no non-human animals have at all or have to a comparable degree. If the anthropocentrist can identify this supposedly universal and unique human quality, the moral principles P2 and P3 used in the anthropocentric argument will no longer lead to absurd or unwanted consequences.

What would this uniquely and universally human quality be like? It has to be equally shared by all members of the species *Homo sapiens*, and by no members of other species. A straightforward proposal is membership of *Homo sapiens* itself. All human beings have this feature to an equal extent, and no non-human beings have this feature. So, we can justify our killing non-human animals for food without implying that it would be morally permissible for some humans to kill other humans for food. So, if membership of *Homo sapiens* is the sole quality in virtue of possessing which something can attain intrinsic value, then all and only all human beings would qualify for intrinsic value. Moreover, all human beings would be equally qualified for intrinsic value, and there would be no unequal human dignity or rights.

But why should membership in the human species be a morally significant property? It is not self-evident that it is by itself a quality by virtue of which a being can attain intrinsic value. It is even less self-evident that it is the one and only morally relevant quality. Even if species membership is morally relevant, it still does not follow that beings who lack such a quality would lack intrinsic value. For there may be other qualities that they have which are morally relevant as well. Anthropocentrism's original appeal to various qualities such as self-awareness,

---

Speciesism

> Racists of European descent typically have not accepted that pain matters as much when it is felt by Africans, for example, as when it is felt by Europeans. Similarly those I would call "speciesists" give greater weight to the interests of members of their own species when there is a clash between their interests and the interests of those of other species. Human speciesists do not accept that pain is as bad when it is felt by pigs or mice as when it is felt by humans.
>
> (Peter Singer, *Practical Ethics* [1993]: 58)

> Pain and suffering are bad and should be prevented or minimised, irrespective of race, sex, or species of the being that suffers. How bad a pain is depends on how intense it is and how long it lasts, but pains of the same intensity and duration are equally bad, whether felt by humans or animals. (*Ibid.*: 62)

---

intelligence, free will and moral sense was exactly a response to the need to provide independent reasons for privileging human beings over non-humans.

In the absence of a good reason, anthropocentrism would amount to bias or prejudice: that of taking membership of just one species as the only morally important quality. Singer has repeatedly made this point, arguing that there are parallels between racism and speciesism. Many have argued that species membership, like membership in a racial group or in a sex group, is a merely biological feature that is irrelevant to an individual's moral standing or rights. The term "speciesism" (originally coined by Richard Ryder) is often used to label views that have the same kind of basis in prejudice that racism and sexism have. For Singer, just as other merely biological features (such as membership of the male sex, membership of certain races) do not confer intrinsic value on people, so the biological feature of being a member of *Homo sapiens* should not confer intrinsic value on an animal. It would be racist, and morally wrong, to attribute more intrinsic value to white people than to black people simply because white people have pale skin but black people do not. So, by analogy (see "Against speciesism", opposite), it would be speciesist, and morally wrong, to attribute more intrinsic value to human beings than to non-human beings simply because human beings are biologically humans: something that non-humans clearly are not.

There are large issues at stake here, ones that cannot be dealt with in detail in an introductory text such as this. One of these is whether demoting humans from the category of being specially different from the animals would involve rethinking the category of the human itself, and what is meant by connected ideas such as *humanism*, being *humane* and being part of a *human community*. Some philosophers have emphasized the importance of our relationship with others in forming our own character and style, especially our response to the way others look at us, in the ways we view the face of the other and in the ways we build and develop ideas, communities and projects through the use of language. The "look of the other" is a central idea in the existentialist philosophy of Jean-Paul Sartre (see Sartre 2000) and the notion that the face of another person already speaks to us is a central component of Emmanuel Levinas's account of how the ethical universe is constituted. Several theorists have wondered what kind of "posthumanist" ethics and philosophy might emerge if we take the animal face, the look of the animal and our communication with animals as the starting-point for theorizing. Such a move might "profoundly threaten the sovereignty of the Western subject of consciousness" (Rohman 2009: 12) and lead to

> **Against speciesism**
>
> P1. Whether an individual has the biological feature of being male or not
> is morally irrelevant to the determination of the individual's intrinsic
> value. [moral irrelevance of being male]
>
> P2. Whether an individual has the biological feature of being pale skinned
> or not is morally irrelevant to the determination of the individual's
> intrinsic value. [moral irrelevance of being pale skinned]
>
> C. Like being male and being pale-skinned, whether an individual
> has the biological feature of belonging to a certain species is
> morally irrelevant to the determination of the individual's intrinsic
> value. [moral irrelevance of species membership, *analogical argument*
> from P1 and P2]

new conceptions of what an ethical theory for the "posthumanist" age should be like (Wolfe 2003). Unfortunately, attempts at depicting an alternative to humanist ethics are often very short on detail, and even those who have been strongest in condemning the imagined boundary between the human and the animal have often been caught reverting to a basically human-centred model of the world (see Clare Palmer's [2001] critique of Foucault). This book is an introduction to philosophy rather than a survey of cultural theory, and so we will not engage further in discussions of whether a posthumanist ethic is likely to emerge in the near future, nor what the parameters of such an ethic would be like.

Ignoring speculations about future worldviews does not come close to solving the problems we now face. Singer's challenge is whether anthropocentrism's privileging humans over all non-humans can be morally justified. Will anthropocentrism one day identify a morally relevant property (or more than one) that does two things? First, the property will be one that all and only human beings possess equally. Second, possession of the property will make all humans much more valuable than all non-human beings. The challenge so far remains unanswered. Although Singer does not make the point, the challenge could also be extended to the general problem of human dignity and equality. In the case of Turmeda's disputation, the problem of specialness of humans was solved by the claim that only human beings are made in the image of God. All the other arguments in favour of human superiority that Friar Anselm tries are refuted by the animals. Remove the religious context, and it is unclear how to argue for the special respect that humans are owed, or how to provide any clear basis for the claim that all humans are morally equal. The problem of whether humans are morally superior to animals is just one aspect of the wider problem of what grounds there are for giving human beings in general a morally important status: one that is shared equally among adults and children, healthy and ill; a status that is not taken away by damage, disease or injury however severe. We shall return to this problem later.

Shifting the onus of proof

Singer's challenge suggests that anthropocentrism has no rational basis for assigning humans a special moral status. But this is not itself a proof that animals deserve equal consideration along with humans, or that at least some animals deserve such consideration, or even that animals have a claim to moral considerability at all. When one position in a debate is already well established, it can be hard to determine where the burden of proof lies in order to argue for a change. Many years ago, when it became clear that smoking not only damaged the health of smokers themselves, but was also likely to be a hazard to other people, there was a great debate about whether smoking should be banned in public places: trains, buses and passenger aircraft, cinemas, theatres and concert halls, bars, restaurants and clubs. Smoking in these places was the norm at that time, so the proposals to ban smoking meant a change in the status quo. At first, the evidence of harms from secondary smoking – breathing in the air polluted by smokers – was inconclusive. This enabled campaigners to restrict the extension of smoking. Smokers who complained about limited availability of smoking compartments in trains found it hard to argue that the areas devoted to smokers should be increased. But since the evidence of the dangers of secondary smoking was not conclusive at the time, there was a problem for health campaigners. In order to justify banning smoking altogether in trains, cinemas, aircraft, buses and restaurants, they had to meet a much tougher standard of proof, and as a result there were years of debate and policy discussions about the degree to which smoking in public should be restricted.

Advocates of animal liberation and animal rights face a problem similar to those who wanted to ban smoking in all public venues. They need not only show that anthropocentrism is unfounded, but need to go on to give positive reasons why animals, or at least some animals, should be given moral consideration, and why the common ways of treating them are wrong. Further, if animals do have a moral status, is this equal for all? Is the suffering of a flea as regrettable as the suffering of a whale or a dog? In answering these questions, the primary consideration for some writers has been the fact that at least some animals can suffer pain.

The capacity for pleasures and pains can do double duty. First, it can be argued that it is wrong for us to inflict pain unnecessarily on human beings and on those animals that are capable of feeling pain. Second, the degree to which an animal is able to experience pain may be a guide to how much consideration we should give to that animal's interests.

The utilitarian ethical approach to animals takes pain and pleasure as central. Basic forms of hedonic utilitarianism claim that pain (or suffering or unhappiness) is the only moral evil in the world, and pleasure (or freedom from suffering or happiness) is the only moral good. The right thing to do in a given situation for the simple hedonic utilitarian is to act in the way that maximizes the pleasure of all concerned and minimizes the pain. Likewise, preference utilitarianism demands we should aim at the satisfaction of people's considered preferences as our target for action. For simplicity, the boxed argument below is put in terms of hedonic utilitarianism. In general, problems for one version of the utilitarian theory translate into problems for other versions, so it is often easier to use hedonic utilitarianism as the standard model.

This time, we will not go over the details of the argument in the box, leaving readers to study its features for themselves. The argument is clearly a compelling one provided we accept the utilitarian principles P1 and UP and once we accept the principle of equality embodied in P3. Singer thinks we should accept all these principles. The claims here recapitulate the points about speciesism already discussed: Singer is challenging the anthropocentrist to give up speciesism unless able to find good reasons to justify counting a biological difference between humans and other species as grounds for a moral distinction. The principle of equality itself is a moral principle, not a factual one. Singer is claiming that no factual difference between two people, or between a human and an animal, is a justification of any difference in the amount of consideration we give to satisfying their needs and interests. Moreover, Singer holds that beings that cannot suffer have no moral claim on us, for things that cannot suffer cannot have interests. Since they have no interests, there is nothing we can take into consideration when we are thinking about what to do with them. As we shall find out later, many environmental philosophers disagree with Singer on this matter.

In further defence of the hedonic utilitarian argument, notice that while intelligence or rationality or the ability to hold moral opinions are all – for Singer – arbitrary ways of marking the boundary of our moral concerns, there is less arbitrariness, he says, about suffering or pain. These apply to a range of beings – human and non-human alike – and since suffering is evil and pleasure is good, then we can follow the

---

Hedonic utilitarianism

P1. We have a moral duty to maximize the overall balance of good and evil – i.e. the overall balance of pleasure over pain. [maximization principle]

P2. The capacity to feel pain and/or pleasure (often called *sentience*) is a morally relevant quality – that is, the pain and pleasure of every being who is capable of feeling them should be considered, counted, and weighed in the moral calculus of utility. [from P1]

P3. Equal pains should be given equal negative moral weight no matter whose pains they are, and likewise equal pleasures should be given equal positive moral weight no matter whose pleasures they are. [equality principle]

P4. How bad a pain is, and likewise, how good a pleasure is, solely depends on its intensity and duration.

P5. Non-human pain/pleasure and human pain/pleasure should be given an equal moral weight, if their intensity and duration are both the same. [from P3 & P4]

P6. Many ways of treating non-human animals (e.g. factory farming, animal experimentation, hunting) cause more pain for the animals than pleasure and pain-reduction for humans. [empirical claim]

UP. It is morally wrong to reduce the balance of pleasure over pain. [utilitarian principle]

C. Many ways of treating non-human animals are morally wrong. [from P5, P6 & UP]

apparently non-arbitrary principle first introduced by Bentham: when counting pleasures and pains, each person or animal is to count for one, and none is to count for more than one.

At first sight, this utilitarian argument looks like a strong one, but there are several problems with it. For example, Singer's use of the word "bad" in relation to pain is ambiguous, having several interpretations. First, think about the idea of "experientially bad" versus the notion of something being "morally bad". There seem to be two distinct ideas of what is bad here. There is a third idea as well, that of "bad for the organism", which can be easily confused with the other two. When he writes that "pain and suffering are bad and should be prevented or minimised", then this may be uncontroversial when applied to the idea of pain as a morally bad thing. But pain is not always bad for the organism; for example, pain can warn of disease, injury or overexertion. So something that is a bad experience can be good for the organism if it stops the organism going on to do further damage to itself. Singer's argument needs some attention here.

There is also a problem about what to say about the arbitrariness of species, race, sex, intelligence and the other marks of difference that Singer dismisses as incapable of grounding moral claims. Why is pain a non-arbitrary marker of where the boundary of moral care and concern is to be drawn? There seems to be more than a hint of circularity in the argument. What makes pain and pleasure plausible properties for determining what is good and bad is that these properties can be found in a wide range of different species. Anthropocentrism, by contrast, focuses on properties such as rationality, consciousness and moral capacity as the properties that determine the boundary of moral concern. And these properties limit attention by and large to human beings only (or to humans and a small number of so-called "higher" animals). But in saying that anthropocentrism draws its moral boundaries in an arbitrary way, Singer is apparently just restating the challenge to speciesism, claiming that speciesists put special weight on properties that are distinctive of humans. Now suppose we encounter someone who thinks that life itself is the foundation of moral value, and that for something to be alive and to be active in maintaining that life are properties that give it moral value and hence require moral consideration on our part. This person may well think that drawing the boundary of moral concern in terms of the capacity to experience pains and pleasures is itself arbitrary. It seems then that the question of arbitrariness cannot be settled independent of the question of what overall moral stance is up for approval.

Animal rights: deontology

Singer's arguments can be tidied up to meet the objections we have just encountered, at least to some extent. They face a deeper challenge, however, from ethical theories that start at a completely different place. The utilitarian takes the value of the consequences of an action as the sole determinant of whether it is right or wrong. In more sophisticated versions of utilitarianism, the focus may be on the probable consequences of our actions, for utilitarians – like everyone else – are well aware that what we hope will happen often does not eventuate. This emphasis on consequences or probable outcomes as the determining factor in what makes actions right or wrong explains why a whole group of ethical theories are described as *consequentialist*. We can say that for consequentialists, the question of what things are intrinsically valuable (good) or disvaluable (bad) is the fundamental moral question. The things in question are states of affairs, for example certain experiences of pleasure or pain, or being happy, or having preferences satisfied. For a different approach to moral theory, deontologists (the term comes from the Greek word, *deon*, meaning "duty") focus on the actions themselves. Think of the moral rules we generally accept, or that other people seem to follow. These can be more or less specific: rules about how to dress, what to eat, how to conduct relations with members of the opposite sex. Sometimes a putative (supposed) moral rule turns out on examination not to be a usable rule at all, and sometimes different rules conflict in puzzling ways. The box "Rules" has a summary description of some putative moral rules and an explanation of how rules are sometimes prioritized.

The basis for accepting a system of moral rules – say the rules that govern the behaviour of people in a particular society – is that certain beings have intrinsic moral status or moral value in virtue of having certain "value-adding" features, and that the moral rules on the list are justified because they protect such beings themselves and their value-adding features. Suppose, for example, that our capacity for determining our own lives and purposes (often called *autonomy*, i.e., literally, self-government) is a value-adding feature. Autonomous beings will be regarded as having a certain moral status (in many accounts, this special status is called dignity, or human dignity). If this status is special, then "respect people's autonomy" is a rule that will help preserve that special status, provided people follow it. "Respect autonomy" is often taken as the most basic, but also the most abstract, moral rule, which in turn justifies more specific moral rules, such as "don't lie". For lying

> ### Rules
>
> Examples of (putative) moral rules:
>
> > "Don't kill or harm innocent people."
> > "Do unto others as you would have them do unto you."
> > "Don't torture anyone."
> > "Stay a virgin until you get married."
> > "Don't lie."
> > "Act so as to maximize utility." [Utilitarian principle]
> > "Don't wear mini skirts."
> > "Respect people's autonomy." [Kantian principle]
>
> Rules, rights and duties are always *parallel*. For every (negotiable/absolute) *moral rule* "do such and-such to X", there is a (negotiable/absolute) *moral right* for X to have such-and-such done to it, and there is a (negotiable/absolute) *moral duty* for moral agents to do such-and-such to X.
>
> The moral rule "do A to X" takes *higher/lower priority* than the moral rule "do B to X", provided, and only provided, *either* X's right to have A done to it is greater/lesser than X's right to have B done to it, *or* moral agents' duty to do A to X is greater/lesser than their duty to do B to it.
>
> To say that "don't torture anyone" is an *absolute* moral rule is to say that it is *always* immoral to torture someone *no matter what*. So, even if by torturing someone we can bring about better consequences for the world, it will still be immoral for us to do so. Why so? Simply because torture in itself is a violation of an absolute moral rule or, equivalently, of someone's absolute moral right.
>
> Different deontologists have different lists of (putative) moral rules/duties/rights.
>
> No (proper) deontologist will regard "act so as to maximize utility" as a moral rule/duty.

to someone is a way of manipulating them and getting them to do what they would not otherwise want to do. Once we do this we have undermined the capacity for self-determination, that is we have undermined the person's autonomy.

It is probably not surprising that some of the strongest objections to utilitarian reasoning about animals come from deontologists. In particular, Tom Regan has argued that it is important to recognize the possession of rights by animals just as we recognize rights in humans. This would mean, taken to its logical conclusion, that it would also make sense to think about the idea of animal dignity. One problem, as the deontologist sees it, is that many of our practices at present do not permit animals to retain any kind of dignity. A second problem is related to the question of interests. The utilitarian believes that animals and people alike have an interest in avoiding pain. Ignore, for the time being, the fact that pain is sometimes enjoyable (for the fitness fanatic, for example, who believes in the principle *no pain, no gain*). And ignore, also, the existence of sadism and masochism, in which people derive pleasure from either physical or emotional suffering. With these exceptions put to one side, what is awful about pain is the experience of it. But in everyday thinking about our moral obligations, it is not the experiences we focus on, but rather the people and other beings who are having experiences. As Regan writes:

> It is a commonplace to say that morality places some limits on how animals may be treated. We are not to kick dogs, set fire to cats' tails, torment hamsters or parakeets. Philosophically, the starting point is not so much whether but why these acts are wrong. (Regan 1983b: 24–5)

The acts are wrong, he thinks, because we do wrong to the animals, not because of some experiences happening inside the animals.

Look at the matter like this. We are each of us vessels or receptacles in which experiences occur: pains, pleasures, sadness and joy. These experiences are what the utilitarian calls forms of *utility*. But the vessel

---

Against utilitarianism
P1. For utilitarianism, utility is the only thing that matters morally.
P2. For utilitarianism, it is wrong to kill an animal (or likewise, a person) only if it the action produces negative utility. [from P1]
P3. For utilitarianism, an animal (or likewise, a person) is a mere *utility-receptacle*, which has no moral status in itself, but is dispensable and replaceable. [from P2]
P4. But, clearly, it is morally wrong to do experiments on an animal (or likewise, a person) because the victim *itself* (as apart from the utility it contains) has a certain moral value/status so that it itself deserves not to be experimented on.
C1. Utilitarianism cannot explain why animal experimentation (or any other harmful practice on animals) is morally wrong. [from P3 & P4]
P5. The *only* reason that utilitarianism can give for thinking that animal experimentation (or any practice) is morally wrong is that such a practice reduces utility in the world.
P6. But animal experimentation will still be wrong *even if* such a practice will actually increase utility in the world.
C2. Utilitarianism cannot explain why animal experimentation (or any other harmful practice on animals) is morally wrong. [from P5 & P6]

itself, not just what it contains, is something of value. This leads to Regan's first objection to utilitarianism. The mistake the utilitarian makes is thinking that utility is all that matters. Someone who cares about the fate of animals is not just concerned about the amount of positive or negative utility in the world. Such a person, Regan argues, is concerned about what happens to the animals themselves. And this leads to his second argument against the utilitarian. Suppose it turns out that what we do to animals actually increases either average or total utility in the world. Would that make it acceptable to treat animals cruelly either in research laboratories, intensive farming units or at home? The answer is in the negative.

Think in particular of people who are opposed to animal experimentation. Suppose it is proved beyond doubt that such experimentation decisively increases utility. For example, it might turn out that the number of cures for diseases – both animal and human – resulting from animal research brings about much higher utility (pleasure) than the

---

Animal rights

The argument to best explanation

P1. It is morally wrong to perform experiments on non-human animals.
P2. The *best explanation* for P1 is that non-human animals have a *moral right not to be harmed*.
 C. Non-human animals have a moral right not to be harmed. [from P1 & P2]

The argument for equal animal rights

P1. Human infants, very senile people, and mentally handicapped people *all* have a moral right not to be harmed that is *equal* to that of a typical human adult.
P2. Like typical human adults, human infants, very senile people and mentally handicapped people are "*subjects of a life*".
P3. Given the truth of P2, the best explanation for the truth of P1 is that (a) all subjects of a life have an *equal "inherent value"* (i.e. non-instrumental value) and that (b) this equal "inherent value" gives all subjects of a life an equal moral right not to be harmed.
P4. (a) All subjects of a life have equal "inherent value" and (b) this equal "inherent value" gives all subjects of a life an equal moral right not to be harmed. [from P1, P2 & P3]
P5. Non-human animals are subjects of a life, too.
P6. Non-human animals have an "inherent value" that is *equal* to that of human beings. [from P4a & P5]
 C. Non-human animals have a moral right not to be harmed that is *equal* to that of human beings. [from P4b & P6]

---

disutility (pain) caused by the experiments themselves. Singer would have a reason to support, rather than object to, animal experimentation. So the utilitarian argument against animal research depends on factual information about just how much pain is caused in the laboratory and just how much pleasure is produced by finding treatments and cures for diseases. Regan thinks that many opponents of vivisection would not be moved by finding that animal research brings about more good than evil in terms of utility. For such people, the concern is with the rights of the animals being used: vivisection is wrong because it violates the animal victims' moral right not to be harmed.

The right of animals not to be harmed, Regan argues, also explains other commonly held views. For example, some objectors to animal research think that people who experiment with animals enjoy the suffering of the animals. That this perception is false has been shown in many studies. In fact, it is quite common for researchers and animal facility staff to form bonds of affection with animals, especially those that are repeatedly handled or observed as part of the experiment. Killing animals at the end of the research is sometimes an occasion for distress for researchers and animal technicians alike. When these facts are revealed to the people objecting to vivisection they change their views, but only partly. They accept that animal staff and researchers are not cruel, and that they do not enjoy seeing animals suffer. Nonetheless, they say, it is still wrong for the experiments to take place. Why? The best explanation is that the animal victims of the research have a right not to be harmed, a right that is routinely violated in the animal laboratory.

If animal rights provide the best explanation for the way critics think about animal husbandry, research using animals and other situations where animals are confined, manipulated and harmed in various ways, then Regan has a non-utilitarian way of justifying objections to such practices. These objections do not depend on facts about how utilities turn out after calculating them, but on the notion that animals are subjects of lives, and – as such – holders of rights. Moreover, these rights will be equal across species: humans are not more or less subjects of lives, and nor are animals. These arguments anticipate Paul Taylor's ethics of respect for nature, which we shall study in detail in Chapter 4. So in this chapter we just summarize Regan's position, confining ourselves to relatively few remarks on it.

At the heart of Regan's deontological position is the concept of a subject of a life. To be a subject of a life is – among other things – to have a centred experience of the world, to hold beliefs and desires, and to have a sense of the future. Even this short list of features seems to leave out more animals than it includes. Most of the animals in the world – where by animal we mean a living organism that can generate its own movement – are smaller than beetles, and most of them probably do not hold anything like beliefs and desires, let alone have any conception – however dim – of a future. Regan's animals are high-level animals, such as dogs, cats, primates and other mammals. We might even object that some of the features Regan mentions are found to different degrees in different animals, thus undermining the thought that animals all have equal rights. Look at the list of features in the box "Subjects", and see if you can think of cases where they are held to different degrees by different animals. There is an Austrian television series featuring a hyper-intelligent German Shepherd called "Rex" with an uncanny ability to understand what people are saying and to solve crimes. If any dog were as smart as Rex, then that animal would have a higher degree of intelligence, and a greater sense of a centred self, than an emu or a panda.

In terms of our earlier discussion of why anthropocentrism has come under challenge, there is a strange complementarity between Singer's and Regan's theories. Physiological studies support Singer's view that animal pains and pleasures are in many ways comparable to human pains and pleasures. It is sometimes said that animals probably do not fear death in the way that many human beings do. The German philosopher Martin Heidegger wrote that humans are the only animals that die, meaning that death is something that we are aware of in a way that is unique to our species. If this is right, then pains that are equivalent in intensity and duration will not be just as awful for animals as they are for humans. Instead, even mild pains that people think may indicate a threat to their lives could be a source of more suffering to them than a similarly mild pain experienced by a dog or an emu. On the other hand, the work of ethologists and biologists who have studied the commonalities of human and animal behaviour seems to support Regan's view that animals are subjects of lives. To the extent that each of us is a knot in a web of wider relationships, then the social lives of some animals seem to run parallel to the social lives of people. Much then can be learned about ourselves individually, and collectively, by studying the lives of animals (see Goodall 1993).

Although Regan's ethic can be argued to give more protection to animals than Singer's, the rights account still leaves open the possibility of occasionally overriding the rights of individuals. While individual rights in general have to be given first priority, according to Regan, there are still some cases in which if the collective interest is big enough, the rights of the individual must take second place to the needs of the collective. For example, to prevent a world war, it may be acceptable to kill or harm innocent individuals, just because the alternative evil – a massive conflagration and enormous loss of life – is so great. So an animal's moral right not to be harmed is not absolute. If several people and a dog are marooned with limited supplies in a lifeboat, then the dog may have to be killed in order to save the lives of the people. Rights can be overridden, but only in special cases.

Neither of the theories dealt with in this chapter give grounds for wider environmental protection, beyond what is necessary to protect human and animal welfare. Endangered species, for example, merit no special protection, since being endangered is not an intrinsic feature of an animal. While there can be philosophical puzzles about whether the loss of species is intrinsically bad, or just instrumentally bad for humans (Palmer 2009), many people concerned with animal welfare and animal liberation may be disappointed to find that neither of the main theories we have looked at has much to say on this issue. What matters for the utilitarian is avoidance of pain; what matters for the deontologist is the protection of individual rights. Members of plentiful species, just like those of endangered ones, are at the mercy of pleasure and pains, and are all equally subjects of lives. Both of the animal ethics theories discussed in this chapter are blind to the wider environmental status of individual animals.

Likewise, neither theory gives any status to collectives, such as populations, species and animal communities. Instead, each theory focuses on individual pleasures and pains, or on individual subjects of a life. Similarly, neither theory has anything to say about the protection of plants, landscapes or ecosystems. While a flourishing environment is important in order to provide food and shelter for animals, such values are instrumental. Plants and ecosystems have no value in themselves in either theory. For this reason, it has sometimes been suggested that the philosophy of animal liberation and animal rights is incompatible with a more general environmental philosophy. For example, when a pest species of goats is out of control and grazing on endangered native plants, environmentalists will often recommend culling the goats to save the native plants. But nothing in either Singer's or Regan's ethic would license this solution to the problem, and Regan himself has coined the term "eco-fascism" to describe the position that individual animals should be sacrificed if this is necessary for the larger systemic good. We shall explore this issue in more detail later, but in the next chapter, we shall keep our focus on the individual, and look at an ethic that extends moral concern and moral rights beyond those of individual animals to encompass respect for all individual living things.

four

Living things: ethics for the non-human world

Individuals, groups and communities

Once the moral circle is expanded to incorporate living beings apart from humans and animals, things get much more intriguing. For not all that lives is individual: termite nests and bee colonies have similarities to individuals in some ways, but at the same time are made up of many individual animals that form a highly organized group or system. Animal and plant populations are holistic, group entities rather than individuals, although again they can be treated – from some points of view – as very large organisms, themselves nested within even larger super organisms. Because of the importance of the idea of groups, communities and systems to contemporary environmental philosophy, we shall devote Chapter 5 to them, concentrating here on the extension of moral consideration to individual plants and other living things.

By treating questions about future generations, animals, individual living things and finally systems as separate matters, philosophy dismantles complexes of attitudes that in the real world are often grouped together. Many people already do think of non-human things as having a significant moral status, yet they do not always separate out their worries about future generations from their care about living things in general. Environmental protesters often talk about the need to protect future generations of people, or even to protect property. Greenpeace activists climbed the 200-metre high chimney of Kingsnorth power station in the UK in 2007 to paint a protest slogan, resulting in £30,000 of damage. Their defence against the charge of criminal damage was that climate change would do far more damage to property than they had done (a defence that was accepted by the court). Eight years earlier, the same organization sponsored a protest aimed at removing genetically modified crops that were being trialled in open-air venues. On this occasion, they argued that their actions were protective of the wider environment and the food chain, so indicating a concern with living things other than humans. This shows how, in common with other environmental groups, Greenpeace is concerned with a range of issues that are somewhat artificially separated in this book. Philosophically, however, it is interesting to see how arguments about future generations, animals, other living things and about systems all share a common structure, and how each extension of value to more and more things does so by using a different value-conferring property. We shall discuss the range of proposed value-conferring properties in more detail in Chapter 7.

Thinking about animals has raised one really significant point: that humans may not be quite so morally special as many people seem to think. Once humans are removed from having a special moral status, then the basis of human-centred ethics starts to dissolve away. If the interests of living things in general are taken as having direct moral significance then we will want to explore the idea of life-centred or biocentric ethics. Just because some living thing makes a moral claim on us – just because it has moral standing – does not mean that its claims will be equal to those of all other living things. Hence we will distinguish in general between biocentric ethics that are egalitarian, and those that are non-egalitarian. Egalitarian biocentrism may look a bit weird at first sight: how can dogs, flies and cabbages ever be thought to have equal moral status in our planning for action? However, philosophers are always interested in following lines of argument even when they lead to apparently untenable conclusions. From this exercise it is often possible to learn something: perhaps that our everyday ideas about what matters and what is important are not usually based on solid arguments and good evidence.

To begin with, we look at one of the most comprehensive and well-articulated theories based on a biocentric point of view: Paul Taylor's biocentric version of a Kantian ethic. After our earlier discovery that Kant regarded even dogs as not worthy of direct moral consideration, there is a certain irony in finding that Kant's own moral system can be used to develop a biocentric ethic. Actually, we learn two things from study of Taylor's work. First, we find out what the general structure of a Kantian ethical system is like. Second, we can find out how plausible this approach to ethics is when applied not just to human beings but to all life in general. For Kant, humans are morally special because they are rational and self-governing. By a free, autonomous (self-legislating) choice, humans can decide to limit their freedom of behaviour. To be moral is to limit ourselves to morally acceptable standards of action. Such a form of rational moral subjectivity is beyond the reach of all animals, including dogs and primates. This kind of humanistic ethic not only puts humans at the centre of the moral universe, but endows them also with a special inherent worth that no animal can have.

It might seem like quite a challenge to take such a human-centred ethic and develop a biocentric version of it. Here's how Taylor does it. First, he develops a biocentric worldview, one that places human beings alongside all other living things, not in a superior position to them. Each individual living thing in nature – whether animal, plant, or micro-organism – is a "teleological centre of life" having a good or well-being of its own that can be enhanced or damaged. The term "teleological" implies that at least the biological activities of each living thing are all goal oriented (the Greek word *telos* means "end" or "goal"). Taylor goes on to argue that all individuals that are teleological centres of life have equal intrinsic value (or what he calls "inherent worth") that entitles them to moral respect. Further, Taylor maintains that the intrinsic value of wild living things generates a *prima facie* moral duty on our part to preserve or promote their goods as ends in themselves. By a *prima facie* duty is meant one that holds "at first sight" and that provides a reason (other things being equal) for us to act in the way prescribed by the duty. Finally, Taylor argues that any practices that treat other living things only as means to human purposes display a lack of respect for them. He concludes that adopting an instrumental attitude to other living things is intrinsically wrong.

Taylor's view is exciting and interesting because it promises to give a defence of a position that people often feel attracted to while being unable to give much rational justification for it. Anyone who has experienced a reverence for life of the sort advocated in the writings of Albert Schweitzer, for example, may turn to Taylor's work in the hope of being able to provide a rationale for the view. Unfortunately, as we show, Taylor's work fails to accomplish its lofty goal, but these failures are themselves educational.

Taylor's biocentric ethic

Taylor's defence of egalitarian biocentrism can be regarded as consisting of three components. At its heart is the attitude of respect for nature, one that recognizes the special inherent worth of every living thing.

Second, what makes this attitude intelligible, and gives it strong support, is the worldview itself: an egalitarian biocentric one that denies any special status to human beings as such. Last, there is the ethical system manifested in the attitude of respect, a system that itself has a structure defining our basic moral duties, the corresponding virtues that dispose us to act in conformity to these duties, and also a set of principles by which conflicts between human and non-human interests can be resolved. This combination of attitude, worldview and ethical system provides a rich and subtle account of how ethics, attitudes and action are intimately connected. So let us start with the attitude of respect for nature, and then explore how – and to what extent – it is supported by the worldview and gives substance to the ethical system.

The box "Respect" shows the formal description of the attitude that Taylor advocates. Taylor does not try to identify properties by virtue of which natural things have moral considerability (that is, he avoids the kinds of strategy taken by consequentialists such as Singer). The alternative to this strategy is to find properties that confer value on the things that possess them. Recall how Regan regards the property of being a subject of a life as conferring value on the animals that possess such subjectivity. For Taylor, the very fact of being alive confers value on each living thing, and thereby gives it moral standing. Notice how radical this idea is. Consciousness, rationality, the capacity for pain and pleasure: these and other properties are neither here nor there in determining the moral standing of living things.

Such things also have a good of their own: because as living things they have the capacity for doing well or doing better, of reaching their natural biological development or being harmed and hindered in attempting to do so. As things progress along their lives' journeys it makes sense, therefore, to consider whether things are going well for them or not. These ideas are fleshed out in the more detailed description Taylor gives to the biocentric worldview, one that has four elements.

Respect

What an attitude of respect for nature involves (Taylor 1981)

For each individual living thing X in nature, we regard X *itself* as having "inherent worth" (i.e., intrinsic value). This consists of the following two attitudes:

(1) We regard X as *morally considerable* – i.e., we give positive weight to X's own good in our moral deliberation about actions that are likely to affect X.

(2) We regard the realization of X's own good as intrinsically valuable, to be pursued *as an end-in-itself* and *for the sake of X itself*.

The biocentric worldview

From the evolutionary and ecological point of view, human beings and all other living things on this planet are equal members of the earth's community of life, and *Homo sapiens* is not a special species (Taylor 1981: 207–9). Taylor is using the terminology of "equality" in a special way. What he means is that the laws of genetics, natural selection and adaptation apply equally to all living things (whether human or not). Humans, in other words, are not immune to the same evolutionary and genetic forces that shape all living things on earth. Further, humans are not *special*, because we are not needed more than anything else. Indeed, some plant life and seaweed are special, given their roles in the cycling of nutrients and elements essential to life. By contrast, other living things on earth can survive and flourish perfectly well without human beings.

In common with other biocentric ethics, Taylor's position has to face the problem of what to say about the planet's biosphere: the part of the earth's surface that consists of living things linked in complex ecosystem relations with each other. What about the biosphere as a whole: does it not have value in its own right? And what about all the non-living components, such as the minerals without which plant and animal life would be impossible? Taylor notes that systems can consist of living things. But it cannot be the case that individual living things are only instrumentally valuable to a larger system in which they are placed. After all, what would make that larger system count for anything ethically unless it is of value to the flourishing of individual things (Taylor 1986: 118)? The fundamental thing for him is the value of individual lives and we only have indirect duties towards larger systems. Taylor also agrees that the survival and well-being of all living things (including human beings) depends on the integrity of the planetary biosphere. As a result, we have indirect moral duties regarding non-living natural entities, but no direct duties owed to them.

What is special, then, is the individual living thing. Each individual living thing has a good of its own and, as we have seen, is a "teleological centre of life". So what is the goal towards which each living thing moves? This is nothing other than the realization of its own good (Taylor 1981: 210; 1986: 121–2), that is, the full development of its biological capacities for preserving its existence, enhancing its well-being and perhaps also reproducing its own kind. To have a good of its own, a living thing needs no consciousness, awareness or even subjectivity. For Taylor, trees and bushes have goods of their own just as much as dogs, emus or human beings. All of these kinds of thing have biological capacities, and for all of them it makes sense to talk about well-being and health, and of what is good or bad for them. Certain food is good for dogs, but other food – such as chocolate – is bad for them. There is nothing metaphorical about such talk. Chocolate poisons dogs and so is bad in the quite literal sense of reducing or damaging their basic biological capacities.

In the light of all this, Taylor denies human superiority: *Homo sapiens* has no higher "inherent worth" (i.e. intrinsic value) than other species. Unless we are to use standards drawn from human values as the only valid criteria for merit in the world, then we will have to recognize that in many ways humans are inferior to animals. We are better at mathematics than monkeys, but vastly inferior to them in tree-climbing. Indeed, it is not simply unfair to say that animals and plants are poorer scientists and writers than human beings; rather, it is nonsense, for there are no common standards against which plants, humans and animals are to be judged as researchers or dramatists (Taylor 1986: 130ff.). To make his case more plausible, Taylor rejects three traditional arguments for human superiority: (a) Greek humanism; (b) the Judaeo-Christian idea of a great chain of being; and (c) Cartesian dualism.

For the Greek humanist, a creature that cannot use reason to master its animal nature and aim to develop nobility and greatness of character cannot achieve a really worthwhile life. But this argument makes the mistake of using human standards as if they are the only ones that count. Even if we agree that a life characterized by reason, nobility and dignity is the best kind of life to which humans can aspire, attempting to judge the merits of plant and animal life by such standards would be nonsensical.

For medieval theologians and philosophers, a further reason for thinking of humans as superior to animals and plants derives from the notion that God created a chain of beings differing in perfection, with God and the angels at the top of the chain and simple forms of life and mere matter down at the bottom. Human beings supposedly occupy a place below the angels, but above all other forms of life on earth. Taylor points out that such a view provides no argument for the superiority of humans over other forms of life but merely restates an anthropocentric prejudice. A similar anthropocentric bias underlies Descartes' view that humans are the only creatures on earth that have minds. Descartes' form of dualism claims that minds differ from bodies, because minds are immaterial while bodies are physical, taking up space and being subject to the laws of physics. For Descartes, there is no possibility that animals have minds; in fact they are just complex mechanisms inhabiting a physical world. This Cartesian dualism also faces the same problems that Greek humanism faces: if bears do not have minds at all, then there is no sense in comparing their value to the value of humans, and no common standard of rationality by which to measure their achievements compared with human ones.

Taking these arguments seriously means that there is no good reason for thinking that members of one species have any higher – or lower – inherent worth than members of any other species. From this it follows that all living things have equal inherent worth, regardless of their species. It is not hard to deduce from this position that since all living things have equal inherent worth, *and* members of *Homo sapiens* have inherent worth, that therefore other living things also have inherent worth and they have it to the same extent as members of *Homo sapiens*.

While many people may feel uncomfortable with the denial of human superiority, Taylor's achievement is to show that this denial can form part of a coherent set of beliefs about the world, a set that is just as philosophically consistent as the much more common anthropocentric attitude that we unreflectingly adopt most of the time. We have already looked at other non-anthropocentric positions. Comparing Taylor and Regan, we may wonder whether *being a teleological centre of life* is a better candidate for being a value-conferring property than is Regan's preferred property: that of *being a subject of a life*. Both writers agree that human beings are intrinsically valuable. So what kinds of being are we, in virtue of which we have intrinsic value? For Regan, it seems that the best explanation for human beings' having intrinsic value is that they are subjects of a life. But since things that have the property of being subjects of a life are intrinsically valuable, it would be mere prejudice to limit the range of intrinsic value to humans alone. It is a fact, according to Regan, that at least some animals are also subjects of a life. Hence these animals too are intrinsically valuable.

Taylor's argument has many of the same features as Regan's, but leads to a very different conclusion. For him, it seems that the best explanation that humans are valuable is that we are each teleological centres of life, striving to achieve the unfolding and development of these lives. But lots of non-human things are also teleological centres of life. So if all teleological centres of life are valuable in their own right, then not only humans but also plants and animals will be intrinsically valuable. In both cases the logic is impeccable, but the conclusions are surprising. In Taylor's case, the result is an ethic that puts extremely high demands on us.

Taylor's ethical system

A worldview on its own provides support for certain attitudes, but unless these attitudes are informed and guided by some systematic understanding of duties, virtues and ways of resolving conflicts, there would be no way of entering into discussions with others in order to evaluate behaviour, persuade people to change the way they act and compare notes on our responses to different kinds of situation. An ethical system tries to provide these resources, and Taylor does this by laying out four basic moral rules of duty, four corresponding moral virtues and five principles for resolving conflict. While his depiction of a biocentric outlook provides a consistent and coherent alternative to anthropocentrism, his ethical system is subject to a variety of problems. Some of these are problems for the system itself, while others raise a question about whether the biocentric outlook underpinning his approach is ultimately viable.

An ethic in which other living things are not mere means to human ends involves some very basic obligations on our parts, and Taylor identifies four rules that are basic, and which apply to our actions towards wild things living in nature. The first duty is a standard one in interhuman relations, and is usually called the duty of not doing harm, that is of non-maleficence. The first prescription that many medical students are taught (supposedly derived from the principles of the Greek physician Hippocrates) is a similar duty: *primum non nocere* (first, do no harm). Indeed the idea that we should not do harm to others is a deep-seated and ancient one, found in many traditions. In the *Analects* of Kongzi (Confucius), for example, it is proposed that one guide for life is a prin-

---

Duties

Taylor's four rules of duty of respect for nature (Taylor 1986: 171–92)

- *Non-maleficence*: Duty not to kill or otherwise harm anything that has a good of its own. In keeping with this rule, we should not cause harm to anything that does not harm us.
- *Non-interference*: Duty not to interfere with natural things. This means not restricting the freedoms of living things, and having a hands-off approach to nature in general.
- *Fidelity*: Duty not to mislead another. This means not breaking the trust wild creatures show towards us, and so not trapping or luring animals into danger by mimicking their calls.
- *Restitutive justice*: Duty to restore the balance of justice between humans and non-humans.

ciple of sympathetic understanding: "Do not do to others what you do not want for yourself."

The duty of non-maleficence is weaker than a duty sometimes confused with it; namely, the duty of benevolence. The notion of benevolence seems to be implied by the Christian "golden rule" that we should always do unto others as we would have them do unto us. If we would like others to do good things for us, then the Christian rule implies that we should reciprocate and do good things for them also. In general, a duty of benevolence asks us to help improve the lives of others, while non-maleficence simply implores us not to make their lives worse. Not only is Taylor's first basic duty towards living things weaker than the duty of benevolence, but it is also weaker than any claim about rights. From the fact that we have a duty not to harm someone, it does not follow that the person in question can claim a right not to be harmed by us. As we saw in Chapter 3, rights are special in that when a person or an animal has a right to certain treatment, or protection, that right can trump other claims and duties. Of course, if an animal has a right to protection – as argued by Regan – then I have a duty to protect it. But the converse does not follow. I can have a duty to protect an animal, even if animals lack rights altogether. Taylor, does not want to make a claim for rights on behalf of animals or other living things; rather, he wants to outline duties we have towards many things, even beings that would not be considered by animal rights theorists as having rights at all.

Taylor's second rule demands that we do not interfere in the lives of wild creatures. When we think about human beings, and our duties to each other, the duty not to interfere is sometimes regarded as part of what is required as a matter of respect for others. What is wrong with being a busybody, or a do-gooder, in the pejorative use of these terms? The obvious answer is that such people interfere too much in the affairs of others. It is one thing to help someone out when they are in difficulty, or when they ask for assistance. It is a quite different thing to set about improving other people's lives when they do not want to be improved and when they have not asked for help. Just as respect for persons means keeping a distance from them, and allowing them to sort out their own issues, so respect for natural living things, according to Taylor, means refraining from too much interference in their lives. A principle of non-interference, whether applied to interhuman relationships, or to relationships between humans and other living things, is always subject to an "other things being equal" clause that is implied. It is not wrong to interfere in the lives of those near and dear to us on some occasions, even when they resent such interference. Children, for instance, are often not good judges of what is safe, valuable or worthwhile and so good parents will interfere regularly in their children's lives. Yet as the children grow older, respect for their gradual maturation into adulthood requires a reduction in interference.

The third rule – fidelity, or the duty not to mislead – is another one of undoubted importance in human relationships. Again, Taylor has chosen to emphasize a weaker rather than a stronger duty. It is sometimes thought that we should show respect to people by always telling the truth, but the duty not to mislead stops short of this. If we always tell the truth, we can do untold damage in many ways and in many situations. If we fail to mislead, then we will do less damage. In our dealings with wild creatures we often engage in deception, and Taylor draws attention to the way hunters will often use fake calls to attract birds and other animals they wish to shoot or capture. Such behaviour, he claims, breaks the third rule, and since hunters generally harm the animals they pursue, their behaviour is in breach of the first two rules as well. The wrongness of hunting is therefore overdetermined.

Finally, the last rule requires us to make amends for the injustices done when the previous three rules have been broken, whether individually or jointly. Reformed hunters, Taylor comments, can dedicate themselves to preserving some individuals of species they have previously harmed or deceived. Since the very business of living, building shelter, constructing leisure facilities, building roads, factories, shops and so on inevitably involves harming other living things, interfering in their lives, and – at least sometimes – breaking the trust they may have developed towards us, then, Taylor tells us, we should try to make amends either to those we have harmed, or to other, related living things. Sometimes we destroy whole systems, and in such cases, Taylor suggests, we can make amends by protecting other systems of the same type we have wiped out, or finding other systems under threat and putting lots of effort into protecting these.

Pretty clearly, Taylor's ethical system is going to make very large demands on those who want to follow it. Whether to adopt his stance is an ethical, not a philosophical, question. But whether the ethic stacks up as a workable system embodying the biocentric worldview with which he starts is a philosophical question of some interest. Further, examining the relations among the four basic rules is also a philosophical issue. For example, we can ask whether some of them conflict with others, and, if so, under what conditions. As soon as we ask questions such as this, we find there is a need to clarify some of the basic ideas, and this sort of clarification is just the kind of quality control that philosophy provides.

For example, take the two rules dealing with non-maleficence and non-interference. Whether these conflict with each other depends on just what is meant by "interference" and what is meant by "causing harm". Here is a story to focus the point. Someone I dislike is about to step on a banana skin. I stand by and watch, hoping the person will step on the skin and slip. Indeed, he does, and I derive pleasure from the fact that, as a result of slipping, he spills the drink he is carrying. That is not very nice behaviour on my part, especially if it would have been very easy for me to call out a warning. What if I excuse myself from any responsibility for the harm that may come to the victim on the grounds that I followed the rule of non-interference? A bystander may say that I should have called out to warn my enemy about the banana skin. But why? One answer would be to cite the duty of non-maleficence. By staying silent, the bystander may say, I actually harmed the person I disliked. Notice that in this case I am blameworthy not because I actively brought about something bad (actually I did not act at all). What I can be blamed for is *not stopping* something bad. In terms of Taylor's duties, I cannot be criticized on the grounds of being maleficent.

The rule of non-maleficence is weaker than a rule that asks us to be benevolent. Calling out to warn the person of the impending slip would be a benevolent thing to do. On the other hand, calling out a warning is a very minimal kind of interference, so should we count that as "interference" at all? In discussing his rules, Taylor points out that failure to interfere in nature will often allow natural harms to occur. However, it is not any of our own actions that bring about this harm. So Taylor concludes that our own lack of intervention would never bring about a harm in nature (1986: 193). But this is precisely the conclusion that the story about the banana skin brings into doubt. In the story, my own dislike of the person who is about to tread on the banana skin plays a part in my deciding not to call out a warning. My inaction seems motivated by a kind of malevolence: of wishing ill to the person I dislike. There is a clear difference in wishing ill to someone and actively doing harm to them, and it is doing, or causing, harm that Taylor is focusing on in his principle of non-maleficence. What he has overlooked are situations in which omitting to take action can be a way of bringing about harms. Taylor's claim that our own non-interference never brings about a harm for which we are responsible is therefore debatable.

Taylor also argues that there are certain priority principles we need to use when thinking about the system of rules. Non-maleficence takes priority over the other rules, and clearly takes priority over the rule of restitution; it is better not to do harm than to do harm and then try to make amends. However, life will be cumbersome and tedious if we constantly need to think about the rules by which we live, the duties they enjoin on us and the relative priority of these in relation to each other. Taylor therefore lays out habits we should cultivate, so that morally right behaviour becomes second nature to us. A virtuous person is someone who engages in right conduct without having to think too deeply about it, for the simple reason that he or she has cultivated morally good habits of character. Not all morally good dispositions and habits are connected with respect for nature. So Taylor identifies first of all a set of moral virtues that make up a morally strong character in general: conscientiousness, integrity, patience, courage, temperance (self-control), disinterestedness (impartiality), perseverance and steadfastness-in-duty. Someone who manifests all these virtues will be disposed to act in morally correct ways. These are general virtues, whereas to each rule of duty, there corresponds a special virtue as shown in the box "Virtues".

By now it should be obvious what kind of system Taylor is advocating and what kind of people he thinks we should aim to become.

Virtues

Taylor's system of moral virtues (1986: 198–218)

- *General virtues*: conscientiousness, integrity, patience, courage, temperance (self-control), disinterestedness (impartiality), perseverance and steadfastness-in-duty

These are the dispositions of a morally strong character. A good character in regard to natural things also requires cultivation of *special virtues* corresponding to the four rules of duty:

- *Considerateness*: To be considerate is not just to refrain from harming, but also to avoid negligence, and to take care to find out if your actions will harm other beings. For instance, a considerate person will not want to release many helium-filled balloons at the start of a big sporting event unless they are biodegradable.
- *Regard (impartiality)*: Having regard means respecting the freedom of wild things, respecting their ways of living and not giving special favour to one species over another.
- *Trustworthiness*: A trustworthy person will not trick or betray wild creatures, nor take advantage of their lack of fear of humans to kill, capture or play tricks on them.
- *Fairness*: A fair person will want to make amends for damage they have previously caused to natural creatures or plants, and will give serious thought to deciding what measure of restitution is appropriate in a given situation, and in the light of the damage done to wild beings.

Becoming a virtuous person is not easy. Human beings are experts in self-deception, good at tricking themselves into thinking they are better than they actually are. We are also prone to weakness of will, aiming to do good things, live better lives and so on, but often failing to live up to the standards we espouse. All that is a problem even before we start to think about our special duties to natural things and the special virtues we need to cultivate to honour these. To be someone who lives a life of respect for nature, we would have to work hard at cultivating the special virtues associated with deep respect for nature, avoiding self-deception and weakness of will. But would such a life be possible for most of us? It begins to look as if Taylor's requirements are too demanding for people living the kind of life to which those in the industrial countries have now become accustomed. The enormous demands of the ethic become clearer when we consider the principles that he advocates for dealing with conflicts between humans and the rest of nature.

Priorities

However noble our ideals, however much we respect and admire natural things, our lives inevitably involve the destruction of the plants and animals we use for food, the killing of countless creatures when we clear land for farming or other development and the harming of yet more living things as our occupation of the planet brings about climate change, pollution, flooding, drought and a host of other consequences of human action. What is at stake, for Taylor, are the competing interests among humans, plants and animals. What serves many human interests will inevitably damage the interests of other living things. And of course, serving their interests will often damage us. There is no win–win solution in regard to nature. The best that an ecologically motivated person can do is try to live as lightly on the earth as possible. Taylor's system, then, can be thought of as putting forward a set of ideals for living gently on the planet, ideals that we may not be able to live up to but to which it may be noble to aspire. Within those ideals, priorities will have to be set, and even if we can never reach Taylor's ideal state, we may still find these priorities worth thinking about.

Taylor lays out five principles to determine the priorities between what is owed to humans and what is owed to non-human living things: self-defence, proportionality, minimum wrong, distributive justice and restitutive justice. We shall deal at length with the first of these, and then very quickly with each of the others.

Taylor's principle of self-defence allows moral agents to harm and even destroy other agents, including other people, but only when the following conditions are satisfied:

(a) the life or basic health of the moral agent is threatened;
(b) the agent has taken reasonable care to avoid being exposed to and endangered by those harmful non-humans;
(c) there is no other alternative to self-defence that is equally effective but will cause lesser harm to the non-human "attackers";
(d) harmless non-humans can also be legitimately harmed or destroyed, but only when it is practically impossible to separate them from the harmful ones and (a), (b) and (c) are satisfied.

There are very interesting implications of these conditions. For example, condition (b) raises the question whether it is right to defend ourselves against attacks from wild creatures when we are on their territory. Wanderers in the wilderness from Aldo Leopold to Bill McKibben have often noted that there is a real risk to undertaking wilderness expeditions, and that there are limits on how much protection we should expect to get from the hazards we may encounter (Leopold 1949; McKibben 1989). Val Plumwood, after suffering serious injuries from being attacked by a saltwater crocodile, argued against the standard practice of trying to find and shoot the animal that had nearly killed her. "I spoke strongly against this plan," she wrote in a magazine article. "I was the intruder ..., and no good purpose could be served by random revenge" (Plumwood 2000: 135). Those who are unlucky or careless in the wilderness often adopt an attitude of acceptance when things go wrong.

There is one problem with self-defence, one that is often not noticed by theorists, and which Taylor leaves in the background of his discussion. Self-defence is an acceptable excuse when first of all we only use force in proportion to the threat, and when, second, what threatens us is itself unlawful or unethical. If someone is trying to pick my pocket, hence doing something unlawful, I am not able to plead self-defence if I use lethal force, for the force is out of proportion to the wrong being done to me. However, it is legitimate to push the pickpocket away, or to snatch back an item being stolen from my person. In general, when I defend myself against another, then that person is doing – or aiming to do – some harm to me, something that is either unlawful or unethical. This condition does not hold for games, or play situations: that is, in cases where our other moral and legal standards are also suspended. In friendly play, bluffing, deception and all kinds of trickery can be fine, even though in everyday transactions with others such behaviour is not morally acceptable.

To make a plea of self-defence is often to attempt to justify violence against another when that other person is engaged in unlawful acts. The classic examples of self-defence therefore are ones where people defend themselves against assault, robbery or other intended crimes. It might seem, switching from law to ethics, that we are therefore entitled to do violence to other living things when they are engaged in unethical acts against us. But how is this to be judged? In Plumwood's case, she seemed to regard the crocodile that attacked her as having done no moral wrong, and that is why she did not want people to hunt it down and kill it. If humans are the only things with a sense of what is right and what is wrong, then other living things are innocents, or – in Mary Midgley's phrase – *natural wantons*. That is to say, they are neither good nor bad, and their actions are neither right nor wrong. On the other hand, if human appropriation of natural resources is wrong, if our expansion of land clearing and pollution is morally bad, then the timber worker who kills the snake or the bear cannot – morally speaking – claim self-defence. For – by Taylor's own ethical standards – it will usually be the case that humans who come face to face with threats to their health and safety from other living things are the ones who are in the wrong. Self-defence, then, gives very little scope for lethal and damaging action towards other living things, and so is not usually a good excuse for violent behaviour towards natural things.

Taylor's other principles apply to cases where the non-humans involved are harmless, meaning that if left alone they will not endanger our life or health. To understand how these principles are meant to work, we need to be clear on the difference between basic and non-basic interests. A creature's basic interests are those the fulfilment of which is necessary for it to live a life fitted to its species-specific nature. The basic interests of a fish, then, are those required for it to live the life of a healthy fish, and so basic interests are different from species to species. Basic human interests are those the fulfilment of which is necessary for a human being to live a meaningful and worthwhile human life. They include: subsistence, security, autonomy (being able to lay down laws to ourselves) and liberty. Humans and non-humans alike will have many non-basic interests, depending on where they are, what courses their lives have taken, and so on.

Taylor's ethic of respect for nature requires us to take a non-exploitative attitude to other natural creatures. For example, raising animals for food, clearing land for a sports ground and the like are actions that he regards as directly expressing an exploitative attitude to nature. In his terminology, such actions are intrinsically incompatible with respect for nature (Taylor 1986: 273–4). Taylor's second priority principle, proportionality, says that basic non-human interests morally override human interests when (a) non-basic interests of humans conflict with basic interests of (harmless) non-humans, and (b) the non-basic human interests involved are intrinsically incompatible with respect for nature. In terms of the principle of proportionality, human behaviour towards other living things nearly always involves disproportionate damage to these things. For we usually damage other animals and plants according to what we want, not according to what we need. Some damage to nature and natural things is inevitable, Taylor claims, if we are to meet our own basic needs and satisfy our own basic interests. But the scale of such damage would be relatively small compared to the actual damage we standardly inflict on other beings. We generally act in a way that ignores and overrides the basic interests of harmless non-humans.

It may seem that asking us to respect the principle of proportionality is just asking too much. For it is very hard indeed to imagine human society developing in a way that allows people to enrich their lives through society, adequate shelter, worthwhile activities with others, and so on, without sometimes putting our own non-basic interests ahead of the basic interests of other creatures. In a gesture towards values that appeal particularly to educated people in industrial societies, Taylor admits that human civilization, particularly the higher forms of civilized life, requires the destruction of plants and animals in order to serve non-basic interests of human beings. The construction of airports, power plants, museums and galleries are all cases where destruction of plant and animal life will be inevitable, and where collateral damage will be done to the interests of living things that are not directly killed by human action. In these cases, Taylor urges us to show a genuine respect for nature by taking all possible steps to minimize the wrong being done. For him, it is only the satisfaction of the most important of our non-basic interests that will justify doing damage to nature, and then only when our actions involve "the lowest number of violations of the rule of non-maleficence" (*ibid.*: 283).

But there is no single way of minimizing wrong done to plants and animals by our behaviour. In clearing land for a new museum building, we may have to choose between two or three sites where different kinds of plants and animals live. Then there is the concert hall and the airport. Where are they to be built, and which particular plants and animals are to suffer so that we can enjoy these amenities? How can we make an environmentally fair decision in these cases while still showing respect for nature? The answer is that we need to consider both individual cases and the combination of impacts that results from several sets of decisions over time. Taylor thinks that there are four methods we should follow here, and doing so exemplifies a principle of distributive justice. One of the methods is permanent habitat allocation: the setting aside of some parts of the planet to be "forever wild" and free from human interference. A second is common conservation, where we let species benefit from the things we build, so that some plants and animals are identified as beneficiaries for every development scheme we put forwards. Third, we try to ensure that our developments do not injure, or damage beyond repair, the ecological integrity of the region in which they occur. Finally, he recommends rotating benefits and disadvantages, by building on some sites with the intention of later rehabilitating them when the useful life of the project has ended. After all the above principles have been applied, Taylor thinks there will still be a case for trying to make good the damage and harm our actions will have caused. For in harming the harmless plants and animals that were sacrificed for the sake of development and civilization, we will have done wrong, and so restitution will be in order. So Taylor sets out as his final principle, that of restitutive justice, based on the simple idea that the greater the harm that has been done, the greater the degree of restitution required. In light of the description of the system, Taylor's whole structure can be set out in terms of Figure 4.1.

One consequence of Taylor's view is that subsistence hunting and fishing are morally permissible, while sport hunting is not. For subsistence hunting is used to satisfy basic human interests. Killing plants for food is also morally permissible when so doing is necessary for our survival. Although he does not spell out the reasoning here, one way of defending Taylor's view of the permissibility of such actions would be like this. Suppose that we are living in a situation where the only way to get nourishment is by killing animals to eat. If we did not kill the animals, then we would die, thereby sacrificing our own lives for the sake of non-humans. But no one is morally required to sacrifice one's own life for the sake of others who are not of any greater inherent worth. So in such cases killing the animals is permissible.

A further consequence of the ethic is that if we have a choice, it is better to kill plants for food than to kill animals if by doing so we cause pain and suffering to the animals. The fact that animals have a capacity for suffering does not make them have more inherent worth than plants. In this way, Taylor's position is very unlike those of Regan and Singer. Yet, like them, he regards pain and suffering as intrinsically evil. And

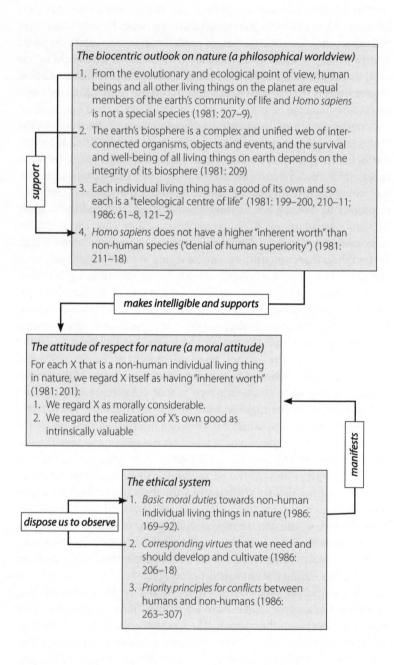

Figure 4.1 Taylor's argument.

it is the intrinsic badness of suffering, not any presumed superiority of animals over plants, that makes it better to use plants for food. Moreover, the adoption of a vegetarian lifestyle will drastically reduce the area we use for raising animals for foods, and those areas can be restored and used as habitats for wild living things. This will reduce our exploitation of nature, and hence would be in accordance with the principle of distributive justice.

Tough though the demands of Taylor's ethic are, we may wonder whether he takes his principles far enough. After all, all life is equally valuable in his view. So why are some human non-basic interests worth supporting when the cost of doing so means sacrificing the basic interests of other, equally valuable, living things? Taylor thinks museums, airports, hospitals and concert halls are worth building, and that the cost of maintaining civilization through such facilities is worth the sacrifice in non-human suffering. Yet such a judgement itself seems relative to interests that themselves need further defence. A sport hunter may argue that the joys of hunting are just as great as the pleasure to be derived from museums and concerts; a gourmand may regard the sacrifice of the animal's interests well worth the pleasure of a wagyu steak or a delicate sashimi. To avoid debates about the relative merits of gourmet food, sport hunting and concerts, Taylor might have demanded much greater sacrifices from us. After all, an ethic that respects all life equally would perhaps not permit the building of libraries, museums and concert halls any more than the construction of shopping malls, theme parks and food courts. An austere version of Taylor's ethic would demand that we change our lifestyles radically, so as to tread lightly on the planet, and bring greater equality into our dealings with other people and other living things.

On the other hand, Taylor's ethic seems to get some things badly wrong. Because he focuses only on individual plants and animals, he has nothing to say about what is wrong with killing the last member of an endangered species rather than wiping out many individuals of a plentiful species. In Australia, for example, many of the smaller kangaroos are endangered, while nine species have become extinct since the European settlement of the continent. At the same time, thanks to land clearing and farming practices that create open range and water dams, several of the larger kangaroo species are more populous now than when the Europeans arrived. From the point of view of an individualistic biocentric ethic, each kangaroo's interest is the same; so Taylor's theory has no resources by which to put priority on protecting an endangered hare wallaby above protecting a kangaroo from a well-represented species.

Some of the smaller kangaroo species are threatened not only by habitat changes induced by humans but by predation from introduced animals such as foxes and cats. Again, for Taylor, the killing of a member of one of these exotic or "feral" species is no more or less morally problematic than the killing of a wallaby. Public opinion in Australia is very different. Among those concerned with environmental protection there is an even bigger dissonance between their attitudes to native species and to introduced species. For many of them, the culling of introduced animals is something to which priority has to be given, and hence not every life and every associated set of interests is equal.

While Regan's account of animal rights emphasized the subjectivity of animals, Taylor's biocentric outlook is strongly influenced by considerations of teleology: that each living thing has a *telos*, or end, towards which it will develop provided nothing interferes. Suppose that every living thing does have a direction of development, and an end-state towards which it inevitable moves. Such an idea may well be doubted, but never mind. Just suppose Taylor is right on this. There is still a puzzle at the heart of his theory. Why does the possession of such a *telos* make something inherently valuable? Taylor's system of ethics has such radical implications that most people will need a strong argument to encourage them to support it. But where is the argument? The absence of the necessary argument is a major obstacle to acceptance of Taylor's position.

Taylor's ethic is focused on individual moral responsibility towards individual living things. In a more comprehensive view of our situation, we need to consider our roles as members of larger systems and groups. In the next chapter, we shall introduce the idea of community, as well as the notion that communities and other groups also need to be considered as morally worthy of consideration. Meanwhile, although Taylor's biocentric ethic looks difficult to adopt and is plagued by a range of problems, it has taught us something about a parallel system of human ethics. If instead of the biocentric outlook on nature, we adopt the view that each of us is a rational, freely choosing (autonomous) being, surrounded by other similarly rational and autonomous beings, then we can develop a standard Kantian ethic. Since, according to Kant, rational autonomous beings have "unconditional worth", an attitude of *respect for persons* will replace Taylor's attitude of respect for nature. An ethical system of basic duties, corresponding virtues and priority principles will then make manifest the attitude of respect for persons. The objections in this chapter to Taylor's biocentric ethic will clearly not have the same force when applied to an ethic for rational beings – which is the one that Kant originally envisaged.

five

Community: how big is our moral world?

In a classic study of corporate managers, Robert Jackall quotes one manager as saying: "What is right in the corporation is what the guy above you wants from you. That's what morality is in the corporation" (Jackall 1988: 103). The chief executive of a major bank was recently heard to say: "What's right is what's right for the bank". So far in this book, we have considered a series of different claims about what is right and wrong, based on ideas about pain, sentience or being a subject of a life, or on respect for nature. None of these views have come close to the view that moral rights and wrongs depend on what other people want, or on what is good for a larger entity of which individuals are only parts. Yet it is obvious that none of us live a life of complete isolation, and our family, the wider society and the natural environment in which we live all play their parts in shaping our beliefs, attitudes, characters and values. Aldo Leopold, an early champion of conservationist thinking, described human beings as "plain members and citizens" of larger biological communities, while in his 1992 book on green political theory, Robert Goodin suggested that: "people want to see some sense and pattern to their lives … That requires in turn that their lives be set in some larger context. The products of natural processes, untouched as they are by human hands, provides precisely that desired context" (Goodin 1992: 37). As we shall see in this chapter, it is not only nature that can provide such a larger context for our lives. Natural contexts are one among many larger systems and structures that can have an impact on the moral views we take.

Holism

Is a house more or less real than the bricks out of which it is built? The question may look like a trick. Surely, bricks and houses are both real, and so it makes no sense to say one is more real than the other. Traditional philosophy, though, does not mind making some distinctions here, based on notions of dependence. Plato, for example, thought that we could not group different things together – a beautiful statue, a beautiful building, a beautiful face – unless there was some common standard of beauty by which the statue, building and face could be compared. That standard – the Idea or Form of the beautiful – would be more real than the things that were individually beautiful. Why? Because, he thought, our classifications depended on the standard, not the other way round. Without the Idea of the beautiful, there would be no beautiful face or building. So the standard was more real than the things that manifested it, and they were less real than it.

Applying the same idea to the bricks and the building we could ask: does the building depend on the bricks, or the bricks on the building? One answer (not the only one) is that the bricks would have continued to exist, even if they hadn't been made into a building. And we can even imagine the building being knocked down, while most of the bricks survive; that is why it is possible to recycle old bricks and make new buildings out of them. So, looked at in this way, the building depends for its existence on the existence of the bricks, but the bricks do not in the same way depend on the existence of the building. In a sense, then, the building is less real than the bricks out of which it is made. In another sense, of course, the building and the bricks are equally real. For to be real is just to exist. And once we transform a pile of bricks and other materials into a house, then the house is there, every bit as real as the bricks from which it is built.

Metaphysical speculations about whether a house is more or less real than the bricks of which it is made might seem a long way removed from environmental philosophy. But our metaphysical notions about what is real and what is fundamental are often closely linked with our moral notions about where the source of value is to be found, and about what matters. What is my body? Is it a collection of tissues and organs, or does it have some separate status? And what is each of us in relation to our social and biological surroundings. To an extent, each one of us is shaped by our place in a wider group: the family, the wider local community, the larger nation and finally all of humanity itself. In each case, the issue of the whole and the part is key. As an integrated functioning human being, I am a whole consisting of many bodily parts, organs, tissues, nerves, blood vessels; I am a system of smaller systems, each of which is important in preserving my life and making possible everything I do. Yet within the larger city community in which I live, and through which I move every day, I am just a tiny particle, carried along in the circulation of buses, cars, trucks, trams, trains and bicycles, stopping for a while now in this building, now in another, passing information to other tiny particles I meet, sharing with them also oxygen, germs and even the atoms that I inhale and exhale each time I breathe. Looked at in this way, I am part of something bigger, just as a red blood cell in my body is part of something much bigger.

Ethics based on an individualistic approach regards the human individual as the most important item in the moral universe. Individuals are regarded as being independent of the communities, cultures and nations within which they live. For the individualists, these larger wholes could not exist without the work, support and cooperation of individuals. So they depend on individuals, not the other way round. Expressed in moral, rather than metaphysical, terms, individualists see the moral value of a company, a town or a nation as no more than the aggregate of the value of the individuals who make it up. By contrast, holists argue that wholes are just as real, and hence just as important, as the parts that make them up. The holist usually wants to make two claims: first, that wholes have their own drives and characters independently of their constituent individuals. For example, I may work for an organization that has a life of its own, a company culture and directions that seem not to be under the control of any individual or group of individuals in the company. This first claim is a factual claim about the status of an organization as an entity over and above the status of the people who are parts of it. The second claim that is typically made by holists is a moral one; namely, that a whole *per se* has a moral value and standing over and above the sum of the moral value and standing of its constituent individuals.

In an essay that became a chapter of his 1949 book, *A Sand County Almanac*, Leopold gave form to a kind of holistic ethic: "A thing is right when it tends to preserve the integrity, stability, and beauty of the biotic community. It is wrong when it tends otherwise" (1949: 224–5). This is the heart of Leopold's land ethic, a version of which has been championed more recently by Baird Callicott. When writing about the biotic community (or "the land", as he often called it) Leopold was referring to the whole community of life on earth, including all terrestrial ecosystems. Humans themselves are members and citizens of the land, and also managers and doctors of it. The inhabitants of the land can teach us

Aldo Leopold's *A Sand County Almanac* inspired many of the ideas that became central in late-twentieth-century environmental philosophy.

L1. "That land is a community is the basic concept of ecology, but that land is to be loved and respected is an extension of ethics. That land yields a cultural harvest is a fact long known, but latterly often forgotten" (1949: viii–ix).

L2. "Every farm woodland, in addition to yielding lumber, fuel, and posts, should provide its owner a liberal education. This crop of wisdom never fails, but it is not always harvested" (*ibid.*: 73).

L3. "We reached the old wolf in time to watch a fiece green fire dying in her eyes. I realized then, and have known ever since, that there was something new to me in those eyes – something known only to her and to the mountain. I was young then, and full of trigger-itch; I thought that because fewer wolves meant more deer, that no wolves would mean hunters' paradise. But after seeing the green fire die, I sensed that neither the wolf not the mountain agreed with such a view" (*ibid.*: 130).

L4. "The land ethic simply enlarges the boundaries of the community to include soils, waters, plants and animals, or collectively: the land … A land ethic … cannot prevent the alteration, managment and use of these 'resources', but it does affirm their right to continued existence, and, at least in spots, their continued existence in a natural state" (*ibid.*: 204).

L5. "It is inconceivable to me that an ethical relation to land can exist without love, respect, and admiration for land and a high regard for its value. By value, I of course mean something far broader than mere economic value; I mean value in the philosophical sense" (*ibid.*: 223).

many lessons about life and ourselves, and at least some of the time they should be left to live in their wild natural state. His sketchy remarks have inspired various forms of holistic environmental ethics, and exemplify what Holmes Rolston III (1988) has called our "storied residence" in nature. They have also encouraged the development of an ethics of place, a sense of bioregional identity (Sale 1985), and a suspicion of economic measures of environmental value (Sagoff 1988; 2004). Despite its wide-ranging influence, Leopold's land ethic looks just as unacceptable as a basis for the good life as the banker's claim that what's right is what's right for the bank. No doubt living in nature – just like working for the bank – gives a larger structure and pattern to our lives, as Goodin remarks. That fact alone would not make either nature, or the bank, the source of the most fundamental ethical principles governing our lives. In a moment, we shall look at some recent attempts to defend Leopold's land ethic against the charge that it is inherently authoritarian, even "fascist".

Holistic views of nature were reinforced by the Gaia theory originally proposed by James Lovelock (1979). The Gaia hypothesis is that the earth's crust, along with its oceans, atmosphere and the biosphere make up one system. This great structure is self-sustaining and self-regulating. In particular, Gaia regulates those features critical for the maintenance of life: the oxygen content of the atmosphere, the salinity of the seas, mean surface temperatures, atmospheric pressure and so on. According to Lovelock, instead of thinking of ourselves as living on an inert planet that "supports" a biosphere, we should think of the whole earth as a single large "superorganism". Its parts include rocks, and structures studied by geology as well as the living communities and the elements – carbon, nitrogen and so on – cycled through them.

The theory that earth is a single living organism had its origins in the work of the eighteenth-century Scottish geologist James Hutton. He was the first person to propose that the planet's crust is a kind of physiological system. The rock cycle, for example, redistributes and changes material belonging to the mantle, crust and surface of the earth. By studying rocks we discover that, over enormous spans of time, mountain ranges grow and disappear, valleys form and close, coasts advance and recede in a process of endless change. The movement of water from sea to land and back again, and the recirculation of nutrition through the soil were, Hutton argued, akin to the circulation of blood and nourishment in the living body.

Inspired by Hutton, Lovelock proposed in a later book to use the term "geophysiology" as a substitute for what he had earlier called "Gaia science" (Lovelock 1988). The idea was that a switch in terminology might make the Gaia idea seem more scientifically respectable. However, the key evidence that we might be part of a larger and self-regulating planetary system came from a number of "daisyworld" models described in the later book. These models provided strong evidence for the view that the more complex and diverse the ecosystems on the planet, the more stable and resilient would be its means for controlling temperature and other variables critical to sustaining life on earth. Even in his early work, Lovelock counted the rocks, air and oceans as part of Gaia. Indeed, in a striking comparison, he points out that just as the dead heartwood of a tree carries the history of its earlier growth, so the atoms of rocks deep in the magma come from the ancestral life that once existed on the planet's surface. If we regard trees as living organisms, then the planet can also be regarded as a living thing: Gaia. It is not easy to derive any ethical guidance from reflection on the Gaia hypothesis. Do we need to make sacrifices, for example, to maintain the planetary superorganism?

Daisyworld

A major achievement described in Lovelock (1988) was to show, by means of a series of simple "daisyworld" models, that an imaginary planet can maintain a relatively constant temperature in the face of increasing solar radiation through the "struggle for existence" among daisies of different shades of colour. In a simple daisyworld model, there are two kinds of plants only: black and white daisies. Each species can survive only at temperatures between 5°C and 40°C. The sun of daisyworld is slowly heating up. In the beginning, the surface temperature of the planet is cool, and the black daisies germinate and grow slowly. Being darker than the soil, the spread of the black daisies produces higher temperatures on the parts of the planet on which they are established. The warmer conditions favour more rapid germination and faster growth, so the black daisies spread more rapidly. This leads to more absorption of solar energy and a generally warmer planet.

Much later, the hot spots created in dense areas of black daisies inhibit further daisy growth as they start to approach the upper limits of the species temperature range. As the sun gets progressively hotter, the white daisies begin to have an advantage. They reflect more of the sun's heat away from the surface of the earth producing conditions favourable to longer life for them and their offspring and better chances for seeds to germinate. Black daisies start dying out, as the whites win in the struggle for existence. At the global level, the success of the white daisies means that the average surface temperature of the planet does not increase. Instead, there is a roughly constant temperature maintained during the changes in daisy populations. From the point of view of the daisies, this is just a struggle for survival between two species with different pigmentation and similar temperature tolerances. But from the point of view of the planet, the change from black to white dominance has preserved a relatively stable mean temperature. No daisy, or population, intended to achieve this result. Despite the appearance of design, there is no need to attribute purpose at any level in the daisyworld system.

The daisyworld models suggested two things. First, that living things in competition with each other for space to grow can work like a thermostat controlling the overall temperature of the planet. In this way, Darwinian biology is incorporated into the theory, not excluded by it. Second, the models provided a possible answer to the question: why is there an increase in biodiversity over time? Increasing biodiversity will ensure greater resilience and sophistication of the temperature-controlling mechanism in the face of fluctuations in solar radiation. In principle, the same story can be thought to apply to mechanisms regulating other important conditions. This would include, for example, the availability of elements essential for the growth and maintenance of living things as well as the factors that ensure relatively constant proportions of atmospheric gases.

Perhaps, but – on the other hand – it may be that what we think of as destructive and damaging changes are not particularly harmful to Gaia. For example, if species reduction brought about by human action leads to major changes in the larger biotic and planetary systems on which life depends, we cannot predict whether these changes will bring about new forms of life, new prospects for prolonging life on earth, or will – on the contrary – shorten the likely tenure of life on earth.

Underlying this puzzle is a deeper puzzle that goes to the heart of much thinking about the environment. The puzzle is another variant on the question: are humans special? Are we one natural species among many on earth, or do we stand apart from nature, as a species with a special potential for damaging and caring for all the rest of life on earth? As we shall find in Chapters 6 and 7, the question of what it is to be part of nature is a vexed one, mired in the ambiguity of the word "natural". And the question of human specialness and human value is a key issue not only for environmental ethics but also for environmental aesthetics. In this chapter, we focus on two much more limited issues related to holistic ethics, exploring these through Callicott's version of Leopold's land ethic, and Arne Naess's philosophy of deep ecology.

More ambiguous than the land ethic, but just as influential in environmental thought, was the claim that Arne Naess, the Norwegian philosopher, made in 1973 that human beings were "knots in a larger web of life" and that we should reject the "man-in-the-environment image in favour of the relational, total-field image". Naess's view at the time seemed to be that individual identity was not a metaphysical given; rather, each person has a possibly shifting relational identity, defined by a network of identifications we can each make with other people, social structures, natural objects (including, in his case, mountains and rivers). Self-realization, on Naess's scheme, involved a wide identification with nature. Naess's position is more ambiguous than Leopold's because it was unclear whether he was mainly advocating a metaphysical change of view: that human beings are essentially relational, and that they lack any clear conditions of individual identity. Such a relational view of the individual is compatible with maintaining respect both for the things in relation and for the system of relations within which the things find themselves suspended and by means of which their identities are defined. In his later writings, Naess moved away from the "total field" view, and from the biocentric egalitarianism that he had originally championed. We shall come back later to look in slightly more detail at Naess's deep ecology and its metaphysical ramifications.

Holistic environmental ethics

For Callicott, one of Leopold's best-known contemporary defenders, the land ethic is right to put primary value on ecological wholes, such as species, biotic communities and ecosystems. Since these things are of primary value, humans, plants and animals considered as individuals, are of secondary importance. When interpreting Leopold's insistence that the integrity, beauty and stability of the biotic community is primary, Callicott famously insisted that:

> What is especially noteworthy, and that to which attention should be directed in this proposition, is the idea that the good of the biotic community is the ultimate measure of the moral value, the rightness or wrongness, of actions. … In every case the effect upon ecological systems is the decisive factor in the determination of the ethical quality of actions.
>
> (Callicott 1989: 21)

Animal and plant lives, therefore, should be sacrificed if they conflict with the system's holistic good. Culling deer that are stripping trees of their leaves might not only be permissible, but actually required in order to save a forest ecosystem. A similar argument would perhaps lead to the conclusion that in Australia the damage done by exotic animals such as cats, camels, goats, rabbits and foxes would justify heroic measures to eliminate these "ferals" in order to safeguard native ecosystems. Callicott never denied that individual living things have interests of various kinds: in welfare, gaining food, avoiding pains and so on. But what he appeared to be denying was that individual things had much by way of moral standing in their own right (as opposed to the contribution they could make to the larger systems in which they lived). This early position is what can be called Callicott's original land-ethical holism, and its key principles are LE1 and LE2.

Not surprisingly, this kind of extreme holism was criticized as "misanthropic" and "eco-fascist" (Regan's term) because it always subordinates the welfare of individual animals and living things to the good of the larger community. A major challenge was whether there are any ways of reformulating this kind of theory to make it less stringent in its moral demands on individuals, and whether it can leave room for a sense of the moral importance and significance of the individual. In later writings, Callicott tried to meet the challenge by developing a multilayered communitarianism of a more nuanced kind. At first, he developed

> *Moral holism*
>
> Callicott's original land-ethical moral holism
>
> LE1. The biotic community *per se* is the sole locus of moral value and moral considerability, and these latter features are not present in individual living things.
>
> LE2. It is an absolute moral duty to protect the holistic good (or well-being) of the biotic community, to which the goods (e.g. welfare, interest, preference) of individuals always ought to be subordinated.

a view that took account of the different responsibilities we have to family, neighbours, our fellow citizens, local and regional species and other systems. Still maintaining the moral primacy of the community over the individual member, he argued that, for each community we are members of, such membership generates a holistic moral principle that says we should protect the good of the community as such. Then he added a clause dealing with individuals. Since we identify ourselves in terms of such community membership, we will come to feel a concern for others who also belong to communities we belong to. And that feeling of mutual belonging generates a sense of responsibility to protect the interests of our fellow community members. In this way, while keeping the interests of the larger community as the primary focus, Callicott was able to introduce a derivative concern for individual interests. Moreover, since neighbourhoods, nation states and other groups to which we are affiliated are not ecosystems, our duty to the biotic community is only one among others. Hence he gives up principles LE1 and LE2 in favour of a much weaker claim:

LE3. It is a *prima facie* (not absolute) moral duty to protect the holistic good of the biotic community. On occasion, the good of individuals can be preferred over the good of the biotic community.

We are simultaneously members of many communities, ranging from the immediate family, neighbourhood and nation to the whole human species, and likewise from different ecosystems and bioregions to the global biotic community. Membership in each distinct community generates a distinct set of duties to protect the interests of that community and its members. As members of the human species, we have duties to maintain the continued survival of our species and also a duty to respect the rights of other people. On the other hand, Callicott argues, as members of the global biotic community we have a duty to preserve its integrity and beauty. The land ethic, therefore, is only one of many different layers of moral codes within a larger range of codes, all of which apply to us. Since it is possible to urge protection of ecological wholes and also respect for human individuals then this looks like an ethic that can be environmental without being either misanthropic or eco-fascist.

Problems with Callicott's ethical theory

The solution of one problem frequently provokes other problems. Callicott's later theory is based on a kind of ethical sentimentalism. For him, something has intrinsic value if a community of people value it (i.e. they share a positive moral sentiment towards it) as an end-in-itself. This is very different from Taylor's view, discussed in Chapter 4, since Taylor's account of value makes no reference to how people feel. By contrast, Callicott's theory reduces facts about values to certain psychological facts about people living in a community. It implies that there are no values without communities of valuers. This kind of view is called value subjectivism: whether something has a value depends on people having a direct positive feeling towards it for its own sake. Leopold himself sometimes talked about our feelings toward the land itself in more specific terms: "that land is to be loved and respected is an extension of ethics" he wrote in the Foreword to *A Sand County Almanac*. Callicott's new version of Leopold does not require anything so specific as love towards things we value: a shared positive feeling towards a lake, a forest or a city will be enough to support the claim that the object of the feeling is of value in itself. While subjectivist theories of ethics come in more and less complex forms, Callicott's version of communitarian ethics is essentially simple: value originates from human feelings directed towards an object (whether an emu, a tree, a mountain, a species or a whole ecosystem). Since he does not focus on humans as being uniquely possessors of value, he regards value as being *anthropogenic* (human-generated) without being *anthropocentric* (human-centred), for, after all, it can be focused on many non-human things. So if a community of people value (that is, feel positively towards) an ecosystem in its own right, then the ecosystem has intrinsic value. What gives values and morality stability or even universality, Callicott suggests, is the simple fact that human beings across times and cultures are similar in their basic needs, affections and aversions. In particular, he believes that people are evolutionarily endowed with the disposition to value the community to which they belong once they recognize their belonging to it. The land ethic, he argues, is just the latest realization of that communitarian disposition in us.

By this stage in his later writings, Callicott has allowed in many different kinds of value. Since people often feel positively towards those they love, those they work beside and many others, then individual human beings will have intrinsic moral value (something that was not clearly stated in Callicott's original defence of the land ethic). But in addition there are dozens of other things that have value in their own right too. Since we feel positively towards many of the communities we inhabit, these communities will also have intrinsic value. So now a big problem faces the theory. Since so many things – individuals, communities and systems – can be intrinsically valuable, how should we prioritize the many competing moral principles generated by our many community memberships? In response to this question, Callicott introduced the principle that duties to communities closer to us (in terms of emotional involvement) take priority over those further away. The rationale for this is that if for a thing to have value is the same as for a community of people to have a positive feeling towards it, then the stronger the feeling, the greater the value, and therefore the stronger the duty to protect it. The first principle is unlikely to support a robust environmental ethic, and certainly not anything like Leopold's original land ethic. As a matter of fact, most people most of the time do not value the biotic communities they inhabit more than they value the human communities that are dear to them. That is why a second principle is required, one that Callicott subsequently introduced: that the stronger the interest at stake, the higher the priority for its protection. This obliges us to sacrifice trivial human interests (e.g. the pleasure from eating whales) for the protection of significant environmental ones (e.g. the protection of endangered species). While the first principle seems to follow from the subjectivist account of ethics Callicott has given, the second one is apparently independent. We can suppose, at least for the sake of finishing off our construction of Callicott's ethical system that he has in mind something like Singer's egalitarian principle, introduced in Chapter 3, that equal interests demand equal consideration.

The introduction of the two principles does not solve the problem of conflicts. What is needed is a further principle that will tell us what to do when the first two principles come into conflict. Suppose I live in a logging community and several of my close relatives and friends are employed in the local timber industry. My own work is in the local tourist bureau, and I happen to be very emotionally attached to the giant karri forest in the locality (karri trees are extremely tall and elegant trees, the Australian equivalent of the great Californian redwoods at the centre of conservation efforts in the early twentieth century). Now I experience conflict. My emotional investment in my family and friends is significant. Nonetheless, I feel also a strong duty to argue for protecting the forests of magnificent trees. If I make the decision on the basis of sentiment, in the end I am likely to favour my friends and families over the trees. On the other hand, the destruction of the great forest will mean death not only to the huge trees, but disruption to ecosystems and the death of thousands, if not millions, of other living creatures. So my attachment to the two principles leads to deadlock. One way out is to adopt a tiebreak rule, one that says that where the two principles collide, then the stronger interests prevail. So Callicott suggested that we should adopt the general principle that the second always takes priority over the first.

Unfortunately, this suggestion faces two major problems. First, it is internally inconsistent, since the second principle – the one that takes priority – makes reference not to sentiments or feelings but to interests. Callicott not only fails to provide any advice on how to measure the significance of interests, but elsewhere in his work attacks Singer's egalitarian principle on the grounds that it takes no account of feelings and emotional investment. He thinks that there is no doubt that duties to our families take priority over our duties to civic charities, to animals, or to those who are unrelated to us. So there is a real puzzle in understanding how he can make sense of using a principle like Singer's to defend natural communities in the face of human disruption. Second, and just as worrying for Callicott, is the fact that the system of two principles and the tiebreak rule no longer looks like a communitarian system at all, and fails to preserve the land-ethic approach. On the contrary, by trying to avoid the charge of eco-fascism, it looks as if Callicott has come up with a system that has marginalized feelings for the land and has given priority to interests that themselves are undefined.

Despite these problems, Callicott's theory, unlike Taylor's biocentric ethics, has left space for the recognition that communities and other

---

Tiebreaker

Principle 1: The more emotionally invested we are in a given community, the stronger our duties towards the community and its individual members.

Principle 2: Stronger interests generate stronger duties.

Tiebreak rule: Principle 2 countermands Principle 1 whenever the two conflict.

holistic entities can have an important status in moral thinking and can themselves be a proper object of moral concern to us. In common with Taylor's theory, Callicott faces a problem of conflicting duties, responsibilities and principles. In the case of Taylor's theory, it is not always clear what priority to give to respect for nature when such respect is in conflict with our respect for human beings. Taylor's radical claims for biocentric equality seem to be undermined, to a very large extent, by his concern to protect important features of human culture, civility and the massive technical achievements of *Homo sapiens*. On the other hand, Callicott explicitly tries to state a rule that will determine priorities, but if we follow that rule, then the original force of the land ethic is seriously diminished. So both Taylor and Callicott face a common problem: their initial theories seem to pose a serious challenge for the anthropocentric outlook on the world. But as their work develops, human interests and cares come back to the foreground and the challenge to anthropocentrism seems to fade away. Do other radical ecological views fare any better?

Deep ecology

As already noted, Naess's original formulation of deep ecology in 1973 postulated that humans and other living things are all knots in a larger web of life. Taking a relational conception of ourselves seriously – one supported by ecological science – meant that we each in some sense extend beyond our physical bodies. Another influential thinker, Rolston, also commented that reflection on ecology shows us that the skin is not a morally relevant boundary: there is as much to wonder at and value in skin-out processes as to admire and be astonished by in processes inside the skin. For Naess, our interconnections with the wider world meant that in a sense that world is part of us. Commenting in his 1986 paper "Self-Realization: An Ecological Approach to Being in the World" on a demonstration against a Norwegian hydropower project that would mean the damming of a river, Naess noted that one of the Sámi people at the protest said: "The river is part of me". The "me" here is what Naess called the larger of ecological self: a self that recognizes its dependence on the natural environment and which cares for, and identifies with, the natural things around it.

Naess's early idea of self-realization involved a set of norms or rules, the following of which would lead to increasing happiness, and protection of the environment. The outline ideas are given in the box below,

> ### Ecosophy T
>
> Norm 1: Aim at self-realization
> *Hypotheses*: (1) The higher the self-realization attained by anyone, the broader and deeper the identification with others. (2) The higher the level of self-realization attained by anyone, the more its further increase depends on the increase of self-realization of others. So (3) complete self-realization of anyone depends on that of all. Therefore:
>
> Norm 2: Aim at self-realization for all living beings.
> *Hypothesis*: (4) Diversity of life increases self-realization potentials. Therefore:
>
> Norm 3: Aim at maximum diversity of life.
> *Hypothesis*: (5) Complexity of life increases self-realization potentials. Therefore:
>
> Norm 4: Aim at maximum complexity.
> *Hypotheses*: (6) Resources of the earth are limited. (7) Symbiosis maximizes self-realization potentials under conditions of limited resources. Therefore:
>
> Norm 5: Aim at maximum symbiosis!

and make up what Naess called "Ecosophy T" (the "T" reminding him of his Tvergastein cabin high in the Hallingskarvet range). The key ideas combine both self-centredness and orientation towards others, since the larger, ecological Self embraces others in its scope. As we aim to realize ourselves (norm 1), we find that our own self-realization depends on the self-realization of others (norm 2), which is itself promoted by increasing the diversity of living things (norm 3) and also complexity (norm 4) and symbiosis (norm 5). To live richly – say the life of an organic farmer – is to live a life that is simple in means (minimizing the consumption of resources) but rich in ends (encouraging self-realization). In his 1986 paper, Naess follows the teachings of Erich Fromm, who denies Freud's view that we only have a limited libido, hence a limited amount of love (Fromm 1973). If this were true, altruism would be self-diminishing and self-depleting, because the more love we spare for others, the less we have left for ourselves.

Fromm's alternative view is that:

> love of others and love of ourselves are not alternatives. On the contrary, an attitude of love towards themselves will be found in all those who are capable of loving others. Genuine love is an expression of productiveness and implies care, respect, responsibility and knowledge.
>
> (Fromm 1973, quoted in Naess 1986: 228)

Naess uses Fromm's example of a self-consciously "unselfish" mother who aims to make herself useful to her children and becomes anxious and stressed over the whole business of devoting herself to their interests, hoping thereby to earn love from them. Contrary to her expectations, the children themselves do not seem to love her. Quoting Fromm again, "the children do not show the happiness of persons who are convinced that they are loved; they are anxious, tense, afraid of the mother's disapproval, and anxious to live up to her expectations". Nothing, Fromm says, is better than being loved by a mother who loves herself. Self-love is not only compatible with love for others, but an important component of it.

What has Fromm's view to do with environmental ethics or ecological philosophy? The case of the anxious mother is a warning to us. For Naess, the love of nature is not to be joyless, anxious, or driven by dislike of human beings (even though he admitted that he himself was a bit "socially apart"). Nor should it be undertaken in an attempt to solve personality problems or compensate for our inadequacies. Although in his early work he championed a kind of biospheric egalitarianism, insisting all living things were alike in inherent value, he rejected the sometimes misanthropic views that conservationists on occasion espouse, which have included calls to stop efforts at famine relief in poor countries as a way of preventing further environmental destruction. Naess, a long-time supporter of human rights, the women's movement and the peace movement, wanted to develop a philosophy of joyful affirmation to counter any notion that his new philosophy of deep ecology would be misanthropic simply because it rejected anthropocentrism.

Ecosophy T was later dropped by Naess in favour of a much weakened position known as "the deep ecology platform". In his own thinking he continued to support the idea that we should develop a conception of our ecological selves that would recognize that the world of people around me is – in some sense – part of who I am, just as the natural world in which I live is also part of me. If these claims are accepted, then it seems to follow that destruction of the natural environment means loss of identity. There are plenty of cases where this seems to have happened, for example where aboriginal inhabitants find their cultural practices forced to change as their traditional hunting and gathering environments have been destroyed. When the Sámi protester said "The river is part of me" this meant something more than "If this place is destroyed then something important to me is destroyed", for the place and me are not meant to be two separate entities. A puzzle about this is the fact that the "internal relation" between *me* and *the river* is not symmetrical: if the river is destroyed then I am damaged, but if I am destroyed, nothing much happens to the river. This asymmetry explains what would otherwise be a puzzling use of the phrase "part of". From a common-sense point of view, humans, plants and animals are all parts of the wider environment. If I use – and live beside – a river, then I might think of myself as part of the river or part of the river country. Leopold's original idea of the land ethic was founded on the idea that we all belong to the land, not vice versa. By turning things around and saying that the river is part of me, Naess, like the protester, conveys the important message that damage to the environment is – sooner or later – damage to ourselves. Elsewhere he comments that when developers and governments press ahead with projects in the face of environmental protests, they often claim a "win" over the opponents. But only in the short term is this a win, for in the long run the reduction of self-realization is always a loss.

We might think that if nature is part of me then I own it, or at least share ownership of it with others. After all, the things I own – such as my bicycle, my body and my books – are easy to imagine at least metaphorically as being parts of me. So why can I not be thought of as owning the land or other parts of the environment? In fact, the tradition of Western ethical and political thought would endorse the idea that we own not only what is literally part of us, but also things that we work with: since we have a primary claim to own our own bodies, and our own work, then anything with which we mix our body's labour can also be claimed

---

Property

Whatsoever then, he removes out of the state which nature hath provided, and left it in, he hath mixed his labour with, and jointed to it something that is his own, and thereby makes it his property … For this Labour being the unquestionable Property of the Labourer, no Man but he can have a right to what that is once joyned to, at least where there is enough, and as good left in common for others.
(John Locke, *Second Treatise on Government* [2004]: II, 27)

The first man who, having enclosed a piece of ground, bethought himself of saying "This is mine," and found people simple enough to believe him, was the real founder of civil society. Humanity would have been spared infinite crimes, wars, homicides, murders, if only someone had ripped up the fences or filled in the ditches and said, "Do not listen to this pretender! You are eternally lost if you do not remember that the fruits of the earth are everyone's property and that the land is no-one's property! (Jean-Jacques Rousseau, *The Origins of Inequality* [1998]: 27)

to be ours. So, at least, argued the seventeenth-century English philosopher John Locke, whose theory of land ownership is central to some contemporary legal regimes of ownership. Locke's view has an important qualification: that we can only claim to own the land we mix with our labour where there is "as good left in common for others". Despite the qualification, other thinkers, such as the Swiss philosopher Jean-Jacques Rousseau, have disputed the idea that natural goods – the fruits of the earth – can properly speaking be owned by anyone. Where does Naess stand on this matter? Like Taylor, Leopold and Callicott, Naess is keen to see wilderness preserved, hence keen to see limitations placed on private ownership of wild areas. But deep ecology is not in general aiming to convince us that we own the land in anything like a legal sense. For the deep ecologist, it is an open question whether private or public ownership of land is best for protecting the environment.

Central to Naess's view is the concept of identification. He describes this through an arresting example (see "The flea", below). Note how he described the flea, as "a non-human being I met forty years ago". Here, we are urged to think about the flea by identifying, however briefly, with it, and by seeing its interests as if they were our own. For Naess this kind of identification, practised towards nature in a general way, is the source of deep ecological attitudes: attitudes that inevitably reflect ourselves. Moreover, self-realization means the development of the self through a network of wide identification with "all life on our maltreated earth". This idea gives a new twist to the idea of the self as relational (Mathews 1991). For Naess is suggesting that we can choose to cultivate a larger self by our own identification with nature and natural things, through expanding our circle of such identification in ways that nourish and enrich us. In this way, the ecological self is not only a malleable kind of thing, but also constructed through the identifications it chooses to make. Just as in Gandhi's notion of enlightenment, derived from

---

The flea

My standard example involves a non-human being I met forty years ago. I was looking through an old-fashioned microscope at the dramatic meeting of two drops of different chemicals. At that moment, a flea jumped from a lemming that was strolling along the table and landed in the middle of the acid chemicals. To save it was impossible. It took many minutes for the flea to die. Its movements were dreadfully expressive. Naturally, what I felt was a painful sense of compassion and empathy, but the empathy was not basic; rather, it was a process of identification: that "I saw myself in the flea". (Naess 1986: 517–18)

Hindu thought, in which the enlightened being "sees itself everywhere", deep ecology is urging us to find fulfilment through identification with nature. Instead of putting forward an ethic that commands us to do our duty, or control our desires and appetites, Naess hoped that his form of cosmic self-realization will encourage us to seek our own good, as its primary directive. Such an ethic will save the world, he hopes, but not by means of making the rule "save the world" our primary norm of conduct.

Ethics and metaphysics

The early deep ecology view just described seems to involve a mixture of both ethics and metaphysics. By "metaphysics" we are referring to the theory of what there is, something also described by using the Greek-derived word "ontology". Whether we talk about metaphysics or ontology, we are referring to the study of what exists, or can exist (often opposed to "epistemology" as the study of what is known, or knowable). In emphasizing the relational conception of the human being, Naess was apparently putting forward a different conception of what it is to be a self or a person. So his view can be seen as a metaphysical rejection of Taylor's approach, which accepts that everything is a separate individual. For the individualist, questions of rights, respect and duties arise when we consider what the appropriate ways are in which different individuals should behave towards each other. Nothing in Taylor's approach suggests that two individuals can be connected as jointly part of a greater whole. While Naess's approach is anti-individualistic in this way, it is not holistic in the way that Callicott's and Leopold's ethics are. Although Naess argued for the benefits of increasing diversity and protecting all forms of life on earth, he did not argue in favour of any kind of communitarian ethic. As a result, deep ecology in its early form, sounded a distinctive voice in the development of environmental philosophy. By simultaneously replacing individualistic metaphysics with a notion of organisms being knots in a larger web of life (hence drawing their identity from their interrelatedness) and also urging the merits of choosing to identify with wider circles of beings, Naess combined an ontological and a value position into a novel philosophy.

Other writers in environmental ethics have also tried to change the metaphysical orientation that underlies much of Western ethical theory. The early work of Naess can be seen as a contribution to both an ethics and metaphysics of place, for he was in essence asking us to rethink the place we occupy in nature. His recognition of the importance of Hindu thought to Gandhi's ethics showed that he was comfortable with the idea of exploring alternative conceptual schemes as a way of provoking us to think in new ways. Later writers, have also argued for the importance of thinking about nature in new ways. For example, David Abram, in his book *The Spell of the Sensuous* used the thought of the French thinker Maurice Merleau-Ponty to query our apparent blindness to the real nature of non-human beings. For Abram, perception always involves a kind of participation, because when we perceive, we are elaborating or recapitulating processes already going on in our bodies. So when we perceive, the world we perceive is already filled with body. Second, when we identify something through perception, then we are in a sense possessed by them just as much as we possess them. Note that Abram does not mean to equate possession with ownership. Rather, the idea that he gleans from Merleau-Ponty is that the subject who perceives and the objects perceived by that subject are all part of a common order (rather mysteriously called "the flesh of the world"). Environmental ethics can be derived from denying the kind of separation that traditional philosophy insists on between the subject who perceives and the object that is perceived. Further, in modern philosophy, this separation is intensified by a dualism that is supposed to exist inside each one of us. According to the so-called "father of modern philosophy", René Descartes, for example, each of us is a union of two very different things: a physical body and a non-physical mind. If once we accept the separation of mind and body, and the separation of subject from the object perceived, then we are able to distance ourselves from our bodies and their surroundings.

In her important contribution to the debate, Plumwood argued that the Cartesian dualism of mind and body, and its related dualism of human subjects and the things around them, led to a "hyperseparation" between humans and nature that lies at the heart of anthropocentrism (Plumwood 1993). To give up on human-centred thinking, we thus have to recognize – she argued – that we need strategies for countering such "moral dualism". Abram goes much further than simply attacking moral dualisms. He thinks Merleau-Ponty's work provides a guide that will enable us to rethink our whole way of being in the world, with the consequence that we re-engage our bodies with the world around us and develop a practice of reinhabitation of the world. While both Abram and his guide Merleau-Ponty are difficult to interpret and understand, their proposals involve a radical rethinking of what we are and where we are. Just as Naess suggests a new theory of what it is to be human, hence a new theory of what exists in the world, so Abram and Merleau-Ponty are likewise critical of standard understandings of what exists. What there is, according to them, is an interaction between subject and objects, a kind of dialogue in which each is alive. Their ontology is one of reawakening, re-enchanting and reanimating.

These claims are as obscure as they are exciting. Nonetheless, Abram is not alone in proposing a revolution in ontology. Many theorists of place have likewise argued that a non-dualist category of *place* can, for many purposes, usefully supplant the traditional category of space. While space is supposedly some objective category in terms of which to describe things and their relations to each other, places are webs of relationship whose description depends on seeing them, as it were, through the eyes of their inhabitants. Place is a more fundamental and less theory-laden concept than the concept of space, and it is a concept that is non-dualist: by being, in a sense, subjective and objective at the same time. Some theorists of place do not find it odd to talk in terms of a dialogue between humans and their surroundings. As Abram points out, our senses co-evolved along with the rest of nature, hence we can be regarded as in a long-term conversation with nature. In terms that resonate both with Naess's total field view, and with the remarks of place theorists, Freya Mathews has written: "this universe is a One, a field of subjectivity, which also self-differentiates into a Many, a manifold of individual subjects. The subjectival dimension of this universe renders it an arena not merely for causality but for communication" (Mathews 2005: 14). For a panpsychist like Mathews, the possibilities of dialogue with nature are immensely important, but these options have been smothered by the impact of a modern culture that simultaneously exploits nature and diminishes human experience.

Like Mathews, the *new animists* have been much inspired by the serious way in which some indigenous peoples placate and interact with animals, plants and inanimate things through ritual, ceremony and other practices. According to the new animists, the replacement of traditional animism (the view that personalized souls are found in animals, plants and other material objects) with a contemporary culture that treats the world as an unconscious stockpile of resources for human ingenuity to transform into economic goods leads directly to the disenchantment of nature. In a disenchanted world, there is no meaningful order of things or events, and there is no source of sacredness or dread of the sort felt by those who regard the natural world as peopled by divinities or demons (Harvey 2005; Stone 2006). When a forest is no longer sacred, there are no spirits to be placated and no mysterious risks associated with clear-felling it. A disenchanted nature is no longer alive. It commands no respect, reverence or love. It is nothing but a giant machine, to be mastered to serve human purposes. The new animists argue for reconceptualizing the boundary between persons and non-persons. For them, "living nature" comprises not only humans, animals and plants, but also mountains, forests, rivers, deserts and even planets. For those people who find the metaphysics of the new animism hard to understand – let alone embrace – it may still be possible to engage with the surrounding world as if it consists of other subjects. This "as if" strategy might bring about a change in attitudes and behaviour, perhaps encouraging the flowering of a respectful attitude to nature.

Problems with radical ecology

The radical transformation in worldview and ethics recommended by some of the writers discussed in this chapter is not without problems. While Naess was innovative in recommending that we cultivate an ecological self, one constructed through wide identification with other living beings, it is not clear how much difference adoption of such identification would make to our actual behaviour. Indeed, while some feminist critics have lampooned the idea of an extended, ecological self as a megalomaniacal masculine fantasy, others have queried whether the route of identification goes far enough in motivating really strong protection for nature. Think of the moral difference between damage to oneself and damage to others. Although we have duties to ourselves to respect and care for ourselves, the breach of such duties is normally not so serous as breaking similar duties to others. For example, although it may be regrettable that someone drinks alcohol or smokes to the detriment of his or her health, this is not nearly so objectionable as finding that a parent has been encouraging young children to become addicted to tobacco and alcohol. In the second case, it would be right to describe the parent as wicked and irresponsible since parents have a special duty to care for their children. Likewise we would normally consider various acts of environmental vandalism to be wicked and irresponsible. Yet, on the conception of the extended self, it is not clear that we can use such strong language. If I neglect my local environment, dump rubbish in it and thoughtlessly kill local trees, then can I not plead the same defence as someone who acknowledges smoking or drinking too much? The local trees, if part of my extended self, are victims of a kind of extended self-neglect, and that may not be nearly so bad as neglect of things that are separate from me but to which I have special responsibilities.

There is a further worry too. Overidentification with others can become a kind of colonization. One form of radical ecological view that draws inspiration from deep ecology as well as animism and panpsychism is *bioregionalism*: the movement to develop environmentally sensitive communities that are in harmony with, and work to conserve, their local biogeographical communities (see the essays in McGinnis [1999] for an introduction to the bioregional idea). Bioregionalist theories criticize contemporary development for being insensitive to the local, to the place in which life is set and to the importance of working in respectful dialogue with the natural environment. While many of the criticisms of contemporary industrial society from a bioregional point of view are telling, the bioregional position itself has to be wary about falling into either of two traps. First, not all small local communities are places in which human or natural self-realization is easily achieved. This is why, for example, many people brought up in small country towns try to escape to cities where they can "find themselves" away from the prying eyes of local busybodies and free from the need to conform to local habits and standards. The notions of separation, segmentation and self-assertiveness are central to many ideas about self-development and the achievement of a moral character, and these are not necessarily compatible with the bioregional vision.

A second trap for the bioregionalist is that we all long on occasion for integration, merger and union with another person, a cause, a project or a place. It is easy to fall under the spell of the idea that bioregional living in dialogue with nature will be life in a cosy Eden, a small cohesive world held together by customs, rules and ceremonies that simultaneously respect people and nature. Such a fantasy has its dangers. Traditional cultures do offer many of the benefits of such cohesion, but only at the cost of reduced individuality and self-assertiveness. On the other side, too much separation and self-assertiveness weaken the ties of community and family and damage the stability and continuity of a society. Bioregionalism has therefore to tread a delicate path between two hazards. If the deep ecologist and bioregionalist are not careful, two lethal mergers will pose increasing threats. There is, first, the submersion of the individual in nature, abandoning the self to the natural other. Second, there is the appropriation of nature by the self, so that what I need and desire is no different from what nature needs and desires. The first merger leads to dispossession, the loss of subjectivity, autonomy and personal identity. The second suffers from a surfeit of self-aggrandisement, in which there can be no question of entertaining a genuine respect for the other as what is not my self. Plumwood quotes Jessica Benjamin to make this point:

> If I completely control the other, then the other ceases to exist, and if the other completely controls me, then I cease to exist. A condition of our own independent existence is recognizing the other. True independence means sustaining the essential tension of these contradictory impulses; that is, both asserting the self and recognizing the other.
> (*The Bonds of Love* [1988], quoted in Plumwood 1993: 157)

It is not only deep ecology that faces this threat. The other attempts to reanimate and re-enchant nature, based on notions of place, integration, dialogue and an ontology that denies the separate existence of self and other, also face the same challenge. Radical ecological views and the desire for community with nature to which they give voice are exciting and enticing. They are not without their own moral and psychological risks.

From radical theory to action platform

In many radical theories, anthropocentric values make a subtle return. Taylor's ethic of respect for nature provided less protection for the interests of natural things than at first promised. It turned out that non-vital human interests were able to override the vital interests of many plants and animals. Likewise, Callicott's early version of the land ethic was modified, as we saw, into a less radical ethical theory in response to criticisms of its totalitarian and "eco-fascist" implications. Whether an ethic of identification with nature, or one based on a new ontology of subjects and objects can motivate greater protection of nature than these earlier ones is also an open question in light of the challenges posed by issues about belonging and separation. While in his early work Naess seemed, like Taylor, to regard all living things as having equal value, by the 1980s he was prepared to support only the weaker claim that the flourishing of all life – human and non-human alike – has value in its own right.

A further weakening of the deep ecology position occurred when, in collaboration with George Sessions, Naess formulated a deep ecology platform in 1984, listing the eight points on which deeply committed conservation philosophies would agree, while leaving up to individuals how best to interpret such principles in specific cases. Another thinker sympathetic to the original philosophy of deep ecology, Stephan Harding, subsequently modified these to an alternative platform. The new platforms were no longer tied to any specific underlying philosophy, worldview, metaphysical assumptions or religious commitments. Instead, they were meant to bring into focus the principles that people with a variety of underlying beliefs and commitments would share provided they all cared deeply about nature and sustainable life on earth.

In both cases, the first three points are similar. In Harding's shorter formulations they state:

1. All life has value in itself, independent of its usefulness to humans.
2. Richness and diversity contribute to life's well-being and have value in themselves.
3. Humans have no right to reduce this richness and diversity except to satisfy vital needs in a responsible way.

The notion of value in itself, intrinsic value, is an ambiguous one, as already noted. That something is of non-instrumental value gives us a reason, in many cases, to care about its preservation and to try to ensure its continued existence. If people are disposed to value naturalness and biodiversity for their own sakes, this alone gives a reason why such values should be protected, independent of their usefulness to humans and other forms of life. The new platform does not give very clear guidance for action on matters that are often critical in discussions of environmental policy. For example, it gives no help in distinguishing the value of native or endemic species from exotic ones. This is a very tricky topic, as we saw in Chapter 3. Being native or endemic does not contribute to intrinsic value in the sense in which such value is independent of any relation that thing has to anything else. Native and exotic animals will alike have intrinsic value, as subjects of lives (as argued by Regan). So what is the value of being native? It may be that the value of being native, like the value of being natural itself, is associated with the fact that some things – individuals, species and systems – have evolved independent of human manipulation and interference. This is something to be investigated in the next chapter, when we explore the whole idea of being natural and the values associated with naturalness.

The move from deep ecology as a philosophy to deep ecology as a platform brought both costs and benefits. Since the eight items in the platform are views likely to be shared by many environmental activists, Naess and Sessions hoped for wide support for the platform. At the same time, much that was interesting and distinctive in Naess's own thought

Platforms

The deep ecology eight-point platform

1. The well-being and flourishing of human and non-human life have value in themselves (synonyms "intrinsic value", "inherent worth"). These values are independent of the usefulness of the non-human world for human purposes.
2. Richness and diversity of life forms contribute to the realization of these values and are also values in themselves.
3. Humans have no right to reduce this richness and diversity except to satisfy vital needs.
4. The flourishing of human life and cultures is compatible with a substantially smaller human population. The flourishing of non-human life requires a smaller human population.
5. Present human interference with the non-human world is excessive and the situation is rapidly worsening.
6. Policies must therefore be changed. These policies affect basic economic, technological and ideological structures. The resulting state of affairs will be deeply different from the present.
7. The ideological change will be mainly that of appreciating life quality (dwelling in situations of inherent value) rather than adhering to an increasingly higher standard of living. There will be a profound awareness of the difference between bigness and greatness.
8. Those who subscribe to the foregoing points have an obligation directly or indirectly to try to implement the necessary changes.

(Arne Naess & George Sessions, in
Deep Ecology for the 21st Century [Sesssions1986])

The deep ecology platform: an alternative

1. All life has value in itself, independent of its usefulness to humans.
2. Richness and diversity contribute to life's well-being and have value in themselves.
3. Humans have no right to reduce this richness and diversity except to satisfy vital needs in a responsible way.
4. The impact of humans in the world is excessive and rapidly getting worse.
5. Human lifestyles and population are key elements of this impact.
6. The diversity of life, including cultures, can flourish only with reduced human impact.
7. Basic ideological, political, economic and technological structures must therefore change.
8. Those who accept the foregoing points have an obligation to participate in implementing the necessary changes and to do so peacefully and democratically.

(Stephan Harding, "What is Deep Ecology?" [1992])

about environmental ethics was lost. There is no need to hold a relational conception of the self, or to share his views on identification and extended self-concern in order to sign up for the platform. In fact, what does the platform achieve other than to identify people who are against anthropocentrism? It does not provide any unifying worldview or philosophy in terms of which supporters of the platform can find common ground, nor does it appeal to the notions of biocentric equality, or to the importance of putting nature first in our thinking. As Mathews (2003) has argued, the platform provides no coherent philosophical rationale for its recommendations, and hence has left the notion of deep ecology open to multiple interpretations and without a shared doctrinal core. This means that the later use of the term *deep ecology* does not itself name a specific environmental philosophy, but rather gestures towards a series of vaguely defined currents of thought.

six

Natural things: the puzzle of what "natural" means, and whether humans belong to nature

From conception to reality

Singer and Regan, Taylor and Callicott, Leopold, Naess and the new animists: all these theorists have tried to expand our moral universe, widening the circle of our duties and responsibilities to include animals, other living things, and even rivers and mountains. When queried about why we should care about rivers and rocks, Naess would often remark that everyone knew what was meant by saying "Let the rivers run free!", even though he never espoused any animist or panpsychist views himself. Here is an interesting phenomenon, little discussed in the environmental ethics literature. Once we conceive, or entertain the idea, that dogs and cats are things to which we owe moral responsibility or some kind of respect, then it seems that an argument is required to show why we should not respect these things. Likewise, once we imagine the *possibility* of trees, flowering plants and fungi having some value in themselves, not just utility for us, then it is easy to conclude that they do have such value. In these cases, we argue from what we have thought about, to what is really the case.

Such arguments have a long history in Western thought, but are generally treated with suspicion. The most famous argument of this sort is the so-called *ontological argument* for the existence of a supreme being. In its simplest form, the argument goes like this. Suppose we hold in our minds the idea of something so great that nothing greater than it can be conceived. In other words, we have the idea of *that thing greater than which nothing can be conceived*. But now we wonder if such a thing exists. For suppose that thing does not exist outside our thought, and is not to be found in the world outside the mind. Then there will be something greater than it; namely, something greater than which nothing can be conceived, and which also exists. But we have just conceived of that too! But it is impossible to conceive of something greater than which nothing can be conceived. So that thing greater than which nothing can be conceived must exist. And so the magic is done, and by pure argument we have deduced the real existence of something just from our idea of it! Anselm's original version of the ontological argument is given in the box below, along with a modern reconstruction due to Alvin Plantinga and we have added a brief reminder of the method of argument by *reductio ad absurdum*.

Philosophers are generally agreed that all ontological arguments involve logical mistakes. Nonetheless, such arguments have exerted considerable psychological force over the ages, not least because it is very difficult to say what is wrong with them. Now although environmental philosophers have not tried to argue for the rights of animals, or for respect for nature, by using explicitly ontological arguments, their argument strategy has had the same kind of psychological force. They have essentially asked us to conceive of a world in which animals have similar moral standing to human beings, or where trees and shrubs share some kind of inherent value that is of the same kind that humans have. At first we may find it hard to make sense of such imagined worlds. The theorists make it easier for us by producing principles and observations that encourage us to take the thought seriously. Animals feel pain, just as we do, plants strive to grow to maturity just like any other living things, we are all alike members of larger biological communities and systems that recycle and reuse waste products and nutrients, and so on. As the narratives unfold, we are drawn into thinking about new possibilities, new ways the world might be, ways that excite and enliven us to new possibilities of wider relationships with other living things, and even with the systems that support life on earth. Once a coherent narrative is given, a *prima facie* case (see p. 69) is established for the rights of animals, or inherent value of all living things. Once such a *prima facie* case is established, it seems that a counter-argument is needed to show why animals do *not* have rights, or plants do *not* have inherent value. The weakness of such a way of arguing, however, is the same as the weakness of ontological arguments. While being aware of the psychological force such theorizing possesses, we have to ask whether there are any logical or conceptual mistakes being made in the reasoning that leads up to establishing the

Anselm

> Thus even the fool is convinced that something than which nothing greater can be conceived is in the understanding, since when he hears this, he understands it; and whatever is understood is in the understanding. And certainly that than which a greater cannot be conceived cannot be in the understanding alone. For if it is even in the understanding alone, it can be conceived to exist in reality also, which is greater. Thus if that than which a greater cannot be conceived is in the understanding alone, then that than which a greater cannot be conceived is itself that than which a greater can be conceived. But surely this cannot be. Thus without doubt something than which a greater cannot be conceived exists, both in the understanding and in reality.
>
> (Anselm, *Proslogion*, quoted in Mann 1972: 260–61)

In modern terms (after Plantinga; see Oppy 2009):
1. God exists in the understanding but not in reality. [assumption for *reductio*]
2. Existence in reality is greater than existence in the understanding alone. [premise]
3. A being having all of God's properties plus existence in reality can be conceived. [premise]
4. A being having all of God's properties plus existence in reality is greater than God. [from (1) and (2)]
5. A being greater than God can be conceived. [from (3) and (4)]
6. It is false that a being greater than God can be conceived. [from definition of "God"]
7. Hence, it is false that God exists in the understanding but not in reality. [from (1), (5), (6) by *reductio*]
8. God exists in the understanding. [premise, to which even the Fool agrees]
9. Hence God exists in reality. [from (7), (8)]

Reminder: a *reductio* argument is one that leads to a contradiction. Because the premises have led to a contradiction, it follows that one of them is false. The principle is exemplified in a famous Stoic argument to prove that you do not know you are dead. Suppose you know you are dead (assumption for *reductio*). If you know you are dead, you are dead (for we can only know something if it is true). If you know you are dead, you are not dead (for to know you must be conscious, hence alive). Hence you are dead, and you are not dead. Since the previous statement is a clear contradiction, then, by *reductio*, you do not know you are dead (rejection of assumption that led to the contradiction).

prima facie case in the first place. This is why analysis of the coherence, consistency and reasoning involved in environmental ethics is essential. The seductive powers of ontological arguments show up the frailty of human psychology. We are quite capable of jumping from imagining that the world is a certain way to the conclusion that the world is the way we imagine it to be. Our only defence against leaping to the wrong conclusions is the patient analysis of the arguments and narratives that lead us there.

The natural

We have already encountered several theories that mention intrinsic or inherent value in nature. But what is nature, and what is it for something to be natural? For Leopold and some other prominent environmental theorists, wilderness is the clearest example of what is natural. Although there is a long tradition of valuing wilderness, especially in literature from the United States, it has sometimes puzzled people in other countries just why wilderness should be seen as valuable. Most human lives are played out on three environmental stages: the city, the savannah and the shores of lake and sea. For the most part, these environments did not feature in the writings of Leopold and other North American wilderness enthusiasts. Instead it was the mountain, the forest and the wild river that attracted most attention. Some critics even suggested that the term "environmental ethics" was a misnomer. Most North American and Australian writers were concerned mainly with the diminishing number of wild places of the planet, and the resulting environmental ethics that emerged in the 1970s and 1980s was conceived largely as a celebration of wilderness and the enumeration of reasons for its preservation. In a remark drawing attention to the gap between European thought about nature and elsewhere, Naess commented:

> In Europe the term "free nature" is more important than "wilderness", and it is increasingly used when discussing very large parts of the Third World. The difference between the two terms is that "free nature" is compatible with human habitation, provided that this habitation is in no way dominant. Thus delimited it is of course a rather vague and ambiguous term – but it is a term which implies a context-dependent compromise between the human and natural habitus. (1999: 327)

One of the most prominent exemplars of North American wilderness ethics is found in the work of Holmes Rolston III arguing that wilderness has both intrinsic and instrumental value. As representative of nature in its purest form, wilderness itself is where the free operation of natural forces places, produces and promotes the development of individuality. Not only are individual living things themselves of intrinsic value, but so are species, and – above them – the ecosystems. Rolston urges that we respect a hierarchy of value, one in which the species is more valuable than the individual, and the ecosystem more than the species. Although he provides no systematic argument in defence of his position, it is tempting to read Rolston as holding a trickle-down theory in which the intrinsic value of the system is carried to some degree in the species, and to some degree in the individual, but not held exclusively at any point or area in the web of life. Because value, as he sees it, is "smeared" across the ecosystem as a whole, he dismisses traditional ethics for holding a "duties-to-subjects-only" position (Rolston 1987: 190). His claim is that if we value human subjectivity, but fail to value the systems that produce lives of rich, conscious subjective experience, then this is like valuing the fruit while not valuing the tree that produces it.

In keeping with this interpretation, it seems that Rolston holds a view like the following. Suppose we accept that centred, conscious intelligent life (that is, human life) is intrinsically valuable. Individual human life is not possible without the evolutionary processes that brought about the human species. So the species has intrinsic value. But without ecosystems there would be no species, no evolution, no new life forms. So the system itself is a thing of value, one that places, produces and promotes the emergence of valuable species and valuable individuals. The conclusions that he draws about the value of species and of ecosystems are problematic. Here is an extreme case to think about. Two people meet, fall in love and build a happy life together (an intrinsically valuable experience for both of them). But they only met because they lost everything in a brutal civil war and ended up in the same refugee camp. Without the war, and the losses they suffered, they would not have found themselves in the refugee camp. Without having met in the camp, they would not have fallen in love and built a life together. But these facts do not show the war to have been valuable, and certainly do not suggest that it was intrinsically valuable. In many cases, what is valuable in itself depends on or results from what is at best valuable only as a means, and in cases where good comes from evil it is strange to use the term "valuable" to describe the evil means.

In urging us to respect wild values, Rolston operates with at least three different understandings of what is natural. While he does not himself discuss the ambiguities in his use of the term "natural", it is helpful to be aware that there is no single property identified by his use of the term. One view that he puts forward in his early work is that nature is the system that gave birth to life, the system governed by laws of nature. In this sense of the natural, what is natural – in humans, plants and animals alike – is what follows natural laws (natural in the sense N1). So humans are at least partly natural, by having one foot in nature even though the other one is firmly planted in culture. In his later work he holds firmly to the idea that humans are in large part natural, by writing about our functional, genetic (hence natural) dispositions, for example to look for food when we are hungry. Since humans have one foot in nature, much of our biographies is natural: being eaten by a tiger in the jungle; breaking a leg when falling off a bicycle; gaining weight when eating too much ice cream and so on. Notice that some of these happenings are also partly cultural, because they involve artefacts (I fell off a bicycle) and technology (we store the ice cream in freezers). They are natural to the extent that our wild inheritance, our genetic mechanism, our physiology, are not under our control.

Now what makes freezers and bicycles different from natural things, given that the laws of physic apply to them too (they can be broken by application of physical forces, for example)? Rolston seems to distinguish between the realm of causes (where physical laws apply) and a different realm, the realm of culture. What happens when we build bicycles or freezers is that we use intelligence, rationality and forethought to build artefacts that serve our purposes. Such behaviour on our part means that we operate within a field of reasons and reasoning, not just a field of physical causation. Culture, the domain of reasons, is not sealed off and separate from the world of physical causes: rather, it emerges from it, just as the iceberg seen from a ship is the tip of a much larger submerged mass

---

Rolston

Rolston's use of the term *natural* seems to take three forms. Something is natural if it is:

N1. subject to the causal laws of physics, chemistry and the "natural" sciences

N2. spontaneously self-originating and self-sustaining in accordance with biological principles of evolution and ecology (in particular, it is not dependent on human intervention for its existence or persistence)

N3. in keeping with its species-specific nature (hence culture may be natural for humans, just as killing mice is natural for an owl).

> ### Autopoiesis
>
> The term *autopoiesis* was coined by the Chilean biologists Humberto Maturana and Francisco Varela to describe the features of living systems, as well as other systems, that have the capacity to produce and maintain their own components through continuous regeneration: "An autopoietic machine is a machine organized (defined as a unity) as a network of processes of production (transformation and destruction) of components which: (i) through their interactions and transformations continuously regenerate and realize the network of processes (relations) that produced them; and (ii) constitute it (the machine) as a concrete unity in space in which they (the components) exist by specifying the topological domain of its realization as such a network" (Maturana & Varela 1980: 78).

of ice. "We do not dramatically emerge out of nature," Rolston wrote, "but beneath the surface life remains nine-tenths natural" (Rolston 1989: 67). As far as physical causation is concerned, Rolston makes a distinction between the laws of nature as described in physics and chemistry (N1-natural laws), and those principles of self-origination and self-maintenance that are central to biology (N2-natural principles). So there are two different ways in terms of which something can be natural as defined by the sciences. Rolston's emergentist view is that self-regulating and self-maintaining *autopoietic* systems emerge from physical and chemical systems, and out of these self-regulating systems there emerge cultural systems. This is why there is a sense in which human life is "nine-tenths" natural even though culture creates an immense discontinuity between human life and the life of all other beings.

In terms of these different senses of what is natural, Rolston's ethical theory distinguishes between our duties to wild animals, farm animals and other kinds of animals, according to the kind of naturalness that can be found in their lives and the context in which we encounter them. Various evils or disvalues drive the system of evolution and selection out of which animal and human life has emerged. But if we value the evolutionary tree that has produced advanced life as its fruits, and if that tree is to be healthy, some subjects have to suffer pain, indignity and death as natural selection and the survival of the fittest drive the development of species and new genetic possibilities. So – as already noted above – Rolston rejects the "duties to subjects only" account of morality. If we encounter a dying animal, harmed as a result of a natural (N1 or N2) event, then Rolston thinks we do no wrong in leaving it to die a painful death. By contrast, theorists such as Singer and Regan would argue that it is our duty to put the animal out of its misery, at least if we can safely and readily do so. On the other hand, Rolston accepts that we should humanely dispatch a wild animal harmed as a result of human behaviour – say after being struck by a car – for that is a case where culture has impacted on nature.

Since he believes that species are improved through the testing and competing that harm and cause suffering to some of their members, and since species are valuable in developing the range of species-specific behaviour (which is natural in sense N3), then Rolston thinks we should allow at least some suffering for the sake of promoting species value. He also believes that farming and agriculture involve – at least on occasion – something like predation on our part. As a result, Rolston suggests that a certain amount of pain and suffering in agriculture is acceptable, provided the animals concerned are not exposed to more pain and suffering than would be normal for their wild counterparts. Similarly, Rolston does not condemn hunting in the way that is common among animal welfare and animal liberation theorists. His views on these matters are not very different from those of Leopold, and this strain of thought within environmental ethics has led to the perception of a split between two camps. On the one side are the animal ethics theorists, whose views on what is right or wrong are based on a concern with pain and suffering as evils (Singer's position), or duties towards subjects of a life (Regan); on the other, those thinkers whose focus is on the flourishing of wilderness and ecosystems give less recognition to the evils of pain and suffering, or lower moral status to subjectivity as such. Later in the chapter, we shall also see that the status of domesticated animals becomes an ever more vexed issue in the eyes of other theorists, who see them as artefacts, not natural things at all.

There is a fourth sense of naturalness that we have not yet discussed. Sometimes, we think of what is natural as what is spontaneous or unreflective, as when we say a certain gesture or reaction is "natural". In many species, the immediate protection of offspring by a mother is regarded as natural in this way, and we forgive parents for being quick to defend their children even in the face of a wrongly perceived threat. In some legal jurisdictions, there has been provision for *temporary insanity* or *crimes of passion*, as pleas that would reduce the normal punishment for serious assault and murder. Someone who makes such a plea would be claiming, in effect, that their action was natural, even if irrational. So, we should add a further sense to the three used by Rolston:

> Something is natural (N4) if it is *not* influenced by, or the result of, reflection or rationality.

Since human reflection and rationality is often exemplified in industrial and technological achievements, or – more simply – in the use of natural forces such as flood and fire to shape a landscape, ecological philosophers have often taken N4-natural things to be of particularly high value, since they are untouched by human hands. It is this sense of "nature" that is invoked by the title of McKibben's book *The End of Nature*, where he laments that we have now destroyed nature. For even in the extreme and apparently untouched areas of the Arctic and the Antarctic, pollutants from human industry are found in the ice and snow. Next time you are caught in a shower of rain, McKibben (1989) suggests, you should ask whether that rain is a natural shower, or one produced by human interference with the climate.

What should now be obvious is that the term "natural" is multiply ambiguous, and so any account of values in nature, or of the natural as a feature that adds value to something, must be treated with great care. Further, many theorists of value in nature give no definition of what they mean by "nature" and "natural", and this will be a source of possible confusion when we come to compare what Rolston says with claims made by other thinkers. In terms of the distinctions made so far, we can – at least tentatively – answer some questions about human action, and the senses in which such action is natural. Note that the senses of natural that we have identified are not exclusive: assuming that some things are still uninfluenced by human planning and purposes, then for these to be N4-natural, for example, will also involve being N1-natural.

What about our own behaviour and actions? First, we can notice that all human actions are natural in senses N1 and N2. For, like everything else in the universe, human beings are subject to the constraints of natural laws (such as those in physics and chemistry), and since our actions depend on autopoietic processes, many of which are devoted to repairing and sustaining our life functions, then our actions are products of N2 biologically natural happenings. A human action is N3-natural provided the action is in keeping with human nature. For Rolston, culture is specific to us, hence part of, and an expression of, human nature. If there is no such thing as human nature, then no human actions are natural in the sense of N3. On the other hand, if it is part of human nature for human beings (from time to time) to act reflectively and rationally, then when they do so their actions are N3. In Figure 6.1, we have shown that all cases of N3-natural things fall inside the class of things that are N2-natural: that is, subject to the laws of the biosciences. But we have let part of the ellipse representing human beings protrude outside the circles of what is N2-natural and also what is N1-natural (subject to the laws of physical sciences). This is because we want to allow for the possibility that human freedom may not itself be subject to any natural law, whether physical or biological, a possibility implied in many different religious frameworks.

Finally, as we have seen, some human actions may be natural in the N4 way, and hence not influenced or produced by reflection or rationality. Some thinkers who believe in the traditional definition of humans as essentially rational may say that it is natural (N3 sense) for humans to be not natural (N4 sense). For them, crimes of passion and other supposedly unreflective and irrational kinds of human behaviour are not correctly described as being of kind N4. Such behaviour, they think, would be better described as less rational and reflective than other actions we undertake. For those who take this view, there is a real incompatibility between N3- and N4-naturalness. Our species-specific behaviour, the behaviour that is in our nature, is (for them) essentially reflective and at least to some degree rational. We thus encounter a philosophical dividing line that separates those on the one side who regard even disordered, psychotic and unreflective human behaviour as rational, and those – on the other – who hold that at least some human actions are not rational at all.

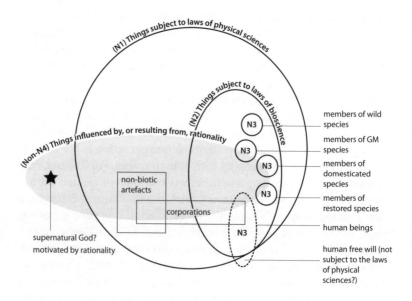

Figure 6.1 Senses of the term "natural".

Figure 6.1, illustrating the various kinds of things that can be natural in the four senses, may look daunting. However, it is useful as a summary of what other writers mean by the term "natural", and is helpful in giving structure to our thinking about the natural. Apart from human free will, the only other thing that is outside the circle of what is N1-natural is the supernatural God of the monotheistic religions. God occupies the shaded area of things that are influenced by or products of rationality and reason, on the assumption that God creates and maintains his own existence. For those who have a different conception of God, it may be necessary to move the symbol wholly or partly out of the shaded area. Since species have their own species-specific natures, they are all labelled as N3-natural. Restored species are also subject to the intervention of rational human planning, and are shown accordingly. Domesticated and genetically modified species are also the product of rational intervention, and we have left them partly outside the shaded area since they are also subject to biological and physical laws (hence both N1- and N2-natural). Corporations include human beings and manufactured goods, so they straddle several classifications since their components are variously subject to physical laws, biological ones and rational planning. All human-made physical things – artefacts – are subject to physical laws while being the product of rational planning and design. As we shall see, some theorists would dispute the way we have represented things, for they would argue that everything touched by human action is no longer a natural object but rather an artefact of some kind.

Nature, value and function

Three different theorists in environmental ethics have speculated on nature value and function in ways that have implications for the merit of ecological restoration and for questions about the authenticity and integrity of natural environments. Individual natural entities (whether sentient or not, living or not), Andrew Brennan argues, are not designed by anyone to fulfil any purpose and therefore lack what he calls "intrinsic function", by which he means the function of a thing that constitutes part of its essence or identity (Brennan 1984, 1988). Brennan proposes that this lack of intrinsic function is a reason for thinking that individual natural entities should not be treated as mere instruments, and thus a reason for assigning them intrinsic value. Furthermore, he argues that the same moral point applies to the case of natural ecosystems, to the extent that they lack intrinsic function. Like Rolston, therefore, he is willing to think of respect for nature embracing respect not just for individual natural things, but also for systems. In the light of Brennan's proposal, Eric Katz (1991, 1997) argues that all natural entities, whether individuals or wholes, have intrinsic value in virtue of their ontological independence from human purpose, activity and interest. Katz maintains a deontological principle that nature as a whole is an "autonomous subject" (a self-governing being) that deserves moral respect and must not be treated as a mere means to human ends. In the ultimate expression of what it means to treat natural things as intrinsically valuable, Robert Elliot (1997) argues that naturalness itself is a property in virtue of possessing which all natural things, events and states of affairs attain intrinsic value. Elliot argues that even a consequentialist, who in principle allows the possibility of trading off intrinsic value from naturalness for intrinsic value from other sources, would not be able to justify such a kind of trade-off in reality. This is because the reduction of intrinsic value due to the depletion of naturalness on earth, according to him, has reached such a level that any further reduction of it could not be compensated by any amount of intrinsic value generated in other ways, no matter how great it is.

Since the notion of "natural" is ambiguous between the four senses just described, it will be interesting to explore whether Brennan, Katz and Elliot are using these senses as part of the account they give of intrinsic natural value, or whether they are assuming a prior understanding of what "natural" means, and then going on to say other things about this. In all three cases, they hold that there is a distinction between what is natural and what is the product of human contrivance. Problems then arise about what to say with regard to the value of those parts of nature that have been interfered with by human artifice, for instance, previously degraded natural environments that have been humanly restored. We saw that Rolston has a problem over how to deal with the question of domesticated animals because they do not fit neatly inside his classifications of what is natural. Landscape and environmental restoration is problematic for Katz and Elliot, although for different reasons. In Elliot's case, since he holds that the properties of being naturally evolved and having a natural continuity with the remote past are "value adding", he argues that even a perfectly restored environment would necessarily be less valuable than an undegraded natural environment. Katz, on the other hand, argues that a restored nature is really just an artefact designed and created for the satisfaction of human ends, and that the value of restored environments is merely instrumental. As we shall see,

it is possible to critique these views provided we admit there is value in
human life and culture, and also that the natural environments interfered
with by humans may have other morally relevant qualities (Lo 1999).

Brennan's view is easily summarized (see "Moral standing", below).
Natural individuals are intrinsically functionless in that their identity
is not defined in terms of their function. Human-manufactured things,
from chopsticks to houses to sports fields are what they are because of
the functions they have been designed to fulfil. In other words, natural
things are not the result of design made to satisfy some end. While
Taylor uses the end- or goal-oriented feature of living things to argue for
their moral standing, Brennan uses a different strategy; namely, looking
for an absence of teleology and absence of design in order to undergird
the claim to intrinsic value. From the ecological and evolutionary point
of view, it makes sense to think about the biological functions of individuals and populations within an ecosystem. But Brennan argues that
it is no part of the identity conditions of a deer that it is prey, or of a wolf
that it is predator. Animals take on ecosystem functions depending on
where and what they do. Some highly adaptable mammals, such as rats,
for example, will fulfil very different functions in a very wide range of
different ecological systems.

If we were to agree with this view, why would we allocate any special
value to individual natural things? To see the force of the argument,
think of things the other way round. What do we say about things that

clearly have specific functions and that are defined in terms of the functions they fulfil? To say that something has a certain intrinsic function is simply to say that it is part of that thing's very essence that it is an *instrument* to serve a certain end. The best that we can say about an intrinsically functional thing is that it has instrumental value. A bodily organ, for example, is defined by its physiological function, and it is a good (healthy, strong, reliable) organ to the extent that it carries out the function well. As many philosophers have previously argued, human individuals lack intrinsic function, precisely because they are not essentially instruments to serve any particular ends. That is, it is not in the nature of any human individual to be only a means to other ends. Anyone who treats another person as no more than of instrumental value shows a serious ethical failure. Another way of thinking about this is in terms of potential. The fact that human individuals lack intrinsic function is closely connected to the fact that people, no matter what social roles and family positions they fill, have the potential to go beyond whatever instrumental roles they happen to serve. The capacity of humans to rebel, to be free from any given instrumental role, to determine themselves (or, in short, the capacity of autonomy – for ruling and governing oneself) is a traditional philosophical basis for attributing intrinsic value and moral standing to each human individual.

In brief, the idea is that if a thing is not by nature a mere means to other ends, then it is wrong for it to be treated as a mere means to other ends. But not to treat it as a mere means is to attribute intrinsic value to it. Thus, it follows that the lack of intrinsic function is a value-conferring quality in virtue of which individual humans acquire intrinsic value and moral standing. Formally, it is easy to lay out the bare bones of this argument, as in the box "Moral standing". To say that natural individuals do not have any intrinsic function is not to say that they do not have any function. For Brennan, the lack of intrinsic function is one, but not the only, value-conferring quality. So his position is compatible with a hierarchical view that some things in the environment are more valuable than others because they also have other value-conferring qualities. The crucial assumption in Brennan's argument is that autonomy is a value-conferring quality. The main point of the argument is that this quality is shared by all natural individuals. While he does not want to share Rolston's value hierarchy, putting the value of species about individuals, and that of ecosystems above species, Brennan does argue that ecosystems, just like natural individual things, have no intrinsic function in terms of which they are defined and so are also candidates for having intrinsic value and moral standing.

Moral standing of natural objects

P1. Only (a) designed objects, and (b) parts of a larger system, are such that certain functions are essential parts of their identity conditions.

P2. No function is an essential part of a natural (i.e. undesigned) individual's identity conditions. [from P1]

B1. So, natural individuals lack intrinsic function.

P3. To lack intrinsic function is the same as to have autonomy (the potential to go beyond any assigned functional role).

P4. Autonomy is a value-conferring quality.

B2. So, the lack of intrinsic function is a value-conferring quality. [from P5]

P3*. If X lacks intrinsic function, then it is not in X's nature to be a mere means to other ends.

P4* If it is not in X's nature to be a mere means to other ends, then X should not be treated as a mere means to other ends, which means that it has intrinsic value.

P5. If X lacks intrinsic function, then X has intrinsic value. [from P3* & P4*]

B2. So, the lack of intrinsic function is a value-conferring quality. [from P5]

C. Natural Individuals have intrinsic value and moral standing. [from B1 & B2]

Restorations and fakes

In the light of Brennan's premises P3 and P4 (see above), Katz has argued that a humanly restored nature is morally inferior to a wild nature (Katz 1992). Katz's view of natural things is predicated on the same core idea we have already come across: what is designed with a function in mind is something that can only be of instrumental value at best. He writes:

> Technology – the design and creation of artefacts – is a central project in the meeting of human concerns, to satisfy human desires, wants, and needs. … Technological products – artefacts – are thus fundamentally anthropocentric … They can only be understood as anthropocentric instruments.
>
> (*Ibid.*: 122–3)

There are three ideas central to Katz's views on restoration. First, he thinks that the purpose behind human restoration of nature, as behind all other applications of human technology, is *always* anthropocentric. "The technological 'fix' of nature", he writes, "merely produces artefacts for the satisfaction of human interests" (1997: 114) and "once we begin to create restored natural environments, we impose our anthropocentric purposes on areas that exist outside human society" (*ibid.*: 98). Human technology applied to nature is, for him, always a kind of human domination of, rather than cooperation with, nature. Second, Katz thinks that technological interference with nature not only reduces but indeed *destroys* the naturalness of nature so that a technologically restored nature is a mere artefact, instead of something lying somewhere between the natural and the artefactual. This view positions him rather differently from Rolston, since his view of restored nature leaves us outside the categories N1–N3 that we have already described. As he himself puts it, "once human intervention occurs, there is no longer a natural system to be preserved, there is only an artefactual system" (*ibid.*: 126). Third, the kind of technological interference that Katz thinks would turn nature into an artefact need not be very complicated or advanced. For example, if someone chooses a place in his or her garden to plant a tree and waters it when the weather is dry, then, according to Katz, this tree is an artefact. Gardening and agriculture may produce pleasant enough landscapes and views, but they are all alike artificial, not natural. So it follows, he believes, that all attempts at restoring nature inevitably result in something inferior to what was there before the restoration. For all restorations of nature result in the creation of artefacts. Katz would therefore be one of the authors who would want to relabel Figure 6.1 to reflect this view of what is artificial rather than natural.

We saw in Chapter 5 that in traditional metaphysics, what was dependent for its existence on something else would sometimes be

---

Katz

K1. Unlike natural entities, artefacts (by definition) are ontologically dependent on human design, interest, labour. [ontological account of artefacts]

K2. The more/less independent, free and autonomous one is, the higher/lower are one's moral value and status.

K3. Artefacts are morally inferior to natural entities. [moral dualism from K1 & K2]

K4. Restored natural entities are artefacts. [assimilation from K1]

K5. Wild natural entities are natural entities.

K6. Restored natural entities are morally inferior to wild natural entities. [inferiority of restored natural entities from K3, K4, K5]

regarded as "less real", while the thing on which it depends is "more real". Katz's ontological account of artefacts (K1) might seem to be a version of this view, as if he takes artefacts to be less real than natural entities. This interpretation would be a mistake. What makes artefacts inferior to natural things, according to him, is the involvement of humans in their manufacture, maintenance or continued existence. Ontological dependence is not a mark of less reality but is instead an indicator of moral inferiority. To be dependent on human craft and design is to be morally inferior to something that exists and maintains itself free from all human interference.

Katz's account seems open to fairly decisive objections. We do not normally call everything that is touched by, or dependent on, human technology an artefact, even when it is relatively unnatural compared to something that has not been so touched. For instance, some people take fertility pills to increase the chance of pregnancy. In unfortunate cases where pregnant women are HIV positive, they may take certain medicines to reduce the chance of their fetuses getting the virus. In cases where fetuses have developed diseases, such as spina bifida, they may need to have *in utero* surgery to correct the condition. The human infants born as a result of those medical interventions have been subjected to human planning and technological control just as much as any small- or large-scale ecological restoration project. So there is a dependency on human technology in each case. In general people who would not have been born, or who would not have survived without medical aids are also dependent on human technology. If, as Katz declares, "the technological 'fix' of nature merely produces artefacts" (1997: 114), don't the medical treatments given to humanity merely produce artefacts too? The absurdity of regarding a human patient as a mere artefact appears to be a *reductio* of Katz's position.

There is a further worry for Katz's position given what he wants to say about the autonomy of natural things. Autonomy literally refers to our capacity for self-governance. In the philosophy of Kant, the German Enlightenment thinker, autonomy involves the capacity of human beings to choose freely to place themselves under the sway of the moral law. In other words, the free autonomous agent is able to choose not to be free, and to govern his or her actions by moral rules that are arrived at by rational deliberation and reflection (something highly unnatural in sense N4). In an extended sense, required for Katz's account of nature's autonomy, we will need to be able to talk of the autonomy of natural living things. Recall Taylor's view that each living being can be conceived as "a teleological centre of life", the:

internal functioning and external activities [of which] are all goal-oriented, having the constant tendency to maintain [its] existence through time and to enable it successfully to perform those biological operations whereby it reproduces its kind and continually adapts to changing environmental events and conditions.

(1986: 121)

Let us then say that *biological autonomy* consists in having the biological capacity to develop in accordance with one's own *telos*. In this sense of the term, all animate members of an ecosystem exhibit this kind of autonomy – at least to some extent.

Human autonomy, in an extended sense, will be – let us say – the *capacity* to act or freely develop in accordance with one's own personality, *telos*, or chosen principles. But notice that such a capacity can be present even when not being exercised. There is a difference between having autonomy and being autonomous. Being autonomous is *actually* acting or developing in accordance with one's own personality, *telos* or principles. A person's autonomy may be limited under many circumstances, such as social and political oppression, or being in prison, confined to a wheelchair or trapped in a broken elevator. In these cases, people still have the capacity: they are just not able to exercise it. Accordingly, someone who possesses autonomy may not be actually autonomous. Under extreme oppression, one's autonomy may also be partially or entirely destroyed, for instance, in the case where the oppressed person is mentally damaged or even killed.

Similarly, human impact on natural creatures and systems can also jeopardize their autonomy. For instance, when humans cripple a pelican so that it cannot fly away from an open enclosure, humans destroy some of its capacities to act in accordance with its biological *telos* and thereby damage its biological autonomy. Nonetheless, animate natural entities often retain their autonomy under human interference, even when technology is involved. For instance, when humans capture a polar bear for short-term zoological study, humans confine, but usually do not damage, its biological and evolutionary capacities. The polar bear is still *able to* live in accordance with its own *telos*, although it may not be *allowed to* fully exercise its abilities during captivity. Hence, it still possesses biological autonomy, although it may be in a situation where its ability to exercise the capacity – its autonomousness – is reduced. Think now of the case of animal shelters where injured wild animals are given medical treatments and released back to their original habitats after recovery. In this kind of case, their biological autonomy is rehabilitated rather than being further damaged. So there are many kinds of human intervention in the non-human world and they are not always destructive.

What about Katz's premise K2? Is it objectionable? Although K2 is not explicitly stated in his work, it seems to follow from what he writes:

> The ethical importance of the distinction between artifacts and natural entities is thus derived from the anthropocentric nature of artifacts, their ontological reliance on human interests, plans and projects. In contrast to natural entities, artifacts, as human instruments, are *always* a *means* to the furtherance of some human *end*. ... If the categorical imperative is applied to a treatment of artifacts and natural entities, we find a crucial difference: artifacts *must* be treated as means, for their existence and value *only* exist in a dependent relationship with human aims and goals; but natural entities, existing apart from human projects, can be considered as ends-in-themselves.
>
> (Katz 1997: 129)

The freedom to exercise our capacities can be impeded by disease, accident or political oppression without the subject of these capacities being any less valuable than someone who is more free. And there is a general worry about connecting moral value to capacity in any case: human dignity is not normally measured in terms of either autonomy or autonomousness. Think, for example of the universal features mentioned in the preamble and in Article 1 of the 1948 Universal Declaration of Human Rights, already the subject of some discussion in Chapter 1: "All human beings are born free and equal in dignity and rights. They are endowed with reason and conscience and should act towards one another in a spirit of brotherhood." The people writing this declaration were well aware that some members of the biological species *Homo sapiens* are born without fully functional nervous systems and so will lack some or all of the very capacities that are constitutive of autonomy, including "reason and conscience". It appears that the declaration is intending to focus on the typical, undamaged and fully functioning adult human being. Were those who drafted the declaration aware that differences in education level, for example, impact on the amount of information that is available to people in taking decisions about their lives? Someone fortunate enough to be well educated and born into a wealthy family may in fact be able to exercise a well-developed capacity for autonomy to a high degree. By contrast, someone with little education and trapped in poverty may have less of a capacity in the first place and may also have fewer opportunities to exercise those capacities. If all human beings are equal in dignity, then this cannot mean that they are the same either in their capacity for free choice, or in their exercise of such choices. Premise K2 thus appears highly debatable.

While Katz's argument is bold, but lacking in detailed justification, Elliot has a straightforward argument against the value of nature restoration, based on a commitment to the idea that being natural in the sense N4 is something intrinsically valuable. Elliot himself holds a kind of ideal-observer theory of value that has some relations to the dispositional theory of value put forward by David Lewis (1989). We shall describe this theory more fully in Chapter 7. Ideal-observer theories of ethics are ones in which decisions about what is the right action in a situation are judged from the point of view of an idealized observer whose response to the situation is not biased by personal likes, dislikes or other personal factors. For example, suppose your supervisor asks you to make a complaint about another worker in your company. If you do make the complaint, you will be promoted, and if you do not you may be fired. Your personal interest in keeping your job may well influence your decision about what to do. In the ideal-observer theory, you have to consider the case from the point of view of an imaginary third party who will weigh up the value of your job for you as well as assessing whether the complaint you have been asked to make is a legitimate one. Appeal to such an observer is meant to encourage us to be impartial in our judgements.

For Elliot something has intrinsic value for a valuing subject (let us call her Sue) when Sue is disposed to value that thing in virtue of the properties it possesses. As in other ideal-observer theories, Sue has to make her evaluation under the ideal condition of "calm reflection", not distorted by anger, envy and other emotions, and on the basis of "as much relevant information as possible". Suppose that she morally

---

Elliot

E1. Naturalness (in the N4 sense of not being the outcome of any rational intent or purpose) is itself a value-conferring quality.

E2. Naturalness can never be restored. [from E1]

E3. Even a perfectly restored natural environment – having recovered all the other value adding qualities (e.g. beauty, integrity) that the original undamaged natural environment used to have – would still lack the value-conferring quality of being natural. [from E2]

E. Even a perfectly restored environment would still be less intrinsically valuable than the originally undamaged natural environment. [from E1 & E2]

approves of the property of being naturally evolved, and on that basis then approves of a nearby forest that seems to be a pristine wilderness. Later, though, Sue discovers and reflects on the fact that the area is actually the result of replantation and reintroduction of animal species by humans after earlier open-cut mining operation. The apparently pristine forest is a fake: the result of nature restoration. For Elliot, it would be entirely reasonable for Sue to revise her earlier evaluative response to the forest. Being naturally evolved – he thinks – is a clear example of a property in virtue of which a landscape or system has intrinsic value for people with appropriate attitudes to nature, attitudes that he believes are widespread. On the other hand, the property of being restored is not one that confers any kind of intrinsic value on the forest.

Elliot's argument against restoration (or "faking nature") seems to go through provided the initial claim about naturalness (E1) is accepted. But in this chapter, we have seen only weak arguments for accepting the claim that what is natural is of value (or value-conferring). Rolston's account of how value is smeared over the system of nature as a whole, and our conjecture that he may regard it as trickling down from ecosystem to species to individual is based on his own expressions of wonder and pleasure at the contemplation of nature. The argument that if we value the fruit then we should also value the tree that produces it has been shown to be untenable. Brennan's claim that natural individuals share with human beings the property that they are not to be defined in terms of their intrinsic functions provides some reason for classifying natural things as having potential and capacities that go beyond those of artefacts, and perhaps provides some persuasive force in getting us to think about the natural world in terms of its capacities for self-repair, self-maintenance and self-development (the very capacities that evoke pleasure and wonder in the writings of Rolston). Katz and Elliot have raised serious questions about the value of restored nature, but their claims are based either on an unsubstantiated claim about the intrinsic value of what is natural, or on a too crude distinction between the natural and the artefactual. Clearly, more work needs to be done to unravel the puzzles about nature and value that environmental philosophy has so far failed to solve, and this will be the task for Chapter 7.

Conceptions of nature

There are many ways of thinking about nature (often with a capital "N") in the fourth sense – N4 – in which nature exists independent of human activity and purpose. Many of the literary and philosophical representations of nature point in different directions: nature, or wilderness, can be a place of terror and horror, of recreation and wonder, of opportunities for commercial exploitation, as a place of unforgiving beauty and awe – or maybe as a place of endless fascination and curiosity. It is hard not to see some of the depictions of nature in literature as a projection onto the world around us of favoured or feared features of humans themselves. In some cases, it will be useful to project onto nature disavowed features of ourselves, or our culture, and these features in turn do more than give us a licence to use nature as we will. In extreme cases, our projections of such features can legitimize an all-out war against the sinful distortions of the earth, the barbarism of a nature red in tooth and claw. When the Pilgrim Fathers arrived in North America, some of their journals describe the howling desolation they encountered: mountains that they saw as a sinful distortion of the earth, forests they regarded as a waste and dismal places requiring to be transformed to productive use. Boston, by contrast, was to be an ordered and civilized city, where humane dealings among righteous people would counterbalance the savagery of the country around them (Short 1991).

It was not long, however, before the new frontiersmen emerged, people who are both attracted to, and repelled by, the new country, at war to the death with the American Indians yet required to be like them in order to survive in the wilds. By the mid-nineteenth century, Ralph Waldo Emerson was able to declare that man, looking at nature with a "supernatural eye" finds abundance, ecstasy, a "cup of enchantments". In a memorable remark, he pronounced "The land is the appointed remedy for whatever is false and fantastic in our culture" (Emerson [1844] 1981). Here Emerson has apparently reversed the early Puritan horror of the wild, transforming into something that he and his protégé Henry David Thoreau could use as a source of self-realization (Thoreau [1854] 2006). These writers anticipated themes in contemporary deep ecology, and some of the other views we have already described.

In the nineteenth century, Darwin shocked Victorian England by assembling with great patience an overwhelming mass of evidence for the naturalness of our origins as a species. He later proposed something his closest disciples and colleagues wanted to deny. This was the claim argued in *The Descent of Man*: that our morality has its prototype in the social instincts of the higher mammals. Both Darwin's bulldog – Thomas Henry Huxley – and the co-inventor of the theory of evolution by natural selection – Alfred Russel Wallace – recoiled in horror from this thought. Huxley and Wallace were both of them distinguished and resolute defenders of the main Darwinian thesis of evolution by natural selection; but neither of them regarded nature as the origin of anything resembling morality. In his famous Romanes lecture on evolution and ethics, Huxley depicted nature as a swamp of barbarity, depravity and evil, a cosmic process that it is our duty to combat. The project of humans is, in his words, to "pit the microcosm against the macrocosm and to set man to subdue nature to his higher moral ends" (Huxley [1893] 1947: 82). The echo of the Boston Puritans is heard in Herman Melville's description of the Galapagos: "In no world but a fallen one could such lands exist" (1856: 291), while even Darwin himself saw "the universal signs of violence" when he visited South America. These are examples of what historians sometimes refer to as the post-Romantic disenchantment of nature. It is to this disenchantment that many contemporary and recent environmental philosophers have tried to find a reply.

There are perhaps three conceptions of N4-nature that are still widely prevalent. First there is a libertine or sybaritic conception: nature (N4) exists to provide pleasure, utility, recreation and produce without limit. This idea involves more than thinking that nature has instrumental value. Rather, it regards the exploitation, ravishing and looting of nature as an activity on which there are no restraints: we are afforded limitless possibilities of satisfaction by the natural world. The exultation of the frontier, the joy of large-scale forest burning, and the unapologetic virility of the miner are expressions of a libertine fervour to exploit the natural world with relish.

> We primeval forests felling,
> We the rivers stemming, vexing we and piercing deep the
>   mines within,
> We the surface broad surveying, we the virgin soil upheaving
> Pioneers, O pioneers!
>   (Walt Whitman, *Pioneers! O Pioneers!*, 1865)

Poised against this model is a second, more obviously puritan, idea. Whereas the first conception pictures nature as a whore, and has no scruples about using her, the second regards her as a virgin and regards virginity as worthy of respect. This conception can motivate an ethic of non-interference, non-intervention, and an attitude of reverence towards a wild nature that is a place of re-creation, self-discovery and awe. Rolston can be seen as vividly depicting just such an attitude to the wild and to the values to be found deep in nature. Instead of a waste, undignified place whose easy virtue is to be plundered for our satisfaction, this other conception regards nature as a place of purity and spiritual significance. The herds of the farmer and the axes of the logger are a desecration of the quiet purity of the meadows and woods. Rolston draws inspiration in his writings from a legacy of American nature writing, particularly the works of the early conservationist John Muir:

> And to think that the sheep should be allowed into these lily meadows! ... One might reasonably look for a wall of fire to fence such gardens. So extravagant is nature with her choices treasures, spending plant beauty as she spends sunshine, pouring it forth into land and seas, garden and desert.
>
> (Muir [1911] 1998: 56)

These two conceptions do not line neatly up with what some people have called the classical and romantic archetypal visions of the wilderness (Short 1991). These archetypes collect two sets of ideas, respectively: first, the "classical" is meant to be the vision of nature as a place of howling waste, desolation and fear, prompting perhaps a dread that might in turn lead to a reverence for nature; second, the romantic vision brings together the ideas of purity, and spiritual retreat, a sacred space unprofaned by humans prompting reverence and care. But fear of the wild can be compatible with both the libertine and the puritan conceptions, and, to a certain kind of temperament, the defiling of what is pure can itself be a source of excitement and exultation. The classical view, according to John Rennie Short, sees nature as filled not only with threats but with even what is evil – painful death piled upon painful death – and mountains as sinful distortions of the flatness of the earth. But there is no need for libertines to regard nature as evil. They can regard the non-human world as amoral. Or they can even acknowledge its goodness as they sully it.

Finally, there is a third set of ideas or conception of nature that can be held separate from both the libertine and the puritan ones. According to this one, nature is a martyr to human greed and exploitation, a place carrying the stigma of inattentiveness and carelessness. The dialogical conception of the new animists and Mathews emphasizes the importance of attention, and of re-enchantment of nature through practices of care and respect. There need be no puritanism associated with the third set of ideas. Even those who regard nature as a legitimate source of resources, goods and services may worry that we have gone too far in our exploitation. So they could depict the environment as oppressed, weakened or having its health undermined by our activities. Like the four different senses in which writers have used the term "natural", these three different groups of ideas about N4-nature – the libertine, the puritan and the victimological – are not exclusive. Some of the thinkers we have already looked at seem to hold more than one of these conceptions, and each of them has its own power to add force to the idea of the values that can be found in nature.

seven

Foundations: can there be a secular basis for the ideas of human dignity and intrinsic value in nature?

Sources of intrinsic value

So far in this book we have explored the writings of environmental philosophers, and have placed these to some extent in a wider historical context. To make any more progress in exploring the idea of value in nature, we need to look specifically at the philosophical and religious contexts within which ideas of intrinsic value or inherent worth have developed. At the end of Chapter 6, we noted the tensions in the ideas associated with nature, for example between nature as a place of dread and awe, and nature as a place of self-discovery and self-creation. Sometimes nature is regarded as a place of sanctuary, and associated with the term "sanctuary" are religious connotations of the sacred. Yet "sacred" is an anagram of "scared", and whether we can retreat to the wild as a place of security, or instead enter it with a sense of danger will very much depend on where we live. Different environments provide different degrees of security and danger. A delightfully sunny morning at high altitude may awaken a sense of wariness in the experienced mountaineer, just as an invitingly calm sea never tempts the prudent sailor to neglect to keep an eye on the weather. There seems to be a gap of a serious kind between these well-known facts on the one side and, on the other, the emergence of claims by philosophers that natural things have intrinsic value, that nature in general is worthy of respect as an end-in-itself, and that we should enter into respectful dialogue with other beings and systems. On the one side is a set of commonplace observations about pleasures and opportunities, dangers and threats, injuries and sufferings, associated with the natural world. On the other are grand claims of universal scope about the presence of intrinsic value throughout all of nature.

We shall later explore the religious idea of the sacred in connection with the notion of intrinsic value. Rolston observes that some human experience of nature is numinous, or mystical, in the way that some religious experience is. Questions about intrinsic value in nature, about human dignity and about the sacred will turn out to be versions of one and the same puzzle: what the theologian Rudolf Otto describes as the great mystery, "*mysterium tremendum*".

On what does intrinsic value depend? We have noted how Elliot claimed that being natural is a "value-adding property", Katz regarded nature as similar to a free, autonomous subject, and Taylor suggested that being a living, goal-oriented centre of life is a source of value. Finally, Callicott, following Leopold, thinks that all constituent parts of the earth's biosphere are intrinsically valuable because they are all fellow members of the Land, a shared community with us. To analyse

---

The numinous

One must also get religion naturalised, not so much in the sense of explaining it (away) naturalistically, as of explaining the numinous encounter with manifest nature. Biology does generate religion: the phenomenon of life evokes a religious response whether or not a functional human society is at issue ... Nature is the first mystery to be encountered, and society comes later, much later, after one learns evolutionary history.   (Rolston 1999: 294)

We are dealing with something for which there is only one appropriate expression, "mysterium tremendum". The feeling of it may at times come sweeping like a gentle tide, pervading the mind with a tranquil mood of deepest worship. It may pass over into a more set and lasting attitude of the soul, continuing, as it were, thrillingly vibrant and resonant, until at last it dies away and the soul resumes its "profane", non-religious mood of everyday experience. It may burst in sudden eruption up from the depths of the soul with spasms and convulsions, or lead to the strangest excitements, to intoxicated frenzy, to transport, and to ecstasy. It has its wild and demonic forms and can sink to an almost grisly horror and shuddering. It has its crude, barbaric antecedents and early manifestations, and again it may be developed into something beautiful and pure and glorious. It may become the hushed, trembling, and speechless humility of the creature in the presence of – whom or what? In the presence of that which is a mystery inexpressible and above all creatures.   (Otto 1927: 12)

these competing theories about the source and location of intrinsic value, it will be helpful to introduce a distinction between two modes of thinking about intrinsic value: a hierarchic mode on the one hand, and an egalitarian one on the other. On the hierarchic conception, intrinsic value comes in degrees, so it is possible for some things to be higher in intrinsic value than others. According to the egalitarian model, however, such value must be spread equally across a given group. For example, it has to be the same across all human beings, or across all conscious and sentient beings, or across all living things, or across all the things that are autonomous, wild and free. Thus, we can ask three general questions about intrinsic value:

- Does intrinsic value vary from item to item according to the extent to which it possesses certain desirable qualities?
- If intrinsic value does vary across items, then how differently (if at all) should we treat things with different degrees of such value?
- What properties or qualities are value-relevant?

It is useful to introduce the idea of *supervenience* at this point. Philosophers sometimes talk about certain properties supervening on some others. For example, an object's colour supervenes on the properties of its surface. This is another way of saying that colour is determined by, or a function of, properties of the surface. As surface properties determine what spectra of light can be reflected from objects, and these properties in turn determine their colours, any two objects having exactly the same set of surface properties will have exactly the same colour. An object's particular set of surface properties ("base properties") is the reason for its having a particular colour (a "supervenient property").

The relation of supervenience is not one of co-occurrence, but one of dependence that is not necessarily symmetric. In saying that Y supervenes on X, we are saying that whenever two objects both have the base property X, then they also have the supervenient property Y, but not necessarily the other way round. For example, the fact that colour supervenes on properties of the surface allows the possibility that two objects having exactly the same colour may differ in their surface properties. A 24-carat-gold-plated object and an 18-carat-gold-plated object may both have exactly the same colour (the supervenient property) although their surface properties (the base properties) are clearly different. In general, when objects have the same base properties they will have the same supervenient property, but objects sharing the same supervenient property may differ in their base properties. Further, the dependence relation involved in supervenience does not have to be a causal one (like the one involving colours). For example, the property of being divisible by the number 3 supervenes on the property of being divisible by the number 6. Here is a mathematical, not causal, form of supervenience. Consider the property of being a president. It supervenes on that of being an elected head of state. The relation of dependence in this case is not causal, but conceptual instead.

Philosophers these days generally believe that a thing's evaluative properties, such as its moral value, or its beauty, must supervene on some other (base) properties it has. Those other properties may include: its intrinsic constitutional properties, such as form, structure, material, shape and size; its historic properties, such as origin, age and heritage; its other relational properties, such as rarity, robustness, location, function; and also its tendencies to elicit certain positive attitudes in observers of some kind, such as desire, love, respect or awe. Indeed, the relevant sets of base properties may be combinations of the above, different in different cases of evaluative properties. If the supervenience thesis is true, then to reject it would be to suggest that two things can differ in their value and yet all their other properties, both intrinsic and relational ones, are exactly the same. Supporters of the supervenience thesis would argue that this is impossible. Why? The obvious point, they would say, is that one thing cannot be better than another for no reason. If two things differ in value, so that one of them is more valuable than the other, then there must be a reason for that. When we judge that a thing has a moral property this must be *because* it has some natural property (Zangwill 2005). It would be unhelpful, to say the least, to maintain that the two things differ in value simply because of their very difference in value. Terms such as "value-adding" or "value-conferring" properties are just other labels for the same idea, namely, that there must be base properties on which value supervenes. Reference to these base properties will provide reasons for attributing value to an object, or greater value to one object rather than another.

Descriptive properties are those that can in principle be detected by naturalistic means (such as the use of vision and the other bodily senses, the use of deductive and inductive reasoning). Many descriptive properties of a thing, for example, the motive, the circumstance and the consequences of an action, are relevant to what evaluative judgement we make of it. The idea that evaluative properties supervene on descriptive ones implies that two cases sharing similar descriptive properties must be judged similarly in evaluative terms. For example, if two courses of action are taken for similar motives in similar circumstances resulting in similar consequences, then if one is deemed morally acceptable, the other must also be so judged. The idea that the evaluative supervenes on the descriptive neither entails nor contradicts the idea that evaluative properties are analysable in terms of, and therefore reducible to, certain descriptive properties, thus bridging the gap that is commonly supposed to exist between "is" and "ought". This reductive view about facts (what *is*) and values (what *ought* to be) is a thesis about the meaning of moral terms (a metaethical claim) which is sometimes called *descriptivism* (see Lo 2009; Pigden 1991). Suppose that descriptivism is right, and that evaluative properties are definable in descriptive terms. This means that an evaluative property is reducible to some descriptive property, and therefore the two are actually one and the same. In this case, the evaluative property will certainly supervene on the descriptive one, and that is so on mere logical grounds, namely that one thing supervenes on itself. But suppose that such reduction is not possible, so that descriptivism is false. In this case, the supervenience thesis still holds. For the supervenience of value on descriptive properties is no more than the requirement that we must give reasons for our evaluations, however minimal. As we have seen, the notion of supervenience requires the identification of some descriptive properties (the base properties) in an object as the reason for attributing value (the supervenient property) to it, and, to be coherent, it requires that such attribution of value must be done consistently in cases where objects share the same base properties.

One of the central questions in environmental philosophy is what exactly the relevant bases would be for attributing value to various things in our environment. Different answers to this question will result in support for either the hierarchic model or the egalitarian model of how intrinsic value or inherent worth is distributed across individuals.

If Katz and Elliot are right in taking intrinsic value as supervenient on naturalness, then two things possessing the same degree of naturalness must derive from it the same amount of intrinsic value. Following the same logic, things that are more natural derive more intrinsic value from their naturalness than things that are less natural. That is why Katz and likewise Callicott (in his early writings) maintain that animals and plants produced by selective breeding, and even those that have come into being as a result of anthropogenic restoration programmes, are of less value than wild animals and plants (see Lo 1999). Likewise, Eugene Hargrove (1989) argues that all of wild nature is beautiful in virtue of being the product of natural wild creative activity. This led him to disagree with John Passmore ([1974] 1980), who had argued that certain kinds of informal gardens transformed nature into something rather more agreeable and beautiful than wilderness.

There are of course other possible base properties – apart from naturalness – on which intrinsic value might supervene. As we have seen, Regan argues that being a conscious subject of a life capable of experience is a relevant basis for attributing intrinsic value (or what he calls "inherent value") to higher animals, be they domestic or selectively bred animals, such as dogs, cats and sheep, or wild animals, such as kangaroos, wolves and whales. For the same reason, he rejects the widespread view that members of an endangered species, by the very fact that they are rare, are more valuable than members of an abundant species.

It is widely accepted, however, that the capacity for conscious experience comes in degrees, where those occupying the higher end of the spectrum of consciousness are called the "higher animals" and those at the lower end "lower animals". So, given the logic of supervenience, if the capacity for being a subject of conscious experience is a base property on which intrinsic value supervenes, then strictly speaking individuals possessing this base property to a greater degree must derive more intrinsic value from it than individuals who possess it to a lesser degree. The hierarchic model of value distribution therefore seems to require that Regan allocate different degrees of value to higher and lower animals.

In contrast, Taylor's biocentrism implies that each living thing is just as inherently worthy as any other. For all living things equally possess the property of being a teleological centre of life: something that does not come in degrees but is a matter of all or nothing. Furthermore, according to Taylor, this property is the sole basis on which an individual's inherent worth or intrinsic value can supervene. In a Kantian fashion, he argues that merits, excellence or any other desirable qualities and abilities – including degrees of consciousness – that an individual may have inherited or developed in later life are all irrelevant to the individual's inherent worth. Admirable and pleasing qualities vary from one individual living thing to another, and naturally our admiration for them varies accordingly. The inherent worth in all living things, however, comes from their being teleological centres of life, something that Taylor maintains is equal across them all and which should call for an equal respect from us to each and all of them.

Therefore, the crucial issue is whether any of the base properties, on which intrinsic value supervenes, admit of degrees. If so, the hierarchic model of the distribution of intrinsic value will follow. Discussions in environmental philosophy are often modelled – at least in part – on discussions in earlier periods of human-centred philosophy, in particular those dealing with the dignity and the status of human beings themselves. These older discussions are recapitulated in arguments regarding the location of intrinsic value in the non-human world, how it is distributed and whether it admits of degree. It is not surprising, then, that – as we indicated in Chapter 1 – environmental philosophy continually forces us back to considering the question of human worth itself and whether there is anything special about humans that places them apart from the rest of nature. To emphasize the commonalities here, to better appreciate the heritage of the new discipline as well as its contributions to the progress in human thought, we shall devote the following section to looking briefly at conceptions of human dignity and the worth of the human being as understood in the traditional context.

Value and dignity in human life

Central to the Universal Declaration of Human Rights are notions of the worth of human beings and the importance of human dignity. Closely associated with the modern notion of dignity are the ideas of *universal human rights*, and the *intrinsic value* or *sanctity* of human life. These rights, and the associated dignity, are meant to be features of all who are born human.

Just as there are two modes of how intrinsic value is distributed across things – hierarchic and egalitarian – there are two traditional conceptions of dignity: an older, classical "meritocratic" one and a more recent "democratic" one. In the classical picture, dignity is contingent on merits and honours. Like the merits and honours on which it supervenes, dignity in the classical picture varies from individual to individual, and it can be lost or ruined for a variety of reasons. In the modern picture, however, dignity is democratized and given an absolute status. It is guaranteed to all human beings in an equal share, regardless of their personal qualities. What plausible reasons does the classical picture provide for thinking that dignity is hierarchical and contingent? Like intrinsic value, dignity is a supervenient property and its possession traditionally depends on the possession of some base properties, such as high birth, virtues and other desirable personal qualities. In both Eastern and Western philosophy, it is accepted that dignity can be acquired via cultivation of virtues, and can also be lost via neglect and degeneration of character. Just as virtues give rise to honour, vices bring about indignity, dishonour and shame. In *The Great Learning*, one of the "four classics" of Confucianism, it is recommended that in order to avoid self-deception, and in order that "what truly is within will be manifested without", "the gentleman must be watchful over himself when alone". By contrast, the petty-minded or unscrupulous man – one lacking in dignity – knows no restraint in private (Legge 1972). So in the traditional conception of dignity, not all human beings are equal in birth, merit or virtue and the possession of such qualities is contingent on features that are not always under our control. The maintenance of dignity is thus a fragile matter.

That older conception of dignity is still present in contemporary usage, especially when we describe people as having a dignified bearing, or putting up with suffering in a dignified way. By contrast, the modern and absolute conception of dignity treats dignity as if it is equal across everyone, and its possession is guaranteed for all human beings. If people's dignity (a supervenient property) is a function of others of their qualities, then in order for people to have dignity to an equal extent, they must also have those dignity-conferring qualities (the base properties) to an equal extent. Further, in order for this equality in dignity to be guaranteed immune from loss or damage, the dignity-conferring qualities must also be damage- or loss-proof. What exactly could such qualities be? Here is the original puzzle which later re-invents itself

---

Dignity

G1. God is all-knowing and all-good. [the Judaeo-Christian definition of "God"]

G2. God believes something if and only if that thing is true. [from G1 & definition of "all-knowing"]

G3. God loves X if and only if God believes that X has value. [from G1 & definition of "all-good"]

G4. X has value if and only if God loves X. [Judaeo-Christian metaethical analysis of "value", from G2 & G3]

G5. God unconditionally loves all human beings equally, in that:

(a) God non-instrumentally loves all human beings equally (i.e. equally love them independently of their usefulness); and

(b) God intrinsically loves all human beings equally (i.e. equally love them for their intrinsic qualities, especially for their origin, i.e. their being God's creations); and

(c) God necessarily loves all human beings equally. (Why necessarily? Because God's love for human beings is independent of all contingent factors in the universe. This means that God's love for human beings is necessary.)

G6. All human beings have an equal unconditional value which is:

(a) non-instrumental (i.e. independent of their usefulness); and

(b) intrinsic (i.e. dependent on their intrinsic qualities); and

(c) necessary. [from G4 & G5]

when environmental philosophers inquire about the intrinsic value of nonhuman things in the environment: what are the base properties on which their intrinsic value supervenes? Now think again about that original puzzle, limiting the focus to the status of humans themselves. Doing so raises a troubling issue about the prospects for defending the democratic conception of equal human dignity shared over everyone alike. Since humans differ in their capacities for consciousness, self-reflection, imagination, emotion, and all the other descriptive properties we can enumerate, would it not be plausible to regard their supervenient value properties as being present in different degrees? While many people are comfortable with taking a hierarchic view of the distribution of intrinsic value across animals, plants and other nonhuman things, few will be willing to think likewise of our fellow humans. Is there a coherent rationale for adopting a double standard here? Using Otto's words for a different purpose, we can say in this case that we certainly face a "mysterium tremendum".

From what does human dignity originate if it is universal, shared by everyone and not dependent on the contingencies of birth, fame and fortune? The traditional Christian answer is that human dignity comes from God's grace. A more recent answer from Enlightenment philosophy is that it comes from humanity understood as rational agency or autonomy. In the twentieth century, existentialist philosophers such as Sartre suggested that it might be based in radical freedom. The problem for modern democratic understandings of dignity is whether they make sense at all if religion is rejected and there is no God. The key is the religious one summarized in the box "Dignity", below. Since the God of Christianity is all-knowing and all-good, he will believe only what is true. Such a God will love things if and only if they are valuable. Given that God loves all his human creations, then it is not difficult to conclude that such beings all have intrinsic value that does not depend on the contingencies of their lives, but is a necessary feature of their very existence.

Premise G4 states that God's love is the origin of all value, and the inference from G4 and G5 to G6 seeks to show that it is God's equal and unconditional love for all human beings that confers equal and unconditional worth on all human beings. Human dignity, according to the modern democratic notion, is nothing but this God-given worth, which is the sole foundation for universal human rights. Since God's love, approval, and commands are traditionally the source and foundation of all values and moral principles, the modern secular notion of moral dignity, value, standing or right as absolute and unconditional inherits the notions of necessity and universality from Christian theorizing. However, for those who lack the faith in the existence of such a loving and powerful God, what rational grounds are there for thinking that all human beings have equal and necessary dignity, which in turn generates equal, universal and absolutely inviolate human rights? What, apart from such a powerful theoretical device as God's equal and unconditional love for all human beings, can legitimize the demanding modern universal and democratized conception of dignity?

In order to provide a secular foundation for the inherent worth or dignity of the human being, some philosophers have tried to replace "God" with various versions of "ideal agents" (usually thought of as fully rational agents). There is a Kantian argument for human dignity, the structure of which is very similar to the religious one, and we give a version of this based on work by Christine Korsgaard (1996). There are serious problems with using this style of argument to support the modern conception of human dignity and of universal human intrinsic value. For one thing, it is arguably not true that rationality is necessarily self-appreciative. There are reasons for thinking that rational agency in the Kantian sense (i.e. autonomy, the capacity to reflect, to will, to make choices for oneself) is not always a good thing. In some tight situations, for example, instinct is sometimes a better response than Kantian reason. Unlike God, then, rationality is not all-good, and so is not an infallible guide to value. That is not the only problem with replacing God by rationality. The modern moral democrats (who endorse the Universal Declaration of Human Rights) are concerned with beings who are biologically human. Clearly, not all biological human beings are rational agents in the Kantian sense. Humans vary widely in their intelligence and intellectual capacities, and there is great physical and physiological inequality among them too.

Many have pointed out the empirical fact of human inequality in rationality, and argued that it follows from the Kantian perspective that beings who lack rationality are excluded from the Kantian kingdom of

---

A Kantian argument for intrinsic human value
K1. Something has value if and only if all rational agents value it.
K2. All rational agents value all rational agents equally and necessarily for their rational agency.
K3. Rational agency is humanity (the essence of being human).
K4. All human beings have equal intrinsic and necessary value. [from K1, K2 & K3]

(Adapted from Korsgaard 1996)

ends (i.e. the kingdom in which all members are always to be treated as ends in themselves and never as mere means). One commentator writes:

> One serious objection raised against Kant's ethical theory is that in claiming that only rational beings are ends in themselves deserving of respect, it requires treating all things which aren't persons as mere means to the ends of rational beings, and so it supports morally abhorrent attitudes of domination and exploitation toward all nonpersons and toward our natural environment. (Dillon 2008)

Here is a vital point for animal and environmental ethics. Not only are most (if not all) non-human beings on earth non-persons (non-rational beings), but so also are people who suffer from a large range of diseases, handicaps and injuries. No typical human beings (whatever "typical" means) are equally rational all the time in the Kantian sense. If rational agency is both necessary and sufficient for dignity, and if we admit that rational agency comes in degrees in human beings, then the Kantian picture for human dignity is not democratic and egalitarian at all. In short, without the foundation of some dignity-relevant quality genuinely and equally shared by all human beings, the modern Kantian conception of equal human dignity lacks plausibility. It is apparently nothing other than a residue of the traditional religious worldview.

We previously made a distinction between having capacities and being able to exercise them. Is it possible to make sense of some of the Kantian ideas about dignity by distinguishing what is true of our capacities from what is true of our exercise of them? In Kant's own account of dignity, and in the work of many of those who follow him, there is a close association between dignity and what we have called extended *autonomy*, meaning more than just the capacity to lay down laws for oneself. In the extended sense, and in application to human beings, autonomy is a capacity to determine one's ends and make authentic choices. To have autonomy in this way is to be self-legislating, self-governing, to make valuations, to be able to respect both oneself and other beings. Dignity, autonomy and respect are all locked together in the Kantian claim that all (and only) persons have a special kind of worth – dignity – that requires respect. The respect that is required by this worth is not a feeling, by the way, but rather (as Kant tries to make clear in *The Metaphysics of Morals*) a duty to behave in a certain way towards others, a way in which we limit "our self-esteem by the dignity of humanity in another person, and so as to respect in the practical sense" (Kant [1797]

1996: 569). This dignity of persons is, for Kant, something absolute and incomparable. Not everyone lives up to their dignity, of course, but simply through possessing it everyone has an equal worth.

In line with our earlier remarks on autonomy and autonomousness, it seems that dignity and intrinsic value, as understood in contemporary post-Kantian writings, relies on both. In other words, the presence of both autonomy as a capacity and the freedom to exercise it are conditions for having value and dignity; by contrast, the absence of either condition can be taken as contributing to loss of value. If autonomy – as a capacity – is the basis of the absolute worth of all human beings, then people will retain this worth even when unable to exercise that capacity. While imprisoned, or under the influence of drugs or disease, for example, people may be unable to be *autonomous* (freely exercising their capacities) while yet possessing these capacities in a relatively intact way. Once released from the confines of the prison, the drugs or the disease, they can return to the exercise of their capacities. So we can make sense of the idea that people can have autonomy, and hence worth, even where they are prevented from freely exercising that autonomy. Indeed, if autonomy is what underpins the claim that people have a special moral status, then certain offences against people – unjust detention, for example – are objectionable not because they interfere directly with the capacities that human beings have, but because they interfere with the exercise of such capacities. For the democratic conception, then, it seems that the possession (or loss) of dignity relies both on having (or lacking) a capacity of a certain sort, and also on being able (or unable) to exercise that capacity.

Secular environmental ethics

In light of our earlier discussion, it should be pretty clear by now that appeals to the autonomy of nature or of natural things largely parallel appeals to the autonomy of persons and human beings. In each case, the autonomy in question is meant to be the base property in virtue of which it is justified to ascribe dignity or intrinsic value either to humans or to natural things. Just as disrupting the ability of people to exercise their autonomy is morally offensive, so environmental philosophers have argued that disrupting the creative functioning of natural systems is likewise morally offensive. There is also in each case a similar puzzle. Take away the religious context in which it makes sense to depict all value as dependent on the goodness and love of God and we are left with no equivalently powerful secular basis on which to build a theory of intrinsic value of humans or of intrinsic value of nature. Rolston, who served as a pastor in Virginia before turning to academic philosophy and theology, is perhaps the most adept among recent environmental philosophers in using the traditional language of religion in application to nature, recognizing the importance of the numinous and the persuasive power of the ideas that first originated in a theological context.

But it is one thing to use the language that draws force from a religious context and quite another to translate that force into naturalistic terms. In the empiricist philosophy of George Berkeley, it was claimed that *esse est percipi*: to be is to be perceived. While Berkeley regarded this as a truth about the world in general – that is, only what was perceived by someone actually exists – the correlate of this doctrine in Christianity is that God's perceiving something to be a certain way is what makes it that way. According to traditional creation stories, God saw that what he had created was good. So His perceptions have a special force in that God's seeing something alone can make something good. If we now try to substitute nature for God, then a puzzle immediately arises. What would it be for nature to "see" that something is good, and thereby make it good? God is supernatural: he can create things out of nothing. But nature is not – according to our best scientific theories – supernatural or magical in any way. So how can nature make something good? Rolston's claim that nature creates value simply uses the traditional vocabulary of Christian theology but does this in a way that is meant to float free of any religious commitment. In the scientific account of the history of the planet, life on earth evolved over time, from simpler to more complex forms. These changes are explained by systematic theories. But the creation of value has no part in the story of science and there is no systematic way to explain its emergence on analogy with the emergence of dinosaurs, mammals and other complex life forms.

Others have aimed for a secular basis that can be described in terms of feelings or attitudes that may be widely shared among many people and across human cultural divides. Callicott, as we have already seen, develops a kind of communitarian ethic. For him, membership in each distinct community generates a distinct set of duties to protect the interests of that community and its members. For example, as members of the human species, we have duties to maintain the continued survival of our species and also a duty to respect the rights of other people, while as members of the global biotic community we have a duty to preserve its integrity and beauty. The land ethic, therefore, is only one of many different layers of moral codes within Callicott's larger communitarian system. By supporting the protection of ecological wholes and also respect for human individuals his system of ethics is meant to be environmental without being either misanthropic or eco-fascist.

According to Callicott, the many layers of moral codes are all theoretically unified under the single idea that community-based sentiments are the ultimate foundation of all values and morality. For him, something has intrinsic value if a community of people value it (i.e. they share a positive moral sentiment towards it) as an end-in-itself. This theory is based on feeling – sentiment – as much as it is communitarian: it reduces facts about values to certain psychological facts about people living in a community. It implies that there are no values without communities of valuers. This must not be confused with the rather different view that people alone are intrinsically valuable. For Callicott, value is anthropogenic (human-generated) without being anthropocentric (human-centred). If a community of people value an ecosystem in its own right, then the ecosystem has intrinsic value. What gives values and morality stability or even universality, he argues, is the contingent fact that human beings across times and cultures are similar in their basic needs, affections and dislikes. In particular, he believes that people are evolutionarily endowed with the disposition to value the community to which they belong once they recognize their belonging to it. The land ethic, Callicott argues, is the latest realization of that communitarian disposition in us. In this theory, the place of an all-knowing and all-loving God is taken by dispositions that natural evolution has placed in all human beings, dispositions that are themselves grounded in basic and universal human needs.

Do these supposedly universal human needs and dispositions do a better job than Kant's appeal to rationality in founding the idea that all people, and all natural systems, have intrinsic value? How, we might ask, do they compare with the religious claim that God can determine values simply by seeing that something is good? Callicott's basis – evolution and common human interests – seems too weak to do the job of founding notions of dignity and intrinsic value. In the religious framework, God cannot be wrong, for it is part of the definition of the supreme being in monotheistic religions that what is believed by that being is true. This gives a powerful basis for claims on behalf of the value and dignity of the human being. On the other hand, there is no reason to believe that the values held by communities, or the values shared across different communities, are founded in feelings that cannot be wrong. History seems to show time and time again that people are disposed to value at one time what people at other times find repellent. Slavery, for example, or sex between adults and children are practices that have been condoned at some times and abhorred at others. However similar their basic needs, affections and dislikes, communities have gone to war over strongly contested values, and whole groups of people have practised discrimination, attempted genocide and other horrors in the name of what they considered to be right. A widespread sentiment that ecosystems or natural things have value in their own right is just not enough to provide any guarantee that there really are inherent or intrinsic values in nature. Nor, in the absence of a framework of belief in a deity, is Rolston's claim that there are objective intrinsic values in nature any more convincing.

A similar issue arises also for Elliot, who holds a kind of ideal-observer theory of value, which also has some relations to the dispositional theory of value put forward by Lewis (1989). Ideal-observer theories held that what is valuable are just those things (experiences, goods, or whatever) that we are disposed to value when we are in ideal conditions for making value judgements. Not everything we desire is good, and not everything we value in moments of excitement are genuinely of value. But maybe if we step back from our involvement in daily activities and ask ourselves not what it is we desire, but rather what we (ideally) would desire to desire, then we can start to find out what is genuinely valuable. For example, someone addicted to drugs or alcohol may desire, above all else, another fix or another drink. Yet, in a calm moment, the very same person might think about these addictions and desires in a different way. Although still desiring the fix, the addict might have a higher-level desire not to desire the fix.

For Elliot something has intrinsic value for a valuing subject (the valuer) when the valuer is disposed to value that thing in virtue of the properties it possesses. As in other ideal-observer theories, the valuer is required to make that evaluation under the ideal condition of "calm

---

Indexing

[T]he attitudes generating indexed intrinsic value might be restricted to [1] those that persist through *calm reflection*, to [2] those that *have as much relevant information as possible*, or to [3] those that we would want to motivate our actions in the future irrespective of our future attitudes. ... [the third condition] suggests that it is at least partly on the basis of *second-order attitudes*, or attitudes we have to our attitudes, that the partitioning is based.

Elliot: Property X is a value if and only if X stands in the approval relation to a "second-order" attitudinal framework that we are disposed to adopt under ideal conditions of "calm reflection" in the light of "as much relevant information as possible". (See Elliot 1997: 15–25)

reflection", not distorted by anger, envy and other emotions, and on "as much relevant information as possible". How do we make sure that people's valuations do not just reflect passing whims, or desires that are idiosyncratic? Elliot proposes that we think of "attitudinal frameworks", which are sets of attitudes shared by groups of people. I, and people who have the same attitudes as I have, will share an attitudinal framework. If values are anchored in, or indexed to, such frameworks, then they are less likely to be whimsical, and – he thinks – more likely to be objective, rather than a matter of individual, subjective preference and feeling. Nonetheless, it is hard to see that attitudinal frameworks can solve the problem, or the mystery, of grounding intrinsic value in a way that makes such value objective and universal. This is beginning to look like an unsolved issue not only in environmental ethics, but also in value theory more generally. In the absence of a religious framework that grounds intrinsic value and dignity in the knowledge and love of the Creator, it is hard to find any justification for the view that there really are in nature values that are not merely instrumental, and that such values are intrinsic and necessary.

Making and finding values

If values exist to some extent independent of our personal, community or even human interests, then they would be objective to some degree. In the religious framework, the beliefs and love of God provide a superhuman – indeed supernatural – source for an objective kind of value. What God thinks, believes and does is entirely disconnected from human subjectivity. In environmental philosophy, the claim that wild places, untouched and unseen by people, may be of immense value is meant to suggest that there are things of value that are not very closely lined up with human concerns. If some environmentalists want to keep logging companies, mineral prospectors and oil corporations away from these areas, then the interest of the environmentalist is in preserving something that does not provide any services to us – other than the pleasing thought that we have kept some part of nature safe from interference. Think about what the appeal to "pleasing" thoughts does in this context. Having the thought itself injects subjectivity back into the picture. Perhaps the best secular attempt at stating what underpins the objectivity of value in nature will inevitably have a subjective as well as an objective aspect. This is the option we shall briefly explore in this section, so as to outline a theory of value that has both subjective and objective elements.

The history of philosophy provides examples of just such kinds of theorizing. Hume, the key thinker of the Scottish Enlightenment, held that there probably were universal features in human nature, and that these would provide a grounding for an ethic that is humanly created, but aspires to a limited objectivity. Hume's views influenced Callicott's thinking, but the original Humean proposal is more sophisticated than Callicott's reworking of it. We shall give a brief outline here of how Hume's theory can provide a story about ethics that will give intrinsic natural value a double status: in part it is discovered, but in part it is manufactured. The resulting theory of intrinsic value lacks the apparent power of the religious narrative, but will reach its conclusions in a way that avoids all appeal to the supernatural. It provides a way of constructing a modest, secular account of intrinsic value: perhaps as much as can be expected.

We have already seen a version of the ideal observer theory of value (nowadays called the "dispositional theory of value"). It has the following core idea:

D. X is valuable if and only if valuers are disposed, under ideal conditions, to give certain evaluative responses towards X.

To satisfy the ideal conditions, those who make the valuations would be impartial, rational, dispassionate and well informed about X (whatever it is). While some writers think that the evaluative responses we make are beliefs about X, Hume took these as feelings, and we shall follow Hume on this. As it stands, D is neutral between universalism and relativism. Universalists hold that only universal values are genuine values, whereas relativists think that what is of value only relative to some people can be a perfectly genuine value. Ancient Greeks made fun of other peoples, calling them "barbarians" because they did not speak Greek, the supposed language of civilization. We can guess that the Greeks regarded the speaking of Greek as valuable since they felt approval towards those who spoke Greek, and disapproval towards those who did not. But the ability to speak Greek is a relative value, and universalists would hold it not to be a genuine one.

Hume is a universalist and doctrine D makes it a question of fact whether there are universal values at all. It might turn out that there is nothing towards which all valuers under ideal conditions would have a favourable evaluative response. In common with other optimistic Enlightenment thinkers, Hume aims to find universal values founded on universal features of human nature. Nowadays we may be a bit less optimistic: some values we cherish may only be relative, and in doing philosophy, running political campaigns, even discussing issues with our friends and relatives, we will be trying to persuade others to adopt our values, hence making some relative values more universal. The recent history of environmental philosophy has probably contributed in part to spreading the idea of intrinsic natural value to a wide audience, and hence encouraging a wider circle of people to embrace this value.

For Hume, an action or character is virtuous if and only if a "spectator" feels the sentiment of approval towards it. It is the opposite – vicious – when a "spectator" feels the sentiment of disapproval towards it. What Hume calls a "spectator" or "judicious spectator" is not just anyone, but a human being who, apart from having a normal capacity for "sympathy" (see Lo 2006, 2009), must satisfy four further conditions. The first is that of having *full knowledge* of "all the circumstances and relations" relevant to the action or character under moral evaluation. This is the first condition on the spectator's judgement:

C1. Having *full knowledge* of all the circumstances and relations relevant to the case under evaluation.

Next, Hume's "judicious spectator" must also adopt what he calls the "steady and general points of view". We often make judgements about things in less than ideal circumstances. A red object, for instance, may appear to have different colours under different circumstances: orangey at sunset, brownish in a dark night, and purplish at dawn. But an experienced spectator judges it to be red because she knows that if the same object were to be placed under standard daylight (the ideal condition for perceiving colours), then it would look red. Similarly, in the case of making moral judgements, we might be in less than ideal positions to have reliable moral feelings, such as approval, attraction or repulsion (what Hume calls "sentiments"). We have strong feelings when the interests of ourselves or those who are close to us are at stake. But this is a distraction from reliable moral judgement, just as poor lighting can interfere with reliable colour perception. So Hume urged us to adopt what he called "steady and general points of view", which amount to the following three conditions:

C2. Being *impartial* in overlooking whether the persons involved in the case under evaluation are our acquaintances or strangers.
C3. Being *disinterested* in overlooking whether one's particular and private interests are at stake.
C4. Making *allowance for* the inevitable aspects of *human nature*: our tendency to self-interest (or "selfishness") and "limited generosity".

Assembling these conditions together, we can state Hume's analysis of virtue and vice quite simply:

H. An action or character is virtuous/vicious if and only if people are disposed, under the conditions (C1, C2, C3 and C4), to have the sentiment of approval/disapproval towards it.

The requirement in H can be weakened to allow for relative as well as universal values. The result is an analysis that shows how moral judgements about values are judgements about the nature of the object under evaluation as well as the moral psychological disposition of our mind.

Virtues and vices are values and disvalues, so it is not hard to take the Humean analysis as providing a general account of value. To say that something is valuable is equivalent to saying that *if* people are in the *ideal* conditions (C1, C2, C3 and C4), then they will feel approval towards it. This allows the possibility that something is valuable but no one as a matter of fact has such a feeling towards it, because it might be the case that no one has yet met all the ideal conditions for forming reliable moral feelings. It follows that the lack of approval from people towards the object does not imply that it is not valuable. According to this theory, values can exist in the absence of valuers, and something can be valuable without being valued. In this sense, value can be thought of as objective, since its existence does not depend on human belief, knowledge or feelings. At the same time, Humean value is subjective, for his analysis is given in terms of human subjects' psychological dispositions to respond under the ideal conditions. If we accept the Humean analysis, then the *concept* of "value" cannot be correctly analysed without employing the *concept* of "subject", which means there is a necessary conceptual connection between "value" and "subject". In this sense, then, value is *subjective*. Given the Humean analysis (and indeed any dispositional analysis in the style of D), values are both objective and subjective. They are objective in terms of their existence conditions, and subjective in terms of response conditions. Since these conditions are complementary to each other, the resulting theory is coherent, making sense of the idea that values are found (in the world) and yet made (because of our psychological responses to them).

Although the dispositional theory of value just outlined has influenced writers in environmental philosophy, including Callicott and Elliot, it still falls far short of the religious account. Although it allows that there may be values that are unrecognized, it also allows that the value of nature, of autonomy, of life may all be relative, namely ones that only some groups of people are disposed to accept. Although the relativity of value makes sense of the continuing disagreement and argument about intrinsic values in nature, it fails to settle the matter in any final way. The ineluctable subjectivity of value means that there can be no final, definitive answer to the question: are there intrinsic values in nature? As we shall see in Chapter 8, there is also a deeper point to be made here: the answer to questions about value, at least if we take the Humean viewpoint, is not one that can be given by philosophy.

What people do under ideal conditions of reflection and judgement, what feelings they come to have in these situations, is a matter to be discovered by factual study, not to be arrived at by *a priori* theorizing. One of the ambitions of philosophy over the years has been to settle questions by appeal only to reason and argument. The questions that can be settled in this way are ones about the consistency of theories, the nature of the relations between one concept and other concepts, the structure of our thought as disclosed to consciousness and so on. The struggle of environmental philosophers to achieve a satisfactory account of values in nature possibly reflects a limitation on philosophy itself. Until supplemented by additional factual information, some of the problems of philosophy are beyond solution.

The aesthetics of nature

The problems described in this chapter have raised questions about how to ground intrinsic moral value in properties that natural things and systems are thought to possess. But you might wonder why we have not so far looked at very important properties that people commonly associate with nature and natural things: properties such as beauty, tranquillity, the awe-inspiring grandeur of an unspoilt valley, or the delightful intricacy of an insect's wing. When Muir first gazed on the lily meadows of the Californian Sierra, he was amazed that anyone would let sheep destroy them. Likewise, at the heart of Leopold's land ethic is an injunction that is as much aesthetic as it is moral, hence challenging the anthropocentrism at the heart of much aesthetic theory. As Leopold put it:

[Q]uit thinking about decent land use as solely an economic problem. Examine each question in terms of what is ethically and aesthetically right, as well as what is economically expedient. A thing is right when it tends to preserve the integrity,

stability and beauty of the biotic community. It is wrong when
it tends otherwise.   (Leopold 1949: 224–5)

For Leopold and those, like Rolston, who have followed his lead, the aesthetic response is an important part of the story about what nature's value involves.

Since the time of Kant, nature has been a focus of aesthetic theory. Kant himself regarded nature as sublime and awe-inspiring, but this did not translate into any ethic of care, respect or duty towards nature. For the Kantian, nature was more important than art as a source of the experience of the beautiful or the sublime. By "sublimity", Kant was referring to the way that nature was able to overwhelm our senses, when, for instance, the seemingly infinite details of a majestic landscape impact on our all too finite sensibility. The vastness of nature escapes the capacities of our bodily senses to take in all the details. We can feel small, trivial or insignificant in the face of the vast expanse of mountain or plain, desert or ocean. At the same time, if we adopt a certain level of detachment, or disinterest (i.e. impartiality), towards nature, we are also able to take pleasure in the way that our minds are able to contemplate the gap between our finite senses and the opulent magnificence of nature. Such disinterested pleasure is, for Kant, at the centre of aesthetic experience. For him, the way in which nature overwhelms our senses provides – ironically – a means of appreciating our own rationality, a rationality that is itself capable of appreciating both the limits of our senses and the infinite wonder of nature.

Aesthetics

As I descended I gazed back, and the lofty summit of the mountain seemed to me scarcely a cubit high, compared with the sublime dignity of man.   (Petrarch, quoted in Nicolson 1959: 50)

[A]t least in the highest examples of art we find functions exemplified and values conveyed which nature and experience are scarcely able to yield. For instance, through art, though rarely through nature, we find ourselves made sharply aware of the splendours and defects of the society in which we live.   (Savile 1969: 103)

Let it be remembered that the subject of the picture – the material object or objects from which it is constructed – [is] the essential parts of it. If you have no love for them, you can have no genuine feeling for the picture which represents them … We love Nature and Beauty – we admire the artist who renders them in his work.

(*The Crayon* [1855], quoted in Hargrove [1989: 97])

Given the way that his account of the aesthetic sublime turns attention back to the human observer, and given the importance of disinterested pleasure in aesthetic experience, it is perhaps not surprising that Kant's aesthetics of nature does not prompt him to develop a philosophy of respect or care for animals or other natural things. To take a disinterested view of any subject matter is to detach ourselves from our own interests, and the interests – if any – of the object that is the focus of our appreciation. Such impartiality can put a wedge between aesthetics on the one hand and ethics or morality on the other. Art can, notoriously, depict what is morally depraved or evil through the use of beautiful structures and colours, as testified by the popularity of scenes of crucifixion and martyrdom throughout early modern European art. The beauty of the art work – discernible to the disinterested observer – may well make it valuable in communicating ideas or emotions and in provoking reflection on morality. Similar points apply to contemporary art. Think, for instance, of the controversy around Fernando Botero's Abu Ghraib series of paintings, where tortured prisoners held by US forces in Iraq are shown in the guise of martyrs depicted in Botero's baroque style and resonating with themes in classical European painting. These are striking artworks that – in addition to their formal and structural qualities as art works – have provoked discussion and comment on the use of torture by those working for liberal democratic states.

Not surprisingly, the emphasis on the importance of disinterest has spawned a debate in environmental aesthetics, with some theorists, for example Arnold Berleant, arguing that a full experience of nature's aesthetic possibilities requires engagement and participation, not just some kind of disinterested standing apart (Berleant 2005; c.f. Brady 2003). From the point of view taken in the previous section, it should be clear that the debate between the aesthetics of engagement and the aesthetics of detachment strikes us as somewhat artificial. Consider, for a moment, the love and appreciation that people feel for each other. There are times when our love for those near and dear to us involves passionate engagement, when our feelings overwhelm us and take control. On other occasions, we are able to stand back from those close to us and consider our feelings and relationships in a more detached and disinterested way. When we do that, we can perhaps reflect on the wonder of love, friendship and commitment, and view the attractive features of those near and dear to us in a more dispassionate way. In any rich relationship, a variety of perspectives and behaviours will be possible. Some of these will involve self-forgetful engagement and participation in worthwhile and enjoyable shared activities. Others will involve the more reflective and detached stance that Kantians consider the hallmark of reliable aesthetic judgement. But it would be wrong to insist that we should engage with a close friend, a lover or a relative only in a detached way, just as it would be wrong to insist that we can engage with a great work of art only in an emotionally detached manner. Just like our friends, lovers and relatives, great works of art are capable of inspiring strong emotional responses in us. The love and appreciation of nature offers equally rich possibilities for engagement and participation, reflection and standing back.

Our own suggestion is to be wary of falling into the *either/or* trap: of thinking that we must choose between one perspective or another. Why should disinterest and detachment be any more or less reliable than engagement and involvement? If we appreciate someone or something from a distance, we may wonder whether that appreciation will survive closer acquaintance. Likewise, if we are strongly attracted to something or someone close up, it will be wise to stand back on occasion to see if the features that so fascinate us are able to stand a more dispassionate scrutiny. Neither the close nor the distant view seems particularly reliable on its own.

The point can be taken further. In a famous essay that attempted to rebut Kant's emphasis on disinterest as a feature of both aesthetic and moral judgement, Iris Murdoch popularized the notion of "a just and loving gaze directed upon an individual reality" (Murdoch 1970: 34). Murdoch's focus on a kind of attention that is both just (that is, impartial) and loving (that is, engaged) seems to offer a way out of adopting an either/or view about the aesthetics of nature or about art and aesthetics in general. To be closely engaged and emotionally affected by someone or something does not mean abandoning what Hume called "steady and general points of view". For Hume, impartiality is not coldness or lack of emotion. By contrast, there is a reading of Kant in which disinterestedness is a kind of emotionlessness. Indeed, in his moral theory, Kant finds a role for only one emotion: that of respect for the moral law. Just as the Humean account of moral values, virtues and vices given in the previous section depicts the emotions as having a central role in any theory of what is morally valuable, so we should expect the emotions also to play a vital part in the story of what is aesthetically valuable. Our appreciation of both art and nature is multilevelled and complicated, but unless it involves emotions, it is hard to see how we can become disposed to approve or disapprove of actions, events, animals, places, people and things in the way that is typical of human beings the world over.

An obvious question arises in response to these reflections: what drives our emotional response to plants and animals, forests and deserts, rivers and mountains? For the Romantic painters, writers and poets who followed in Kant's footsteps, there was the love of the scenic: the grand view, the inspiring mountainscape, the large-scale canvas of nature on which the human being could be depicted as a small and relatively insignificant creature.

Later writers were less interested in the scenic, as such, and often drew inspiration instead from natural science, building up a narrative of nature's complexity, subtlety and self-regulation that itself might motivate feelings of respect, awe and love. This is exemplified clearly in Leopold's essays, where attention to detailed description of animal behaviours and ecological interactions helps build up a picture of the land as a community to be loved, one that can nurture human beings, and whose distress can be relieved by what he called "land doctoring". Leopold's merger of morality and ethics in his land ethic, inspired by knowledge of natural processes themselves, constitutes what has been called a positive aesthetics, one where untouched nature is regarded as essentially beautiful. For many writers, it is knowledge of geology, natural history and ecology that can best support such a positive view, and can draw our attention to what is wonderful and beautiful in nature (Hargrove 1989; Carlson 2008). Positive aesthetics has been characteristic of the approach to environmental value by many of the most prominent North American theorists, including Callicott, Carlson, Hargrove, Katz and Rolston, but it has also been adopted by writers in other countries. For example, as we have seen already, Elliot argues by reference to the historical facts that faking nature through restoration processes always involves producing something of lesser aesthetic and moral value than what was originally present. Without knowing the history of a landscape, we may be led to believe it is naturally beautiful. If once we find, however, that it is not original but the result of restoration, then we recognize that this is something that is artificial and hence of less value than the original. Elliot's argument parallels an argument that can be made about works of art. Even art experts can be fooled by good forgeries. Once it is known that a painting is a forgery, then its value is reduced, as a result of that very knowledge. According to this view, aesthetic qualities, then, are not something inherent in the work itself, but are instead not separable from facts about the history of production of the work.

While in this section we have only brushed the surface of environmental aesthetics, we need to be aware that it explores a notion of value that is just as mysterious as the one found in environmental ethics. It is certainly not clear that knowledge of ecology or natural history, for example, will inevitably drive a positive evaluative disposition towards what is natural. Look at the passage by Dale Jamieson in the box "May". This shows clearly that there *may* be occasions when contact with natural environments brings about transformations in people. But such transformations are not guaranteed. No amount of reading of natural history books, and viewing of David Attenborough documentaries is guaranteed to bring about a change in the way people think and – importantly for a dispositional theory of value – how they are disposed to feel. Hargrove has argued that because of the creative power of nature at work in the production of species, landscapes and ecosystems, there is no ugliness in nature. Yet no amount of study of nature's creativity is likely to ensure that all students will agree with Hargrove's verdict. Moreover, if beauty and ugliness are supervenient properties, ones that pictures, landscapes and vases possess in virtue of other, base properties, a further problem obtrudes for us. Will beauty be at the same level as intrinsic value, so that nature's creativity, or the presence of life, simultaneously produces both intrinsic value and beauty? Is intrinsic value itself a base property on which beauty supervenes, or is beauty itself something on which intrinsic value depends? These are not easy questions to address, and so the field of environmental aesthetics looks likely to provide challenges to thinkers for some time to come. Unfortunately it seems to have provided no solution to the tremendous mystery to which this chapter has been devoted: the foundation of intrinsic value itself.

eight

Origins: political, religious and cultural diagnoses of environmental problems

How dangerous are our ideas?

The study of ethics, politics, history, the sciences and literature is dominated by claims about significant thoughts, great books (dealing with "great ideas") and even "dangerous ideas". Daniel Dennett called his book on evolutionary theory *Darwin's Dangerous Idea*. Visions, ideas and ideals are often said to have driven our cultural and intellectual progress. Ideas can be socially or emotionally unsettling, or can be at the centre of waves of progress. In a three-volume study of the growth of Western science, A. C. Crombie announced that the "history of science" was the "history of a vision and an argument initiated in the West by ancient Greek philosophers, mathematicians, physicians" (1994: vol. 1, 3). It is not only progress that is driven by ideas and arguments. Feminists claim that patriarchal modes of thought have structured not only men's relations with women, but have been a component of colonial exploitation and have played a part in developing and maintaining social class divisions and even the exploitation of nature and animals.

Can ideas, beliefs, visions and arguments really do these things? People obviously hold – and claim to act under the sway of – beliefs and ideals. Writers, political activists and philosophers often assume that their words, ideas and theories have spurred people into action on occasion. But sometimes the words come after the deeds, and some theories maybe reflect rather than create social, cultural and political reality. Theories may also reflect and maintain social and political realities, thus propping up structures of behaviour that the theories did not themselves create. In this chapter we shall look at the claims that environmental problems have been the product of certain ideas, worldviews and attitudes. Removing or changing these ideas will – so some writers argue – help reduce the impact that humans have made on the rest of nature, and contribute to saving the planet. One common theme will emerge from looking at these diagnoses of our environmental plight: human-centred thinking appears over and over again as one of the key issues.

In a 2002 article, John Gray bewailed the influence of religious beliefs, in particular their association with further beliefs about the importance of human beings in comparison with the rest of the natural world. Gray's complaint was not that religion is inconsistent. "To my mind," he wrote:

> such religious beliefs have caused an immense amount of harm, but at least they are coherent. It is perfectly reasonable to think humans are the only source of value in the scheme of things – so long as you retain the theological framework in which they are held to be categorically different from all other animals. (Gray 2002)

Our analysis in Chapter 7 of the dim prospects for a secular account of dignity and intrinsic value supports Gray's remarks. Gray's complaint also mirrors the charge made originally by the historian Lynn White Jr in a famous article in the journal *Science*. Struck by the anthropocentrism that is central to Christianity, even in spite of its worship of a supernatural being, White wondered if the ideas promulgated by Christian thinkers and ministers were part of the problem we now face. Could Christianity be at the root of the environmental problem?

Central to the rationale for White's thesis were the works of the Church Fathers and the Bible itself, which, he argued, prescribe anthropocentrism: the view that, humans are the only things on earth that really matter. Of course, for a believer, God, Satan and the angels are all important too, but these are not earthly beings. Genesis (1:27–8) says that because human beings are created "in the image of God", they should "replenish the earth, and subdue it: and have dominion … over every living thing that moveth upon the earth". The full quote is given in the box "White", below. Remember how the claim that God appeared in human form was the only consideration Turmeda could muster to win the debate with the animals in the "Disputation of the Donkey". Likewise, in his *Summa contra Gentiles* (bk 3, pt 2, ch 112), Thomas Aquinas stated that non-human animals were "ordered to man's use". According to White, the Judaeo-Christian idea that humans are created in the image of the transcendent supernatural God, who is radically separate from nature, also by extension radically separates humans themselves from nature. This ideology opened the way for untrammelled exploitation of nature. Modern Western science itself, White argued, was "cast in the matrix of Christian theology" so that it too inherited the "orthodox Christian arrogance toward nature" (White 1967: 1207).

Without technology and science, the environmental extremes to which we are now exposed would probably not be realized. But these are not innocent either, according to White, for Christianity has provided the right kind of separation between humans and nature to promote the development of the modern sciences:

> I personally doubt that disastrous ecologic backlash can be avoided simply by applying to our problems more science and more technology. Our science and technology have grown out of Christian attitudes toward man's relation to nature which are almost universally held not only by Christians and neo-Christians but also by those who fondly regard themselves as post-Christians. (White 1967: 1206)

So the claim is that given the modern form of science and technology, Judaeo-Christianity itself provides the original deep-seated drive to unlimited exploitation of nature.

The second premise of White's argument also has a central place in many rival theories in the field. Indeed, the structure of many major theories diagnosing the roots of environmental crisis is regularly of the same pattern as White's: (1) X leads to anthropocentrism; (2) anthropocentrism is very harmful to the environment; therefore (3) X is the origin of environmental crisis. We shall look at just three other cases: the *disenchantment of nature, ecological feminism* and *deep ecological relationalism.* The disenchantment theory goes like this. Traditionally, animist views have held that personalized souls are found in animals, plants and other material objects. As we have already seen, panpsychists and the new animists argue that dialogue with a living nature is possible even when we stop short of claiming that the non-human world is full of souls. Of course, if humans are the only special, ensouled beings on earth, then the denial of any kind of similar status to everything else on the planet leads to anthropocentrism and thus provokes environmental crisis. In a disenchanted world, there is no meaningful order in natural things or events, and there is no source of mystery, sacredness or dread of the sort felt by those who regard the natural world as peopled by divinities or demons (Stone 2006). A disenchanted nature commands no respect, reverence or love. It is nothing but a giant machine, the most inner secrets and operations of which are to be revealed and manipulated by human science and technology.

Broadly speaking, a feminist issue is one that contributes in some way to understanding the oppression of women. Feminist theories attempt to analyse women's oppression, its causes and consequences, and suggest strategies and directions for women's liberation. Feminist theorists have claimed that the origin of environmental woes has a different factor: patriarchy and its radical separation of male and female into two evaluatively opposite spheres. Patriarchy leads to male-centredness (androcentrism) as well as anthropocentrism. Plumwood writes:

> Many environmental critiques have shown how control over and exploitation of nature is linked to control over and exploitation of human beings. High technology agriculture and forestry in the third world which is ecologically destructive also strengthens the control of elites and social inequality, increasing for example men's control over the economy at the expense of women, and it does these things in a way which reflects structure, not co-incidence. (Plumwood 1993: 64)

Patriarchy associates the male with the rational, active, creative human mind, and civilized, orderly, transcendent culture, and the female with the emotional, passive, determined animal body, and primitive, disorderly, immanent nature. It assigns superiority to everything on the male side but inferiority to everything on the female side. Such a patriarchal mode of thinking, according to the ecological feminist, sustains all forms of oppressions in the world, including the human exploitation of the natural environment. Since patriarchy leads to anthropocentrism, it is the favoured feminist target for explaining why the environment is in a mess.

Deep ecological relationalism (or holism) blames atomistic individualism as the origin of environmentally harmful attitudes and behaviours. As we have already seen, in his early work Naess contrasted the individualism of traditional philosophy with the alternative relational conception of humans as knots in webs of interrelatedness. Just as Christianity, according to White, depicts humans as apart from nature, so too according to the early versions of deep ecology does the adoption of the individualistic picture of isolated people pursuing their separate projects. The result of individualism is human selfishness towards nature. To counter this form of egoism, deep ecologists argue that people need to adopt an alternative "relational" (or "holistic") metaphysics of the self, an extended, ecological Self. By recognizing our interconnections with each other and the wider world, we start to take better care of nature and the world in general. In each story, then, the same ingredient is present: anthropocentrism. What is different is the trigger that leads to human centredness and our sense of separation from the rest of the living world: religious doctrine, disenchantment, masculine egoism or a mistaken belief about the nature of individuals and their identity. Even if anthropocentrism is not the only cause of the environmental crisis, each of these theories insists that it plays a part in maintaining structures of thought that make it difficult for us to find a way out of the pattern of dominating and exploiting nature that is characteristic of the contemporary world.

Despite the fact that White's thesis and the other three views of our problems all share a common structure, much of the debate in environmental philosophy has been among and between the proponents of these views. In the heat of such debate, the various parties seem to have overlooked the commonalities between them. Deep ecology and feminism, for example, have come into collision in spectacular ways. While deep ecologists urged the importance of developing an extended sense of self, many feminists disagree. They argue that the idea of nature as part of oneself would be quite the wrong one to adopt and might be likely to justify continuing exploitation of nature. For details on the arguments, see the heated exchanges reprinted as part IV of Brennan (1995).

Fact and philosophy

All four theories just described not only claim that anthropocentrism is at the heart of the problem of environmental destructiveness, but also have a solution. The solution, as we have already seen in earlier chapters, is *non-anthropocentrism* instead. However, just like the notion of "natural", there is some ambiguity about what this term means. There seem to be two very different claims, each of which can be thought of as a version of non-anthropocentrism. One of these is an evaluative thesis, the one that should now be familiar as a key claim in many environmental philosophies: that natural non-human things have intrinsic value, that is value in their own right independent of any use they have for humans. This means that humans are not special in having value in their own right: other things are also valuable in this way, and if this is true then the anthropocentric theory of value must be rejected.

This evaluative claim on its own would hardly make a difference to the world unless we were able to act on it in ways that help the planet recover from the insults of climate change, pollution, species loss and the rest of the litany of environmental destruction. Although enormous ingenuity and effort has been expended in spelling out alternatives to the anthropocentric view of the world, this has apparently been based on the implicit assumption that a recognition of intrinsic value in nature is likely to change people's behaviour. We should try, then, to spell out this implicit thesis of non-anthropocentrism as a separate claim about human psychology and behaviour. The hidden thesis is this: that people who believe in anthropocentrism (the ones who think humans are special) are more likely to be environmentally damaging, whereas people who reject anthropocentrism are more likely to be environmentally protective.

The rejection of anthropocentrism can only be a solution to the problem of environmental harm if something like the hidden thesis is true: let us call it the "psycho-behavioural" thesis, and contrast it with the evaluative claim to the defence of which much of the last three decades of environmental ethics have been devoted. By contrast, the psycho-behavioural thesis is seldom discussed, remaining hidden as part of the tacit background of environmental ethics. When the thesis does get explicit mention, this is often in the introductions or prefaces of books, or in reference works, for example when it is said that deep ecology's "greatest influence … may be through the diverse forms of environmental activism that it inspires" (Taylor & Zimmerman 2005: 458). If the psycho-behavioural thesis is true, then it is important in two ways: (i) in providing a rationale for both the diagnosis and solution of environmental problems, and (ii) in giving practical justification to environmental philosophy itself (conceived as the mission to secure converts to non-anthropocentrism).

Now, if the psycho-behavioural thesis turns out to be false, what should we say? Suppose it turns out that those who think humans are special do not act in particularly damaging ways towards the environment, or that those who think there is much intrinsic value in the non-human world are not particularly careful about their own environmental impact. This would have quite an effect. A question would have to be asked about environmental philosophy itself and about why it has spent so much time examining the question of values in nature. In addition each of the four theories we have just examined would be rendered less interesting. Each of them assumes that anthropocentrism disposes people to be environmentally damaging, a supposition we are imagining to be false. As we have formulated premise W2 in White's argument, it is the psycho-behavioural thesis that does important work. The same is true in the other three arguments. A major reason for undertaking study of environmental value and attitudes would be undermined if it turns out that the psycho-behavioural thesis is false.

Is there any reason to think the thesis might be false? In a significant study of agricultural practices in Latin America, William Durham showed that families who held animist views about nature, and who were careful to ask forgiveness for land clearing that disrupted indigenous vegetation and animals, had a worse effect on the environment than families who aimed to maximize their income from farming and had no particular conception of the land as intrinsically valuable or sacred. It turned out that the economically oriented families had ecologically superior land rotation practices (Durham 1995). In other cases, groups of indigenous people in South America were shown to be more or less implicated in land clearing according to whether their economic activities were more or less integrated into the wider market economy. Here, then, are cases that point in two ways. Given that indigenous cultural beliefs often invoke the importance of taking care of the local environment, it would be expected that the less integrated an indigenous group is, the less it is likely to engage in extensive land clearing. The *a priori* expectation is vindicated in the one case, but not in the other. The conclusion to be drawn here is that it can be dangerous to jump to the conclusion that people's beliefs and values will translate directly into actions that exemplify such beliefs and values. Facts and theories do not always match in the way we expect.

Another reason to take care is the problematic assumption of rational agency: the idea that if people rationally or intellectually believe that they have a duty to do something, then they will actually do it (or at least do it more often than not). The psycho-behavioural thesis is just a particular case of this more general thesis, one that is a factual claim about human cognition and behaviour. Again, the truth or falsity of this theory cannot be decided by purely *a priori* philosophical reasoning. In fact, the four major philosophical theses already mentioned are committed to the truth of empirical claims about social and cultural reality. To be credible, then, they must be able to stand up to empirical testing. If we believe we have a duty to respect nature, for example, or believe that natural things are intrinsically valuable, then will we in fact act in ways that are eco-friendly? This question about the relation of belief to action looks no different in kind from the sorts of questions that social scientists regularly ask.

So far, there has been little experimental testing of the four theories. White's is the only one to have been empirically tested by sociologists and other social scientists, with generally inconclusive results. One reason for this is that social scientists themselves make the same mistakes as philosophers, by jumping to conclusions about the connection between anthropocentrism and anti-environmental attitudes and behaviours. For example, one of the best-known and most widely used survey instruments in the field is the revised new environmental paradigm (NEP) scale of Riley E. Dunlap *et al.* (2000). That survey instrument was developed from an earlier questionnaire – the original NEP scale – developed in the 1970s. Both the original and the revised scales use indicators of anthropocentrism to measure the presence of un-environmental attitudes. So the designers of the survey already assumed that anthropocentrism determined an un-environmental attitude.

When some feminists attacked deep ecologists for projecting what they saw as a masculinist view of the extended self onto the world, they were concerned that such a view would lead to less, rather than more, care for the environment. But in his early work, it is clear that Naess thought just the opposite: by urging that we take the self-realization of the extended self seriously, he thought it clear that we would care more for the environment. Here is a disagreement that again depends on facts, not philosophy, in order to be resolved. Jumping to conclusions has apparently led people to think that anyone who thinks humans are superior in value to non-humans will be inclined to show little care for non-humans. But this just does not follow. Since there is nothing in the definition of anthropocentrism that refers directly to environmental destructiveness whether in attitude or behaviour, there is bound to be a gap between identifying someone's attitudes as anthropocentric, on the one hand, and as environmentally destructive on the other. This is not to say that there is no connection to be found here. There may be circumstances where, other things being equal, having an anthropocentric system of beliefs and associated feelings will dispose someone towards environmentally damaging behaviour. Investigation of just what these circumstances are, however, will require more than philosophy, and will necessitate some study of facts.

These problems about the White thesis are independent of further, logical issues that can also be raised. Think again about the three key ingredients listed in the box "White" above, in the argument linking Christianity, anthropocentrism and environmental harm. Let us label the three key factors here as (A) Christian beliefs, (B) anthropocentric beliefs and (C) environmental harm. White's argument is not even logically valid when thought of in terms of the claimed interconnections between A, B and C. First, suppose there is a strong association between factors A and B (say, 70 per cent) and also a strong association between factors B and C (again 70 per cent). In other words, suppose that 70 per cent of those holding Christian beliefs also hold that there are no intrinsic values in nature, and then suppose that 70 per cent of those who think there are no intrinsic values in nature are disposed to act in environmentally harmful ways. By simple arithmetic, it is obvious that these figures do not show that even a majority of Christians are disposed to act in environmentally harmful ways.

On its own, this logical point may not be too serious. White probably did not intend his argument to be a deductively valid one and, in any case, he was writing about general cultural trends, not about the behaviour of actual groups of people. In this context, a lack of deductive validity is not a problem for White's argument, so long as it was intended as a merely cogent argument in the first place. What he was probably aiming for was an argument in which, given the assumptions, the conclusion was more likely to be true than false. For any argument to be cogent, its premises need to have a relatively high chance of being true, and their being true should make the conclusion more likely to be true than false. That means that in order to test the cogency of the argument, we need to separately test all of the three claims involved. Oddly enough, as far as we can ascertain, no sociological studies of White's thesis have taken this approach. Again, the probable explanation for this is that people have jumped to conclusions rather than subjecting the issues involved to rigorous factual examination.

The considerations about White's thesis can be readily transferred to the other theses as well. If there are doubts about the factual grounding and cogency of White's analysis, then the same has to be said of the three other cases: the *disenchantment of nature, ecological feminism* and *deep ecological relationalism*. In all cases, there may well be connections to be made between deep-seated worldviews and belief systems on the one side, and people's attitudes and behaviour towards the environment on the other. In all of these cases, it will be necessary to supplement pure and inspired theorizing with some factual information too. This is a task that can be undertaken either by sociologists, or by people working in the new field of experimental philosophy (where surveys and other empirical techniques are being used to complement philosophical theorizing).

The domination of nature

Whatever empirical discoveries show about the plausibility of the diagnoses of our environmental problems, the new animists – just like the feminists – are concerned that our attitudes to natural things make it easy to justify domination and exploitation of them. As natural processes fall more and more "under technology's thumb" (Leiss 1994), the need to understand and explain our subjugation of nature has become more urgent. But the explanation for this can be given in a number of different ways: by appeal, for example, to philosophy, politics, anthropology and a number of other disciplinary perspectives. Since nature's domination is likely to be a result of the operation of complex factors, no single explanation drawn from a particular perspective will be adequate. A prudent course would be to look at a range of theories with a view to seeing if they can separately provide part of the answer we seek.

While classical Marxists regard nature as a resource to be transformed by human labour and utilized for human purposes, the critical theorists Max Horkheimer and Theodor Adorno saw Marx himself as representative of the problem of "human alienation" (Horkheimer & Adorno [1969] 1972). At the heart of the problem is the conception of "instrumental rationality", a concept developed from the work of Max Weber at the beginning of the twentieth century (Weber [1920] 2001). In his book *The Protestant Ethic and the Spirit of Capitalism*, Weber argued that the project of mastering the world required the development of a certain kind of personality, one that sees work in a way influenced by the religious inheritance of Calvin: namely Puritanism and Protestantism. In the attempt at world mastery, capitalism also encourages, he claimed, a certain kind of calculative and rational approach to things, and takes observation, measurement and the application of purely quantitative methods to be capable of solving all problems. Reason becomes an instrument of manipulating other people and the world in pursuit of supposedly good ends. Nature (and, likewise, human nature) is thus no longer regarded as mysterious, uncontrollable, or fearsome. Instead, it is reduced to an object strictly governed by natural laws, which can be studied, known and employed to our economic benefit.

The critical theorists argued that under the impact of this kind of instrumental rationality, our relationship with nature has been disrupted, encouraging the undesirable attitude that non-human things are nothing more than items to be probed, consumed and dominated. According to Horkheimer and Adorno, the oppression of the natural environment (what they called "outer nature") through science and technology has been bought at the cost of suppressing our own "inner nature" (Horkheimer & Adorno [1969] 1972). Modern industrial society, they claimed, has ignored and subdued human creativity, autonomy and the manifold needs, vulnerabilities and longings at the centre of human life. To remedy such an alienation, the project of Horkheimer and Adorno was to replace the narrow instrumentalist model of rationality with a more humanistic one, in which the values of the aesthetic, moral, sensuous and expressive aspects of human life play a central part. Thus, their aim was not to give up our rational faculties or powers of analysis and logic. Rather, the ambition was to arrive at a dialectical synthesis between reason and feeling – Enlightenment and Romanticism – to bring us back to an appreciation of freedom, spontaneity and creativity (see the critique of this in Eckersley [1992: ch. 5]).

In his later writings, Adorno advocated a rather obscure doctrine of "sensuous immediacy" towards nature, as a way of re-enchanting the aesthetics of nature. If we can find ways of re-enchanting the world through aesthetic experience, he argued, then this would also be a re-enchantment of human lives and purposes. If Adorno is right, then one of the main problems with our attitude to nature is a loss of engagement and sensuous immediacy, these features having been supplanted by the calculative approach to the world that is the hallmark of industrial societies that use instrumental rationality as the key method of approaching the discussion and solving of problems. This way of interpreting the work of the critical theorists suggests a commonality between them and the new animists, since both groups of theorists are suspicious of reason and of rationalistic and rationalizing approaches to the world. It is precisely this kind of calculative and rationalistic approach to the world that makes the new animist position at first seem absurd: how can thinking about the other beings in our world as if they are persons be fitted into the rationalistic framework? Recall also the ideas of phenomenologists such as Abram, who argues that we should see ourselves as part of the "common flesh" of the world: that we are in a sense the world thinking itself. His work too can be taken as trying to undermine the overdependence on reason and calculation that has led to a one-sided way of thinking about nature.

Although the problem of the domination of nature has been treated in this section as if it results from a problem of attitude – an over-rationalized way of thinking about the world – it also raises urgent practical questions about how we should change our ways of thinking about political, economic and social policies. These matters will be dealt with in the final chapter. However, it is worth remembering that if Weber is right, and if instrumental rationality is a key feature of modern capitalist societies, then it is going to be extremely difficult to introduce anti-rationalist ways of thinking and feeling into policy debates at local, national and international levels. One of the main virtues of instrumental rationality is that it fits well with the highly bureaucratized nature of modern states. In these structures, it is important that all considerations that bear on policy can be dealt with in a common coin, the most obvious being costs and benefits measured in terms of dollars.

If we can reduce all our discussions and decisions to a common coinage, this seems to make our decisions apparently open to rational justification by being objective in the sense of being free from partiality. Such impartiality is one of the common aims of the sciences, and also appeals to the moral philosopher. One reason for the success of utilitarian reasoning, of the kind used by Singer, is that it aims to reduce questions of good and right to matters that can be assessed using one measure: pleasure, welfare, preference satisfaction, or some other simple measuring property. Bernard Williams called particular attention to this problem:

> [There is] an assumption about rationality, to the effect that two considerations cannot be rationally weighed against each other unless there is a common consideration in terms of which they can be compared. This assumption is at once very powerful and utterly baseless. (Williams 1985: 17)

Like the critical theorists, Williams believed that this demand was not itself a new one (it is "as ancient as Socrates"), but in an echo of Weber he also regarded it as an expression of "modern bureaucratic rationality". Bureaucratic rationality, then, may be another factor to consider in explaining our contemporary domination of nature.

Feminism and the mastery of nature

Weber's term "mastery" of the world is well chosen according to some feminist writers who see anthropocentrism as a result of patriarchy (Plumwood 1993; Warren 1994). In the scheme for White's thesis, the feminist version substitutes "patriarchy" for "Christianity" in the first sentence:

W1. Christianity leads to anthropocentrism.

A more elaborated version is given in the box "Feminism", below, where the core claims are written out as F1 to F5. You will see that we have here another argument of the sort that has now become quite familiar: an argument to the best explanation. If F1 and F2 are both true, then this gives grounds for taking seriously the idea that patriarchy is the best explanation of a kind of oppression that reinforces a number of interconnected forms of domination. If these forms of domination are genuinely interconnected, then it is likely that to eradicate one of these forms of domination, all the others will also have to be eradicated.

What, then, is patriarchy, and how does it come to play a part in such a diverse range of evils? While the term "patriarchy" literally means the form of family organization in which the father (or some other male) is head of the household, we shall treat it as a theoretical term used in

---

Feminism

F1. Under patriarchy, women are subordinated and exploited by men. [*misogynist reality*]

F2. Under patriarchy, non-humans are subordinated and exploited by humans. [*anthropocentric reality*]

F3. Patriarchy endorses an oppressive dualism which facilitates different, but mutually reinforcing, forms of domination. [feminist theory of patriarchal dualism]

F4. F3, given the truth of F1, best explains the truth of F2 and all the other forms of domination (e.g. racism, classism) under patriarchy.

F5. No one form of domination can be properly eradicated without the others also being eradicated.

---

feminist analysis to denote a kind of social and cultural structure that systematically privileges and empowers males at the expense of females. To use the term in this way means that we shall find more about what patriarchy is meant to be by exploring what theorists have to say about the nature and structure of patriarchal culture. Since there are many kinds of feminism, and not all of them agree on the analysis of patriarchy, we shall focus mainly on those feminists who have contributed to the debates on environmental philosophy. For these ecological feminists, feminism is itself a form of *ecological* philosophy for two reasons. First, it rejects (traditional) anthropocentrism: the view that non-human nature is, and should be treated as, nothing more than a mere means to human ends. Second, it endorses the environmental movement, and also the animal liberation movement, both for non-anthropocentric reasons. In common with other forms of feminism, it takes the view that the oppression of women exists, is wrong and should be stopped. To analyse and eradicate oppression of women, feminists say, it is important both to identify the causes of such oppression and also advance strategies for women's liberation.

For ecological feminists, there are important parallels and connections between the oppression of women and the oppression of non-human nature under patriarchy. In particular, they maintain that the twin dominations of women and non-human nature are mutually reinforcing so that we cannot properly eradicate the one without eradicating the other. At least in the Western philosophical tradition, women have been the target of misogynistic comments from antiquity to the present, where the supposed female closeness to emotion and nature has not been deployed as a compliment. It is easy to spell out the main features of the polar opposites employed in the dualistic thinking referred to in premise F3 of the feminist argument. Patriarchal thinking treats the male or masculine qualities in the lefthand column in the box "Dualisms" as superior to the female or feminine qualities on the right. Only the interests of the superior beings count, or if the interests of the inferior beings are allowed to figure, then they are given much less weight. In consequence, this pattern of dualistic thinking privileges one side over the other and licenses domination of the one by the other. Once the pattern of dualistic thinking is well established, then racism, sexism, social class discrimination, the exploitation of animals and ecological destruction can all be rationalized far too easily. In each case, a particular race, sex, social class or species is privileged over another, and the favoured "higher" items are then supposed to enjoy a special status relative to the "lower" items.

Once such dualistic modes of thought are in operation, it is hard to find a perspective in which care for others and a concern for their suffering or their problems can be properly expressed. As a result, it becomes hard to foster real connections and healthy relationships between the sexes, or between people of different races or social classes, between people and animals, or between people and the wider non-human world. The three features – care for, concern about and connection with others – are ones that feminists have tried to recover in their accounts of ethics, these being the very features that patriarchal modes of thought and discourse make it hard to consider or express. The fundamental problem with dualistic and hierarchical modes of thinking is not just that they are unreliable and lead us into errors of belief or knowledge. Nor is it just that the dominating party often falsely sees the dominated party as lacking (or possessing) the allegedly superior (or inferior) quali-

---

Correlations

Ecofeminism is the position that there are important connections – historical, experiential, symbolic, theoretical – between the domination of women and the domination of nature, and understanding of which is crucial to both feminism and environmental ethics. ... any feminist theory and any environmental ethic which fails to take seriously the twin and interconnected dominations of women and nature is at best incomplete and at worst simply inadequate.   (Warren 1996: 19)

Many environmental critiques have shown how control over and exploitation of nature is linked to control over and exploitation of human beings. High technology agriculture and forestry in the third world which is ecologically destructive also strengthens the control of elites and social inequality, increasing for example men's control over the economy at the expense of women, and it does these things in a way which reflects structure, not co-incidence.   (Plumwood 1993: 64)

Dualisms

The male	The female
male, master, colonizer	female, slave, colonized
culture, human, humanity	nature, non-human, animality
reason, rationality, mind, mental	emotion, feeling, body, physical
transcendent, universal	immanent, particular
production, activity	reproduction, passivity
civilized, developed, order	primitive, undeveloped, chaos
freedom, autonomy, independence	necessity, inescapability, dependence
subject, the self, perceiver	object, the other, perceived

ties, or that the dominated party often internalize false stereotypes of themselves given by their oppressors, or that stereotypical thinking often overlooks salient and important differences among individuals. These factors all combine into a cognitive structure that patriarchy encourages. That structure encourages denial of the interdependence between the two sides of the duality; masters depend on slaves, after all, just as slaves depend on masters. The structure also encourages an exaggerated separation (in Plumwood [1993] this was called "hyperseparation") of the two sides, so that racists, for example, often act as if there is no common humanity between them and the people they attack, or sexual chauvinists think of men as wholly rational beings and women as wholly emotional ones. Finally, the structure of thought in question encourages stereotyping, as if all those on one side have the desirable qualities (all humans are rational) and all those on the other side entirely lack the desirable qualities (all animals are merely instinctive).

In a crude way of thinking about the history of feminist thought, it is possible to distinguish three waves of analysis. So-called *first-wave feminists* attacked the cognitive structure just described, arguing that women belonged on the side of reason and civilization just as much as men did. *Second-wave feminists* tried to argue that the supposedly inferior side of the dualism was actually not inferior at all; emotion could be superior to reason in many cases, for example, and being closer to nature was a plus for women, not a sign of anything inferior. For *third-wave feminists*, the fundamental problem is the very notion of a prescriptive dualism itself. They deny that there is any sensible way of setting up a classification of properties so that the attributes on one side are really of higher value that those on the other. The challenge for third-wave feminism is for us to find ways of transcending dualist modes of thought, which are very easy to slip into, and which can colonize and structure our thought about ethics and values in dangerous ways.

Feminist theorists also have deployed the idea of "the other" to capture some of the weirdness of dualistic thinking. Under patriarchy, women are seen as the *other* while men occupy the central place in the system. This also happens in anthropocentric thought, they claim, where non-human beings are seen as the other while the human subject occupies the centre. Anthrocentrism and androcentrism (male-centred) thinking are just two sides of the same coin. Among the questions that feminist theorists address are to what extent a genuine other can be said to exist in various contexts, and, if so, how communication with the genuine other is possible, and what constitutes the respect for the genuine other, where that genuine other is recognized to be radically different from oneself. Think, for example of our various ways of communicating with animals in different contexts and often under very different conditions. Proper communication should be attentive to the particular characters and needs of the animals with which we are interacting. Plumwood, for example, described the very different ways in which it is possible to engage with a range of animals – including snakes and lyrebirds – in ways that respect what she called the "etiquette of an interspecies encounter" (Plumwood 2002: 190–94).

On the basis of this outline of feminism in application to ecological philosophy, it is possible to see the commonalities that might exist between the feminist and the deep-ecological approach to our situation and the resonances between ecological feminism and some of the other theories of domination that we have discussed. Is the feminist argument one that lends additional weight to these others? Does it contradict any of them? Does it do a better explanatory job? Feminists have claimed that F3, the feminist theory of patriarchal dualism, provides the best explanation for all forms of domination under patriarchy (argument to the best explanation again!). We have already encountered a number of other such arguments that supposedly explain the domination of nature. How should we go about comparing these with each other? If they are rival theories, then proponents of one theory may be able to show how the other theories can be subsumed under theirs. For example, in the early deep ecology work, it was argued that an individualistic conception of the self led to a detachment from other people and nature resulting in a sense of separation between "man and the environment". Some feminist theorists might want to argue that a relational conception of the self – the self as a knot defined by its place in a web of wider relationships – is one that is best articulated in a feminist account of identity and relation. If this argument worked, then the deep-ecological understanding of the self might turn out to be a version of a feminist conception of the self. But now what is to stop someone who supports the idea of an ecological, extended self from arguing that the fundamental insight of connectedness is due to deep ecology, and that the feminist conception of the self is one that derives from a deep-ecological vision of a profoundly interconnected world?

Such arguments would not be easy to settle because we do not have adequate criteria by which to judge and compare the different theories. Any criteria we put forward for comparison are likely to be disputed, and they are likely themselves to draw on existing theoretical points of view. There is no view from nowhere in these matters, and no perspective that is absolutely independent of all other perspectives. Again, there are factual or empirical issues at stake as well, not just philosophical and conceptual ones. Think of F5, the claim that one form of domination can only be eradicated simultaneously with a range of others. This looks as if it is meant to be a direct consequence of F3. Since one form of domination underlies a range of other kinds of domination, sweeping away one of the forms will sweep away the others. Now, if patriarchy is the common cause of a range of other forms of domination, then sweeping away patriarchy will probably finish off the other forms of domination, in as much as they are just expressions of patriarchy. But it is not clear that this would necessarily be the case. Would it be possible, for example, to imagine a society in which patriarchy is abandoned, but racism still flourished, or one where patriarchy and racism are wiped away, yet animals still suffer exploitation and the environment is not protected? This looks like an open question that might be tested in the course of history, not a question that can be finally answered by philosophical argument alone. Further, it is possible to imagine patriarchy as an institution surviving even when racism, classism and anthropocentrism are eradicated. This again looks like a historical possibility. But if that were so, then patriarchy would not necessarily lead to anthropocentrism, and if anthropocentrism is the source of the domination of nature, then patriarchy would not be to blame.

These ideas lead us back to the problem faced at the start of the chapter, and the question of the extent to which factual matter is presupposed in philosophical theorizing. Feminism represents a radical challenge for environmental thinking, politics and traditional social ethical perspectives. It promises to link environmental questions with wider social problems concerning various kinds of discrimination and exploitation, and fundamental investigations of human psychology. So also do the other theories we have considered, all of them offering to explain the domination of nature and the reasons for our environmental damage. What we have seen in the case of feminist theories is that there may be all sorts of connections between various forms of oppression, including philosophical or conceptual ones, but also questions of cause and effect and historical fact. Theoretical speculations about the cognitive structures, worldviews and thought processes that underlie our understanding of the world and the values we hold are stimulating and provocative. But without some factual evidence as well, it is unlikely that we can prove a real connection between certain modes of thought on the one hand, and our behaviour towards nature on the other.

nine

Beyond individual responsibility: governance and the affluenzic society

Many contemporary industrial societies are characterized by the condition some writers call "affluenza". In the affluenzic society, the continuous growth in material wealth and consumption of material goods sits at the centre of human life and aspirations, rapidly reducing and replacing other goals and values of human fulfilment (James 2007). Constituted by a set of robust positive feedback mechanisms, affluenza is the larger system under which many local and global economies now operate, and which shapes the personal values of many indivduals and the social priorities of many nations and governments. Although globalization has very effectively rapidly expanded the territory of affluenza and further strengthened its already vigorous structure, it has not been analysed or studied by environmental philosophers. In this chapter, we look at what affluenza might be, speculating about its structure and causes. If you think we are right about affluenza, and if you think it may be a problem that obstructs us in tackling environmental problems, then we hope you are able to give some thought to the obvious question: is there a way of controlling the damaging and destructive tendencies that are present in affluenzic societies? This may be one of the most important environmental questions facing us in the twenty-first century.

While much of the emphasis in philosophy and policy discussions is on how individuals can respond to the challenges posed by environmental catastrophe and climate change, our analysis of affluenza poses a new problem. For if we are right, it is not individuals alone who are at the heart of environmental problems. Rather, things that are larger than individuals – things like governments, business corporations and non-government organizations – are major players in causing environmental damage, and affluenza itself is a system-level phenomenon. One major driver of affluenza is the transnational corporation, an entity that wields disproportionate economic and political power in relation to its social and legal accountability. Much of the emphasis in public policy discussions is put on how to motivate individual citizens to better respond to the challenges posed by environmental problems and climate change. By contrast, very little is usually said about how policies can and should be shaped to steer corporate behaviour so that they respond to social needs and environmental problems. We therefore explore at the end of this chapter the idea of constitutional corporatism, a new form of political arrangement which might be needed to limit the power and influence that corporations now wield over governments and societies. While this may not be the only way of tackling problems in the affluenzic societies, we suggest it as one way in which to make corporations more responsible to the citizens and more protective of the environments of countries where they operate.

Since the 1990s, globalization has very effectively spread the grip of affluenza beyond the developed and income-rich regions of North America, north-western Europe, Japan and Australia, to the developing and relatively income-poor regions in the world, most notably to China and India, which jointly constitute more than a third of the world's pop-

---

Footprints

The idea of the ecological footprint was developed in 1992 by William Rees. It gives a neat measure of carrying capacity by comparing the human demand on the planet with the regenerative capacity of ecosystems. For people counted individually, or by town, country or region, it is possible to estimate the demand their consumption and pollution places on nature. For each of us, we can ask how many hectares of productive land it takes to grow our food, absorb and recycle our wastes, break down the toxins our industry produces. This form of ecological accounting can also be applied to products, to give comparative ecological footprints for bottles, cars or bibles. The carbon footprint is a way of measuring just the greenhouse gas emissions that are caused by a group, an organization or an event.

For example, the average person in the UK who drives regularly and eats meat has a carbon footprint of 11.2 tonnes of carbon dioxide and an ecological footprint of 5.7 hectares (or global hectares, using a normalizing calculation to permit comparison across the globe). If the whole population of the planet lived at this level of consumption and pollution, then 3.5 earths would be required to sustain the current world population.

Source: http://www.ecologicalfootprint.com/

ulation. Like their rich counterparts, individuals living in the emerging industrial countries aspire and work hard to achieve the same material goals as everyone else. The main difference is that they have started a bit later and are now in a hurry to catch up. As the global population now approaches seven billion people, with a forecast of nine billion by the middle of the century, a real issue arises owing to the high ecological footprint of materially rich lifestyles. More than forty years ago, theorists were warning that the planet faced a difficult choice: either we could maintain our energy-intensive lifestyles and reduce population, or maintain population but only at the cost of adopting much more modest lifestyles for everyone (see e.g. Meadows *et al.* 1972; Hardin 1972, 1974).

As we have already seen, deep ecologists and other environmental theorists have advocated the importance of adopting styles of living that are simple in means and rich in ends. But over the past half century, the main direction of economic policy in most countries has been to focus on increasing the income and purchasing power of the citizens. While income per capita has increased in several European countries, in Japan, Australia, and – most spectacularly – in the United States, the differences between those living in the income-rich countries and those living in the income-poor countries have widened. While extreme poverty has decreased in the past thirty years, as the World Bank explains, the number of people living on less than $2 a day has hardly changed at all:

> Global poverty measured at the $1.25 a day line has been decreasing since the 1980s. The number of people living in extreme poverty fell from 1.9 billion in 1981 to 1.8 billion in 1990 to about 1.4 billion in 2005. The number of people living on less than $2 a day has changed little since 1981.
>
> (World Bank 2008: 10)

The countries that had the highest proportion of people living in poverty forty years ago are much the same today, and Africa south of the Sahara remains one of the planet's poorest and most disadvantaged regions. The development of the global economy has failed to tackle the big inequalities between rich and poor countries. There is no moral argument that implies that individuals living in some parts of the world are more entitled to live a materially rich life than individuals living in some other parts of the world. So a huge challenge remains: how to modify global economic and political structures and institutions so that an increase in material wealth for the average person can be attained without giving away other precious goods that are essential to human fulfilment. If affluenza continues to hold the rich countries in its grip, we may wonder if there is any way of helping to save the planet while also meeting the legitimate expectations that many people have for a better life.

Structure of affluenza

Positive feedback occurs in a process where part of the output is fed back into the same process itself, thus amplifying its effects, and then the amplified output is further fed back into the process, producing even more amplified effects, and so on. For example, in some models of climate change, increasing global temperatures are thought to be causing melting of the permafrost in polar and alpine regions. This melting releases carbon dioxide and methane into the atmosphere,which is thought to cause further global warming, producing yet more carbon dioxide and methane, which then further speeds up the rate of melting permafrost, and so on. According to this conjecture, there is a positive feedback between increase in global temperature, melting of permafrost and release of methane and carbon dioxide. Unless elsewhere in a system there are negative feedbacks to counteract or other mechanisms to break them, positive feedbacks will have destabilizing and potentially irreversible destructive effects on the system itself.

Affluenza, we conjecture, operates like a large system of such positive feedback loops, ones that threaten to destabilize and destroy the system itself as well as the many lives that depend on it. We have seen that deep ecologists, ecological feminists and a variety of environmental philosophers argue that humans are relationally constituted: who we are is a function of where we are and the history of our interactions with other people and wider world. By contrast, the structure of affluenzic societies encourages and rewards the development of highly individualist people. As we shall try to show, these people – people like you and me – are peculiarly single-minded and primarily motivated by the immediate and short term, unable to learn from past experiences or be moved by responsibilities towards the future, and whose basic hedonistic features are manipulated and exploited to feed and boost the affluenzic structure itself. The 2008 global financial crisis was the direct result of the behaviour of such people cultivated under the structure of affluenza. This system, whether local and global, is only one part of a much larger structure of positive feedback mechanisms, which characterizes many contemporary industrial societies. We have chosen to name this system

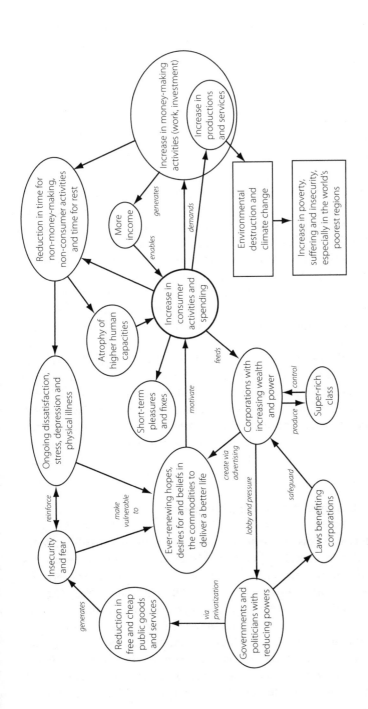

Figure 9.1 Structure of affluenza

using the popular label "affluenza" (De Graaf *et al.* 2005). Although some writers regard affluenza as a condition of individuals – one defined as a dysfunctional condition characterized by addiction, anxiety, depression and ennui (James 2007) – we prefer to think of it as a property of a larger system.

Figure 9.1 shows several of the loops in the system of reinforcing feedback. Under the influence of skilful advertising, amplified by status anxiety and the need to provide for family education, healthcare and other benefits, people come to develop special hopes in, and desires for, commodities and services they think will deliver a better life for them and those near and dear to them. Corporations with increasing wealth and power are the source of this advertising, while at the same time they also put pressure on governments and policy-makers to reduce subsidized public services and replace them with market-priced private alternatives. Meanwhile, consumers pursue their desires for the things that will lead to a better life, and this leads to increasing consumption and the gaining of short-term pleasures and quick fixes. At the same time, this pursuit of commodities promotes discontent and dissatisfaction. Why? Quite simply, because to get more and more goods and services, the individual has to make more money, hence spend more time working. This then pulls individuals in two directions: ideally they want to spend more time with their friends and families, enjoy the fruits of their labours and relax amid the products and services they have worked to obtain; but at the same time, their ongoing dissatisfaction with products, and their fears about the uncertain future of life in a privatized society with little provision of public welfare, gives them an incentive to work harder and longer, leading to stress, depression and physical illness.

Atrophy of higher human capacities

It is not just stress, depression, obesity and a tide of other lifestyle illnesses that characterize affluenzic societies. We argue that these societies also undermine and diminish some very basic human characteristics, leading to a fading away or atrophy of some of the most valuable capacities humans possess. We can see how this comes about by thinking about why commodities that seem to promise so much to consumers end up being unsatisfying to them. There is a line of sociological theory that argues that the consumer society mostly feeds off individual vulnerability. For example, some sociologists suggested that the shopping mall is a kind of "parasite café" (Pfohl 1990), where individual consumers are infected or "parasitized" by the system of commodities that shapes every aspects of their lives, and pushes them to seek ever more intense and fantastic satisfactions, by which they measure their status, success and self-worth against each other. But why keep on buying ever new products, and consuming ever more services? Why is there never enough? Some time ago Chellis Glendinning argued that the consumption of, and dependence on, technology is an addiction at the heart of industrial life (Glendinning 1995). The pleasures of such consumption seem not to be intrinsically satisfying. Consumer goods, as such, are always updateable, upgradeable, upscalable. To update, upscale and upgrade is always possible, so long as you have the money to do so. It is the fate of any consumer product to become unsatisfying and therefore need replacement. Consumer goods are not meant to last or provide long-lasting satisfaction. On the contrary, the ideal commodity is something that people initially lust after, and then quickly become dissatisfied or bored with, and therefore soon seek a better replacement.

There is little by way of clear explanation of just why such technological or commodity addiction comes about in the first place. For ourselves, we think the answer lies – at least in part – in the nature of commodities themselves. There appear to be two conditions that are necessary for something to be a successful commodity. First, it must be intrinsically deficient, in that it is designed not to deliver complete satisfaction to the consumer. Typical examples of incompleteness are found in cosmetics, for example, where a multiplicity of skincare products are prescribed by manufacturers for a range of skin problems and nourishing needs. Instead of applying a single product that nourishes and protects, consumers are expected to experiment with different layers of serum, toner, moisturizer and so forth. There is a second feature, namely planned (and sometimes accidental) obsolescence. This has been the subject of examination since the 1930s and theorists have distinguished various types of obsolescence (see Packard [1978] for a classic study). For example, some mechanical parts have a designed lifetime, and then fail, needing replacement by a new part. In other cases, a fully functional piece of machinery is still in good shape after years of use, but comes into competition with newer and supposedly better models. In the computing industry, the upgrading and replacement of software by newer versions ensures that operating systems and programs that are adequate for many purposes are no longer supported because they have become incompatible with current industry standards.

There are other forms of intrinsic deficiency apart from incompleteness and manufactured obsolescence. These two alone provide plenty of opportunity for marketing new products, the promoting of competition among products many of which serve extremely similar purposes and the development of brand diversity in the marketplace. In addition to all this is what René Girard (1977) has called "mimetic desire". According to this theory, marketing shows us a "model" who is associated with a commodity. A famous sporting personality advertises a shaver, or a car; a beautiful and scantily clad woman stares lovingly at a watch or a camera. The consumer wants to be like the model, or to be associated in some way with the model, and the advertising dupes him (or her) into thinking that buying the product will bring about that assimilation. Alas, after purchasing the shaver, the watch, the camera or the car, life is made happy for a short time, and then goes very much as before. The consumer does not become the model, and the acquired object loses its shine. Never mind, though, for there is always another object, associated with another model to whom the consumer can aspire, and maybe this time purchasing the object will bring about the desired change. But that, too, fails to happen. And so the cycle continues, based on the illusion of false hope and belief.

This problematic condition is represented by another loop in Figure 9.1 that links discontent, desire, hope and belief in an endlessly frustrating cycle of addiction. It is consumers' dissatisfactions with what they currently have, and their desire for, and belief in, better prospective products that maintain the flow of the market. It follows that successful product marketing must not only create desires and beliefs but must also create dissatisfaction by building its seeds into the very consumer products themselves. Accordingly, we have an everlasting cycle that runs from discontent through to desire, hope, belief and then back to discontent. For many people, the cycle of yo-yoing emotions from the low ends of disappointment and boredom to the high ends of excitement, hopefulness and optimism is a psychological equivalent to a physical addiction resulted from drug abuse. In all forms of addiction, the highs are short-lived, and when they give way to the lows the addict is compelled to seek the highs again to ease the pain, the void and emptiness inside. Affluenza apparently promotes addiction. The highs it offers and the lows it generates coordinate and feed into each other, so that the addict is locked into the cycle.

While seeking pleasure, convenience, wealth and status is one central aspect of human nature, we claim that in the affluenzic system this group of drives becomes the sole action-guiding principle by which people live. These addictions are focused by the system on a range of instant pleasures and satisfactions that are relatively narrow in comparison to many uniquely human capacities that normal human beings are capable of developing. Against the vivid and intense lure of the new forms of pleasures presented as purchasable from the market, many enjoyable things that used to be regarded as essential for human well-being – and which are mostly free – are forgotten or pushed aside, for example the building of friendship and trust with other human beings, self-realization through meeting challenges, and communion with nature. Ironically, so essential to human well-being are such forgotten activities that they are, after a long period of neglect by entrepreneurs, now freshly marketed as "extraordinary experiences" obtainable only through commercially guided adventures, such as wilderness adventures, white-water rafting and eco-tourism, presented and marketed as accessible only by a minority of elite consumers (see the Arnould & Price [1993] study of white-water rafting). The affluenzic society manages to commodify experiences that were previously some of life's freest and most shareable goods. This atrophy of higher human capacities is one of the great harms of the affluenzic society, which provides a host of gadgets and commodities on which to focus consumer desires and hopes that are inflated and deranged by intense marketing and advertising.

Time starvation is another feature of the increasingly frenzied lives that people now lead in the world's most advanced affluenzic systems. Like physical capacities, emotional and intellectual capacities and other valuable skills also decline if people fail to regularly exercise those capacities. But the exercise of capacities to play and enjoy music and dance, to develop solidarity and friendship with others, to become skilled in arts and sports, to study in order to become wiser: these things all take time, something that is rare in the fast moving affluenzic society where such skills do not pay as much as the capacity to make quick money in the stock or property markets. The skills of making quick money are ones that can themselves be learned relatively quickly, and are very different from those required in developing the deeper satisfactions of friendship, empathy, generosity, forgiveness, self-reflection, self-critique and the moral virtues. The reward structure of the affluenzic system, however, is blind to the skills and capacities that take time, that are difficult to master and that can become lost when not exercised. The danger is that the growth of affluenzic systems will threaten to atrophy higher human sensitivities and capacities, and hence lead to a loss of the richness that makes human life, and the human psyche, so valuable in the first place. We wonder whether this may actually be the source of the peculiar kind of frustration felt by people living in affluenzic societies. Their material needs and security are well met, but they are not much happier than their counterparts in the poorer regions where material needs and security are much lower. What keeps people happy despite the material adversity in their lives? Perhaps it is the exercise and development of those very higher human sensitivities and capacities, which are in danger of withering away under affluenza.

A self-destructive system?

What stops a system exploding when it is full of positive feedback loops? Just as in climate systems, there are features of national and global economic and political systems that have the potential for dampening down some of the tendencies of the positive feedback cycles. At the end of David Guggenheim's 2006 film *An Inconvenient Truth*, Al Gore suggests a number of ways to help to save the earth. The focus is on actions that individuals can take such as changing to energy-saving light bulbs, walking more and driving less, recycling more, keeping your vehicle tires fully inflated, washing clothes in cool water, planting a tree and so on. These, although valuable, ignore the structural and institutional facts of environmental destruction already discussed in this chapter. Think about replacing traditional incandescent light bulbs with energy efficient ones. Australia has 0.32 per cent of the global population but produces nearly 1.5 per cent of global carbon dioxide emissions, equivalent to a total of 560 million tonnes of carbon dioxide per year. The country is the first in the world to force domestic consumers to purchase energy efficient light bulbs, which will reduce carbon dioxide emissions by an estimated 2–4 million tonnes each year – well under 1 per cent of emissions. Every little helps, but action on light bulbs can be a distraction from action on serious inefficiencies in industrial and transport energy use, especially in a country that relies on poor quality brown coal for much of its electricity production, and which is also the largest exporter of coal in the world. In a set of institutional structures that rely on corporations, governments and advertising to control, manipulate and direct individual behaviour, each person has only a limited part to play in a wider scheme of environmental disaster.

If individuals cannot provide the necessary negative feedback, what about the organizations that can limit the activities of big companies: governments, non-government organizations, trade unions, religious groups and other collectives? By focusing on light bulbs rather than the coal industry, the Australian government was taking action that impacted on individuals in order to limit some of the damage being done to the environment. But governments can also control corporations, set emissions standards, establish trading schemes for emissions and engage in a range of other actions that affect corporations and their profits. A tricky question arises when we ask what we mean by talking about government action (or inaction), and the relations between governments and corporations. Individual human beings are capable of forming intentions and motives, and adopting goals and commitments. That is why human individuals are responsible for their actions. When a person has done wrong or harm to others, or broken a law, it is appropriate for that person to be held accountable. The fact that people are capable of reflection and decision makes them appropriate subjects of law and morality. That is why when they are found culpable, it is appropriate to subject them to blame, and in the case of law-breaking and criminal behaviour, it is appropriate to subject them to proportionate punishment that fits their crime.

Should we think of a corporation also as an agent who is capable of decision-making and acting, and is accountable for its actions? When we say a company acted or had an intention, exactly what are we saying? There are different ways of answering this question. At the beginning of Chapter 5, we asked the question whether the bricks of which it was built were in any sense more real than the house. It seemed clear that in a sense the bricks are just as real as the house and vice versa. However, the question of the reality of corporations or organizations may seem at first a bit more complex. In one way, there is no more to a company than the staff, computers, factories, office buildings, machinery and webs of communication and information that link these together. According to this view, the organization is nothing but the aggregate of the individuals on its payroll, running its business, and making decisions in its name. By contrast, human actors have responsibilities and commitments, and live according to values that are incorporated into their daily lives. On this form of individualistic reductionism, the corporate actors are possessors of projects and values in only a metaphorical way. When we say the company acted, or had an intention, we are saying something metaphorical that is shorthand for saying something much more complex: that a manager, or a group of people in the company, acted individually or jointly, and had formed, individually or jointly, certain intentions.

Such reductionism is driven by a mistaken thought: that the most basic description of a situation is the only one that gives the truth about it. Such a thought gives a very special meaning to the word "true", as if the only thing that can count as truth is a literal statement about the fundamental things that make up the situation or system we are describing. Each person in a corporation is a mix of tissues, nerves, organs and sinews. On the reductionist view, there would be no people, only the biological components. But these in turn are composed of other simpler things. So perhaps there are only atoms and molecules: no people, no corporations and no governments. Such extreme reductionism would not be helpful in enabling us to talk about people and their relations to other people and to the larger organizations and systems to which they belong. The notion of truth encompasses our capacity to make appropriate statements about a range of things – including our assessment of people, actions, governments, companies and so on. Extreme reductionism about corporations also ignores the fact that companies – and other organizations – are, in the eyes of the law, legal persons, who can act, sue people, and take steps to protect various interests, and can be described in moral vocabulary. Within the legal system, companies and universities are just as much fundamental things – legal entities – as people. Once we have recognized the legal reality of the corporate person, then it makes sense to enquire whether a corporation is good or evil, and whether an organization sets high or low ethical standards for those who work in it. In keeping with the idea that the corporation or organization is a person at law, we will assume in what follows that what is true of the human individual is also true of corporate or social actors – motivation, responsibility, action, character, interests, behaviour, belief and so on.

Accepting that corporations are just as real as the buildings they occupy and the staff they employ does not settle all the philosophical worries about them. For example, what about the individual shareholders? Are they part of the companies or corporations in which they invest, or separate from them? There is a legal argument for regarding them as quite separate, thanks to the device of limited liability. In this type of investment, investors' financial liability is limited by law to a fixed sum, usually the sum of money they have invested. The maximum possible loss that investors can suffer will never be greater than the amount they have already invested. As well as not being personally liable for any of the company's debts or fines, investors are not held personally responsible for the company's actions in the event where the company's actions cause harm to others or break the law, notwithstanding the fact that the investor financially supported and stands to gain from the company's actions. If a company with limited liability is sued, then it is the company, not the shareholders, that is sued. Limited liability is a form of legal protection provided by the government to the investor against the risk of their investment going terribly wrong, especially the risk of it causing serious harm to others. This legal device was a fairly recent invention. It is good as a device to encourage business ventures, by stimulating investments from small investors. It is a very good deal from the investor's point of view: limited loss and liability on the one hand, with the possibility of unlimited growth and profit on the other.

The invention of legal devices such as limited liability – which dates from the mid-nineteenth century – and the loosening of company laws throughout the twentieth century made possible the emergence of giant multinational corporations after the Second World War. The late twentieth century also saw an unprecedentedly rapid growth in personal wealth of individual investors, and also the creation of mega-rich managers and senior executives. However, in many instances, the success of such business ventures and creation of wealth in the developed countries depended heavily on their success in avoiding paying for the human and environmental cost. Many cases can illustrate this, and we have chosen just one, the Urrá Dam, where the costs of the development were borne by displaced people and the natural environment, a situation that is all too common in many cases of "economic development", which often entails cheap labour, child labour, poor working conditions, environmental costs, population displacement and the widespread destruction of lives, communities and cultures.

Cases such as the Urrá Dam show that not only are big companies often implicated in both environmental and social destruction, but that they are also not the only players in the game. As well as the individuals who are involved in economic and political decision-making, there are a number of other actors, just as real as individual people, and in many ways more influential (Porter & Brown 1991). It is the interaction between these actors and the corporations that might be thought to hold the key to stopping the affluenzic system of the rich world running away out of control. The most important legal persons in such cases might be thought to be the nation states, which can legislate on environmental issues, and through their governments can lead or support reforms or regulation. But nation states are often weak and powerless in the face of the economic muscle of corporations who may represent far more wealth than the state in which they operate. In fact, by the beginning of the twenty-first century, of the top hundred economies in the world, half were corporations, not countries. Within the nation states themselves, there are often many levels of bureaucracies – each charged with their own separate missions – and the failure of these to share common goals can further weaken the ability of a national government to control the operations of corporations within its borders.

Urrá Dam

This mega-dam project in Colombia was first mooted in the early 1950s and finally took place in the 1980s without consulting the local indigenous people, the Embera Katio. The filling of the $800 million hydroelectric dam inundated 7,400 hectares of fields and hunting grounds, destroying homes, cemeteries and sacred areas. The subsequent sedimentation and contamination of the river has vastly reduced the quantity of fish, the Embera Katio's main food supply and symbol of their culture. Medicinal plants have also disappeared. Children have increasingly suffered from malnourishment and respiratory diseases, and the standing water created by the dam has allowed malarial mosquitoes to propagate. One of their representatives said: "We, the Embera, don't appear in the studies of 1951 or in the following studies. In 1977, the zone, including our territory, was declared a public utility without asking us. ... The country first knew about our problems through our declaration against the Urrá Dam in 1994."

The Colombian government has a law stating: "Interested people must have the right to decide their own priorities in the development process while this affects their lives, creeds and institutions, and the lands that they use or occupy". But none of this was applied in the Urrá Dam case.

In 1994, after major protest events, representatives of the Embera Katio people were granted an audience at the environmental ministry, only to be told by the then minister that "the construction of Urra will continue, because it offers more development opportunities than ecological ones".

Since then, bitter confrontation continued: the Colombian government and the multinational consortium in charge of the dam project versus the indigenous and fisher people. The ten-year development of the dam project took place against a background of civil war, in which the Embera Katio people refused to take sides. The dam development depended on finance from European countries. Many traditional leaders of the Embera have been killed, and the dam has produced only 340 megawatts of electricity.

Intellectuals who protested against the project, such as Alberto Alzate, author of an independent study warning of the social consequences, were assassinated. Mario Calderon, the former parish priest of the area, became a researcher for CINEP, the respected Catholic human rights NGO. He too was murdered, with his wife and father in law in their family home on 9 May 1997, thirty-three days after having organized a forum denouncing the Urrá project. Efraín Jaramillo, the anthropologist who worked with the indigenous people of the Sinú River, had to go into exile in Germany. Hector Mondragon, adviser to the national indigenous movement, was likewise forced out of Colombia.

Sources: www.foei.org/en/publications/link/97/e972223.html; www1.american. edu/ted/ice/urra.htm; www.colombiasolidarity.org.uk/articles/bulletin-archive/47-bulletin-issue2-julyseptember-2001/342-the-urra-i-project

Stakeholders: Embera Katio people; Colombian Ministry of the Environment; paramilitaries working with wealthy local landowners; Empresa Multiproposito Urra SA, the multinational consortium in charge of building the dam (consisting of the Colombian government, Scandinavian entities Skanska and Nordic Investment Bank, Russia's Energomachiexport and the Export Development Corporation of Canada); foreign construction companies such as Australia's DecoTEC; and the World Bank, the underwriter of the project.

In the Urrá Dam case, the Colombian ministry of the environment was apparently unable to work in keeping with the existing legislation that was designed to protect the rights of indigenous people. Such people, when let down by their own government and its agencies may turn to international organizations including the big aid agencies, human rights groups, the United Nations and various financial agencies such as the World Bank, the International Monetary Fund and the development banks. Like national governments, each of these actors has problems in dealing with corporate activities. Often international development funding is targeted on projects that have problematic social and environmental aspects. So the very same organization can be pulled in two ways, having a mandate to protect the interests of poor people and indigenous populations on the one side, but also on the other having a responsibility to support sustainable development aimed at ameliorating poverty.

As long as the big corporations are single-mindedly driven by the desire to maximize profits, they have an advantage over all the other groups with which they negotiate. For if the World Bank, the United Nations and the aid agencies are at the mercy of mixed motives and honest doubts about what is the best option for a region or a country, they will be less effective in maintaining a position against those organizations whose motives are purely geared to profits. For this reason, negotiations about development projects in the income-poor countries of the world often come out in favour of the transnational corporations and the interests of their shareholders. Those shareholder interests are also protected by the governments and organizations of the income-rich "northern" countries; notice, for example, how Canada's Export Development Corporation was one of the initial investors in the Urrá Dam Consortium along with investment from Scandinavia and Russia. It is not surprising that some writers now regard the transnational corporations as the new rulers of the world (Karliner 1997; Korten 2001). As the box "Urrá Dam", above, shows, issues involving human rights and indigenous people – often the poorest people in a country – warfare, environmental sustainability and international finance draw the various organizational actors together into webs of negotiation, collaboration and conflict. If corporations generally come out best in such cases, then this means the other actors in the situation are not limiting the power that corporations wield, and therefore there is a risk that the positive feedback loops in affluenzic systems will drive these systems to self-destruction, bringing devastation to social and natural environments alike.

Rich nations and poor regions

The nations that are dominated by affluenzic systems are the industrialized income-rich countries of the world. These countries were profoundly affected by a financial crisis that spread around the globe in 2008. Government injections of liquidity into national financial systems all over the world showed that even in an era of intense globalization and unparalleled corporate power, the nation state was still alive and well, and capable of taking heavy-impact financial and economic actions. National governments took major roles not only in internal political and economic matters, but also in ways that affected the global economy. This should be a lesson for those theorists who have been somewhat premature in declaring the retreat or death of the nation state (Hobsbawm 1990; Appadurai 1996). Our later suggestions about changing the corporate charters as a way of limiting the damage corporations can do to the globe and dampening their effects on affluenzic systems are actually inspired by the example many national governments set during and after the financial crisis of 2008.

In the months following the crisis, the economies of the United States and Europe paid $10.2 trillion in order to bail out banks, prop up financial institutions and stimulate recovery. This kind of expenditure puts a new perspective on climate change and the costs of its amelioration. Late in 2009, the World Bank issued a report indicating that the cost of protecting developing countries from a two degree increase in average global temperature would be in the region of $75–100 billion per year for the period 2010–50. Before the crash of 2008, such a sum may have seemed too large to be realistic as a cost that should be borne by the industrial world. By comparison with the expenditure that shored up the world financial system, the sum now seems modest: $100 billion, after all is only 1 per cent of $10 trillion. There is little evidence, so far, of even this amount of support being provided to control and provide amelioration for climate change.

In the light of what we have said in this and previous chapters, it should now be clear why the financial crisis stimulated rapid action, while climate change is met with dithering, scepticism and even outright denial (Adam 2005; Revkin 2009). Put crudely, the global financial crisis is one that mostly affects the wealthy nations. But the catastrophic effects of global climate change are first and foremost suffered by the world's poorest. Most people in rich countries receive various forms of regular income, be it wage, pension, social welfare, interest from savings, return from investments or business earnings, the stability of all of which depends on the continual growth in various financial markets. It is the people in the income-rich countries who stand to lose the most under the collapse of local and global financial markets and systems. By contrast, the financial crisis had relatively little impact on the poorest in the world, who own next to nothing, let alone any financial investment in any market. But as we saw at the start of this book, these are the people who live in the regions on earth most vulnerable to the detrimental effects of climate change, such as extreme weather, sea-level rise, water and food scarcity.

Unlike the rich and powerful, those in the income-poor countries have few resources to deal with catastrophic changes and their countries lack the resources to engage in big civil engineering projects to match the Thames Barrier in the UK or the flood defences of the Netherlands. At the same time, it is the income-rich nations, and the corporations based in them, that are largely responsible for climate change. Land clearing, forest removal and major mining and construction projects in the income-poor countries are financed – like the Urrá Dam – by funds and capital from corporations and organizations outside these countries. While people in the world's least advantaged societies often experience extreme environmental decline, the money and consumer desires that drive the ecological impact come from far away. Ironically, there is even evidence to suggest that in northern Europe and parts of North America, the effects of climate change may lead to some increased crop yields. Climate change is thus disproportionate in its environmental impacts, exacerbating already existing inequalities and making them worse. No wonder the rich countries show relatively little sign of panic or worry in the face of huge environmental changes, compared to their determined efforts to control the 2008 financial crisis.

Where do environmental philosophers stand in this matter, and what solutions have they advocated? It is not uncommon for environmental writers to be accused of misanthropy. In his *Desert Solitaire*, author and essayist Edward Abbey, much loved by many wilderness advocates in North America, famously wrote that "I'd rather kill a man than a snake" (Abbey 1968: 20). It was even more shocking to find the father of modern American environmental philosophy, Rolston, writing in a 1996 article that:

> [T]he growth of culture has become cancerous. That is hardly a metaphor, for a cancer is essentially an explosion of unregulated growth … Feeding people always seems humane, but, when we face up to what is really going on, by just feeding

> people, without attention to the larger social results, we could
> be feeding a kind of cancer.   (Rolston 1996: 258–9)

Rolston represents the opposite extreme to David Korten, whom we mentioned at the end of the preceding section. For Korten, the corporations represent a form of planetary cancer. What leads Rolston to claim that the poorest in the world are the "cancer" eating away the planet, while in fact it is mainly the individuals living in the wealthy nations who eat and consume away the planet's resources and choke it with the wastes they produce? The average ecological footprint in the UK, as we have seen, is nearly 6 global hectares, while the average for Pakistan and Zambia are only 0.6 hectares. The United States, Rolston's home country, has an ecological footprint of nearly 10 global hectares per person.

Rolston's view seems to be that an overriding focus on poverty and its attempted eradication can lead to action that would undermine the attempts to conserve and protect natural habitats, especially the increasingly rare areas of wilderness, which he believes are of tremendous intrinsic value. Environmental conflict situations can occur when groups of poor or displaced people move into national parks or other set-aside areas, causing damage through firewood collection, farming, gathering and hunting. Rolston reminds his readers that wilderness preservation is not something that can be tackled after social evils such as poverty have been eradicated. His argument is that poverty has always been with us and will also be with us, and so "if we did nothing else of value until there were no more poor, we would do nothing else of value at all" (*ibid.*: 250). This last statement may seem to be obviously true. After all, there are many valuable goals we can set, and if we set ourselves to achieve just one of them we would inevitably neglect the others. But this truism cannot be what Rolston's rhetoric is directed towards defending. Rather, his concern is likely to be that conservation and species preservation have an urgency about them that requires them to be prioritized above other worthwhile goals. We cannot defer saving species or conserving wild areas, for once these things are lost, they cannot be restored.

Rolston's rhetoric, and that of other conservationists, has annoyed some writers who see such protests as part of a new form of colonial discourse. After all, many of the resources on which income-rich countries depend are sourced from income-poor countries. Luxury goods such as hardwoods, coffee, cocoa, tea and exotic fruits are not only cropped using low-paid labour, but also take up land that could be used for local subsistence farming, or small-scale industry that would benefit local communities. Surprisingly, the international companies that profit from resource exploitation for overseas markets are seldom the target of environmentalists' complaints. Ramachandra Guha, in a famous attack on "green missionaries", bewailed the fact that foreign environmentalists would regularly visit India with the same gospel: to expel indigenous people from forests and national parks in order to protect and conserve iconic species such as the tiger (Guha 1999). Indigenous people, as shown by the Urrà Dam case, are also often the victims of large projects aimed at securing energy supplies or extracting oils and minerals. The poor are not just likely to suffer most as a result of the global economy and its voracious demand for resources, but are also simultaneously the target of misinformed attacks from conservationists (Guha & Martinez-Alier 1997). In some ways, this may not be surprising, given the historical findings that modern environmentalism has its roots in colonial practices (Grove 1995; Brennan 1998; Anker 2001). Historical origins are not an excuse for a continuing blindness within environmental philosophy to the role of corporations. It is imperative to tackle problems in a well-informed way, making sure that information is available about all the relevant forces and actors at work in a situation. Yet again, it appears that the role of a particular class of actors – the big international companies that dominate world trade – is mainly overlooked by writers on environmental philosophy and policy.

Constitutional corporatism

The challenges of the affluenzic society are hard to overcome. As we saw earlier, theorists have advocated the importance of connecting spiritually with nature, of finding ways to re-enchant the world and recognizing the sacredness of the earth. However, such ideas seem puny when compared with the massive wealth and power of the corporations, and their ability to manipulate consumer preferences. Attacks on the utopianism of deep ecology have emphasized the fact that most people would find it hard to give up the many benefits of advanced technology, modern medicine and urban living. If the power of the modern corporate business culture is to be directed into sustainable futures in which humans flourish in harmony with natural systems, then new ideas are needed: ideas that will be just as powerful and motivating as the beliefs and desires from which affluenza feeds. We are not the first writers to turn the spotlight on organizations and structures and away from individuals. While the major focus of philosophical and ethical theorizing has been on individuals and their own moral responsibility, a minority of thinkers have looked at other features that set the agenda for individual action.

Among the writers who seem to have anticipated the problems of the affluenzic society is one whose voice was notable in the early development of environmental philosophy in the United States in the 1950s and 1960s, the social ecologist Murray Bookchin. His approach to environmental problems was rooted in a combination of Marxism and the anarchist thought of Peter Kropotkin, whose work on mutual aid influenced Bookchin's early thinking. More than forty years ago, Bookchin issued warnings in his writings about global warming, the crisis of ever-expanding industrial capitalism and the obsession with economic growth at the expense of the fulfilment of real human needs. The ecological imbalances we now face, he conjectured, are a result of social imbalances. One example he gave – along the same lines as Rachel Carson's bestselling book *Silent Spring* (1969) – was the pursuit of profits by the chemical industries that led to the simultaneous poisoning of human beings and nature, thanks to the insertion of unnecessary industrial chemicals into food, and their continuing accumulation as environmental pollution. Indeed, Bookchin thought capitalism was able to use human technology against nature so effectively because modern capitalism grew out of the use of technology to enable the domination of workers by employers and the majority of the working population by a smaller number of bourgeois. His solution was decentralization:

> In decentralization exists a real possibility for developing the best traditions of social life and for solving agricultural and nutritional difficulties that have thus far been delivered to chemistry. Most of the food problems of the world would be solved today by well-balanced and rounded communities, intelligently urbanized, well-equipped with industry and with easy access to the land ... The problem has become a social problem – an issue concerning the misuse of industry as a whole. (Bookchin, writing as Herber 1952)

While some aspects of Bookchin's diagnosis match our own, we are not convinced that the introduction of decentralization is a realistic solution to the problem.

Kropotkin's arguments about mutual aid – like the vision of William Morris's 1890 utopian fable *News From Nowhere* – paint the beguiling picture of a comradely society in which the profit motive is absent, and people work for mutual benefit and from a sense of enjoyment in their labours. Self-government replaces the normal suite of laws by which societies are ruled. Unfortunately, the utopian visions of these socialist and anarchist writers is not accompanied by any detailed description of how the envisaged utopia is to be reached, or of systems and processes by which its stability can be maintained in the face of natural and human-made threats (Brennan 1998). While belonging to this tradition, Bookchin differed from his precursors in accepting that highly technological and urbanized societies provided many desirable benefits to human life and conviviality. He also rejected as impotent some of the approaches already discussed in earlier chapters, such as certain forms of nature religion or mysticism, or anything that smacked of deep ecological "eco–la-la" (Bookchin [1987] 1999). Are there resources in Bookchin's thought that may help us see a way out of the problems posed by the corporatized planet?

As well as founding the political ideas of social ecology, Bookchin is sometimes described as an ecological humanist, because he accepts that humans are both in nature and in culture. Unlike many nature romantics, he did not write with disdain about cities, but rather, influenced by the historian Lewis Mumford (1961), he saw possibilities for cities as "organs of love", provided their development encourages life-giving, sociable and nurturing functions as well as expansive, and competitive ones. Like Mumford, Bookchin did not advocate any kind of return to nature, or rejection of technology, but instead urged us to live as if we are nature rendered conscious: as "unfinished animals", we have possibilities of developing systems of life and government that simultaneously nurture and develop us culturally and naturally, and this means protecting and caring for both natural and human beings.

For eco-anarchists, a troubling tendency with much socialist thought is the emphasis on centralization of government and control in order to limit the development of too much inequality among citizens (or at least to limit the harms that can befall those who are weak and vulnerable). By contrast, anarchy (literally "absence of government or laws") aims at finding ways to set conditions under which people can govern themselves without imposition or direction from a central authority. While Bookchin is happy to think about ways in which technology can be used to help people and nature, he – just as much as deep ecologists – is committed to drawing up schemes for futures in which people live in much smaller communities (small, rather than large cities) and in which community identity, mutual sympathy and shared commitments to common goals can be fostered. The vision of small, supportive communities linked by mutual respect, commitment to shared ideals and free from regulation and other impositions by central government, is not one that is appealing only to anarchists and utopian socialists. Many of those on the political right are also critical and suspicious of government interference in the lives of individuals, giving them common cause with thinkers on the political left. We hope that our brief account of the traumas of the affluenzic society has drawn attention to the fact that it is not just big government that can interfere with, and structure, the lives of individuals. Big money can do that too, structuring and managing the lives of individuals and communities in ways too diverse to enumerate. Those who worry about the power and control of government over the individual should, to be consistent, also be concerned about the amount of influence corporations also wield over our lives.

Decentralization and bioregionalism provide structural solutions to the problems we have described. Life in small communities would be more democratic, less frenzied, lives, lived more in place than those in the big anonymous cities that focus and channel the workings of the global economy. But such a change in structure requires also a reduction in the size and influence of the great corporations that have so recently started to dominate the world socially, politically and environmentally. Other structural solutions are also possible. Korten's claim, as we have seen, is that the global economy has become like a malignant cancer, advancing the colonization of the planet's living spaces for the benefit of powerful corporations and financial institutions. He is not opposed either to the corporations as such or to the financial sector as a whole. Rather, he regards the global economic system overall as having made what were once useful institutions into instruments of a market tyranny that feeds on life in an insatiable quest for money. While we have speculated earlier on the compulsive nature of status-seeking, addiction to consumer pleasures and the dominance of affluenzic modes of behaviour, Korten places blame on a deregulated global economy and rogue financial systems that put making money, particularly in terms of shareholder returns, well ahead of commitment to sustainability, community building or any other large social interest. Although we differ in emphasis from him, Korten's analysis is complementary to ours and adds depth to the suggestions already made.

Unlike Korten and the decentralists, we propose a solution that focuses on just one item in the system: the corporations themselves. As we have shown, companies, governments and non-governmental organizations are all important players in the system, and each of them can be seen as having important roles in amplifying or dampening some of the forces that propel the system to destruction. We propose that one way of dampening some of the positive feedback within the system we have described can be achieved by limiting the power of the corporation, and by revisiting earlier understandings of corporate charters. An analogy may be helpful in this case. Think of how democracy glimmered for a while in ancient Greece, and then was tried at various times throughout Europe, but only as occasional experiments. Although the democratic ideal was known, the practice itself was lost, in the main, for more than a millennium.

Something good – like democracy – is vulnerable to loss, can easily be destroyed and can be recovered only with difficulty. But the loss of democracy was not permanent, and a recovery was made. From the Magna Carta in 1215 to the passing of the United States Constitution in 1787 there was a prolonged struggle to regain democracy, often involving a series of negotiations and compromises with the tyrannical power of monarchies. In the nearly six centuries of effort, what was happening was a gradual limiting of the power of tyrants and the result was that in those democratic countries where a republic was not established an accommodation was made, often in the form of a constitutional monarchy, where the absolute power of the ruler was held in check through government limitations of that power. This idea of limiting absolute power is one that can now be applied to corporations given their role – despite their many benefits – as instruments of global social and environmental destruction.

Constitutional corporatism – an accommodation that may have to be reached through prolonged struggle against corporate power and influence – would use legal instruments, both nationally and internationally, to limit the powers of corporations. In opening up this possibility for exploration, policy theorists, political scientists and philosophers would be recognizing that the fears expressed by earlier writers and thinkers were well founded. There is dispute about whether Abraham Lincoln himself wrote in one letter that:

> I see in the near future a crisis approaching that unnerves me and causes me to tremble for the safety of my country … corporations have been enthroned and an era of corruption in high places will follow, and the money power of the country will endeavour to prolong its reign by working upon the prejudices of the people until all wealth is aggregated in a few hands and the Republic is destroyed. (Quoted in Shah 2002)

But there is no doubt that Adam Smith looked with concern at the possible monopoly and secrecy powers that corporations might wield

(Korten 2001). More recent writers have given readable accounts of the rise of the corporation and the way in which legislation abetted the abandonment of the originally restrictive – and socially responsible – charters under which early corporations operated (Hartmann 2004).

As economic entities of enormous scale and influence, corporations are able to set their own agendas aimed at securing huge wealth for their chief executives and senior management, good returns for their shareholders and non-negotiable control over their suppliers. Corporations have been credited with installing and removing heads of state in both the income-rich and income-poor countries, and, as Joel Bakan points out in his book *The Corporation* (later made into a successful documentary film of the same name), "The corporation's dramatic rise to dominance is one of the remarkable events of modern history" (2004: 5). It may seem to be a simple idea to limit their role in amplifying the destructive features of contemporary economic systems.

However simple the idea, its implementation will be very difficult. Many corporations are adept at avoiding tax, secure connivance in their schemes by funding political parties, bring inappropriate influence to bear in the awarding of contracts, fail to give any lasting benefits to the communities and countries within which they operate, and pour vast sums of money into legal action designed to fight claims against them for environmental and social damage. These are all behaviours that need to change if environmental destruction is to stop or significantly reduce, but the precise steps towards such change are unknown. If the corporation is a key problem, then we need to understand a great deal about it, and to study in detail how such powerful organizations are able to operate, flourish and rapidly expand in the global market. There is no single problem of the corporation, as such, but instead a tangled skein of interlocking issues, many of them involving other aspects of the world economy. Such complex challenges are sometimes called "wicked problems". A wicked problem is one that resists reduction to familiar categories, allows for a plurality of – and synergies among – theories and potential solutions, and is usually encountered at the early stages of developing new forms of understanding. There is no test in such cases for what are the correct solutions to such tangled and interlocking sets of problems, for there will be changes in the situation, and in our understanding of it, as we proceed in tackling the wicked problem. As a result, investigating such problems will usually lead us far from our starting-point and into new territory (Brennan 2004; Norton 2005).

The awareness of the existence of wicked and tangled problems provides a practical complement to the intellectual quest to resolve foundational problems in philosophy. Think of dollars and pounds, or kilometres and miles. These provide alternative ways of measuring cost or distance. Each can be expressed in terms of the other if we know the exchange rate or the conversion factor. But there is no obvious way to convert values of different kinds into each other. Think, for example, of the various bodily pleasures we can enjoy, the different sorts of intellectual satisfactions, the delights of great music and art, friendship, health, moral virtues. All of these are valuable, and utilitarianism assumes that all of them can be measured in one common coin, namely "utility". As we have already seen, the assignment of utilities has always been something of a mystery, left to students to figure out for themselves. The logic of the philosophical idea of "utility" is rather like the logic of money, which some people take to be a universal measure for the worth of everything. But we must be wary of the idea that one measure can provide a standard for everything. Some environmental philosophers have denied that there is any such single scale for measuring all the values in human lives, or that there is any single system of duties and principles that can adequately deal with the problems and complications in ever-changing and unpredictable human affairs. The possibility that there exists one single scheme for comparing all the even more diverse values in the wider environment, and for guiding human behaviour in it and towards its other inhabitants, is an even more far-fetched idea.

A number of environmental thinkers have argued that we need to draw on different sources of value and obligation in order to guide action in different situations. Such *moral pluralists*, as they are called, stand in clear opposition to others who seek a single set of values or a univocal or monistic worldview on which to found an environmental ethic (see Zimmerman [1994: 187–95] for a useful discussion on the debate between moral pluralism and monism). Among the pluralists we can include Naess (1984), whose deep ecology platform is both holistic and pluralistic, and also Christopher Stone (1987), Gary Varner (1991) and Brennan (1992). On the other side stand Bookchin (1990) and Callicott (1990), the latter arguing that any coherent ethical system must be expressed in terms of a single overarching value or principle (see Lo 2001 for a useful discussion).

The deep ecology platform has struck many people as being a pragmatic attempt to bring divergent standpoints into agreement on the need for environmental action, and a number of environmental pragmatists have argued that priority should be given to practice over theory so as to avoid the drawbacks often associated with merely theoretical or "top-down" solutions to practical problems (Light & Katz 1995; Norton

1994, 2005; Weston 1985, 1992). The trouble with solutions driven by a monistic principle and ideology, they say, are that these are likely to suffer from limited perspectives and result in poorer policies than those reached through wide consultation and engagement with a diverse range of views. Such practical experience suggests it is not wise to regard any single theory as able to supply a measure for all the different values at play in our environmental and social choices, especially when such decisions involve not only individuals, but also government agencies, multinational companies and groups. Environmental pragmatists regard it as plausible to take a pluralist understanding of ethics and matters of policy as the best way to theorize the tangled problems we now face.

Wicked problems aside, governments are naturally unwilling to interfere with corporations, given not only the huge influence of the private sector but also because of the dangers associated with changing to something new. The 2008 financial crisis did not lead to action to substantially reform the financial system in any fundamental way, but rather to shore it up and keep it running. To contemplate controlling or limiting the power of the big corporations raises the spectre of an intervention that may make things go worse rather than better, and this fear is acute in countries with a horror of socialism or communism (seen as the obvious alternatives to free-market capitalism). Such a picture of the present leads to a final question. Is there hope for the future? Other social commentators in recent years have been affected by gloom and despair at the failure of the Enlightenment vision, which promised a modern age of limitless progress and unbounded freedom. One of the gloomiest of these writers is the political philosopher Gray, who has attacked the naive progressivism of modernity in a number of works (e.g. Gray 2003, 2007). He has argued that any optimism that globalization and the corporate culture will ameliorate environmental destruction and liberate the poor over the next few decades flies in the face of the historical record. Further, Gray thinks that Western culture has run out of steam, and once went so far as to propose that "any prospect of cultural recovery from the nihilism that the Enlightenment has spawned may lie with non-Occidental peoples, whose task will then be in part that of protecting themselves from the debris cast up by western shipwreck" (1994: 184).

While Gray's work resonates well with recent critiques regarding the delusions of affluenzic addiction, the point of these studies is that we have to take limits seriously, limits that define our own humanity and which will protect both social and ecological structures from the damage that arises from the pursuit of infinite growth. Limiting the power of corporations would be a way, we have suggested, of stopping the damage the contemporary structures of economic power do to humans and environment alike. Yet in many leading industrial democracies, revolutionary change is not up for discussion. Political power operates over relatively short periods of time, and governments have to face re-election before long-term policies have a chance to be evaluated. The pressure on governments is thus to favour incremental and gradual change, change that is small rather than dramatic. As far as environmental conservation is concerned, this looks like bad news. It is likely to be business as usual as far as the voters' consumption patterns are concerned, and there will be no incentive to contemplate big changes to the economic system or the massive corporations that dominate it. By contrast, in countries where capitalism is not the predominant mode of thought or social organization, there may be fertile soil for more creative thinking, and opportunities for exploring a greater role for government in developing new mechanisms of constitutional corporatism which will constrain the current explosion of unregulated growth. Gray wonders if hope can be found in nations other than those where affluenzic capitalism has permeated the entire fabric of social and political thinking and organization. We need not turn exclusively to non-Western constituencies (as Gray does) in this search. Successful innovation in any countries that are not under the sway of affluenza and corporate control may provide new ideas in the struggle to envisage a sustainable future.

We hope that the ideas explored in this concluding chapter have encouraged you to think about global environmental challenges in ways that are different from what was described in the earlier chapters. For the most part, they focused on matters of individual ethics. We saw through them that, as predicted at the start of the book, our journey into environmental philosophy repeatedly drew us back to the creatures who are always at the centre of our own thinking: human beings themselves. Puzzles about respect for other animals, living things and nature provoked basic puzzles about human worth itself, what that worth depends on and whether humans are especially different from the rest of the living world. In this final chapter we have looked beyond the individualistic perspective to consider the larger structures and organizations that shape our lives and possibilities. These wider political and economic systems within which our lives are set contain the seeds of both destruction and salvation. Greatness consists in the capacity and willingness to look beyond our own self-interest and embrace those who are weaker. The question is not whether human beings are born above other species in worth and dignity, but how and whether they will rise to that status.

Questions for discussion and revision

one Introduction: the place of environmental philosophy and its basic concepts

1. Is a whale no more intrinsically valuable than a pig, a fox or a kangaroo?
2. It is considered humane in some situations to kill an animal to put it out of its misery. Reflect on why there is much more controversy about the mercy killing of human beings.
3. It is said by some writers that people have no right to pollute the planet, but that equally people have the right to a decent life and to the means of subsistence. Is there any conflict between these two claims?
4. Do you think the notion of dignity can be applied to animals or plants? If so, explain what it means in your imagined context. If not, explain why only humans can have dignity.

two Future generations: what consideration do we owe them?

1. Vegetarians, vegans, cyclists and in general people who restrain their energy and material consumptions often claim that their lifestyles are better for the environment than those of meat-eaters, car-users and average consumers. Do you think people without children are likewise justified in claiming that their lifestyles, as people without children, are better for the environment than those of people with children? Do you think sacrificing your opportunity to have children is a virtuous way to do good to the environment? Why or why not?
2. If it is predicted that in thirty years' time, up to 80 per cent of the human population living in your country will have to endure horrific suffering owing to large-scale ecological disasters and warfare, do you think individuals who

are in the reproductive age now will be morally justified, or even required, to not have children or at least to reduce the number of the children that they are going to have? Why or why not?

3. Do you think we have direct responsibilities to the future generations of non-human living things on earth? If so, what kinds of non-human living things and why? If not, why not?

4. Do you think the last people's plan to destroy everything non-human on earth after their own demise is morally wrong? Why or why not?

three Animals: are they as morally valuable as human beings?

1. (a) Are *sentient beings* necessarily subjects of a life? If so, explain why. If not, give some counter-examples.
   (b) What about the other way round? Are subjects of a life necessarily sentient beings? If so, explain why. If not, give some counter-examples.

2. (a) Will some animals be given moral consideration under Singer's utilitarianism, but not under Regan's deontological theory of rights? If so, give some examples. If not, explain why not.
   (b) What about the other way round? Will some animals be given moral consideration under Regan's deontological theory of rights, but not under Singer's utilitarianism? If so, give some examples. If not, explain why not.

3. (a) Are all animals morally considerable and *equally* so under utilitarianism? If so, explain why. If not, give some counter-examples.
   (b) What about equality among human beings? Are all human beings morally considerable and equally so under utilitarianism? If so, explain why. If not, give some counter-examples.

4. (a) Do all animals have *equal* rights (e.g. the right to life and the right not to be harmed) under Regan's deontological theory of rights? If so, explain why. If not, give some counter-examples.
   (b) What about equality among human beings? Do all human beings (including those who are not subjects of a life) have equal rights under Regan's deontological theory of rights? If so, explain why. If not, give some counter-examples.

5. (a) Are there situations under which, all things considered, utilitarianism will permit, or even require, the horrific treatment of an animal (e.g. the infliction of suffering on and the killing of the animal)? If so, describe those situations. If not, explain why not.
   (b) What about the treatment of human beings under utilitarianism? Are there situations under which utilitarianism will permit, or even require, the horrific treatment of a human being (e.g. the infliction of suffering on, and the killing of, the human being)? If so, describe those situations. If not, explain why not.

6. (a) Are there situations under which, all thing considered, Regan's deontological theory of rights will permit, or even require, the horrific treat-

ment of an animal (e.g. the infliction of suffering on, and the killing of, the animal)? If so, describe those situations. If not, explain why not.

   (b) What about the treatment of a human being under the theory of rights? Are there situations under which the theory of rights will permit, or even require, the horrific treatment of a human being (e.g. the infliction of suffering on, and the killing of, the human being)? If so, describe those situations. If not, explain why not.

7. Anthropocentrism claims that human beings are much more intrinsically valuable than animals and non-humans in general. Do you agree with this anthropocentric claim? Why or why not?

8. Is there some morally relevant quality that is equally distributed among all and only human beings, so that all human beings are equally intrinsically valuable and all human beings more intrinsically valuable than all non-human things and beings?

9. Is it possible to consistently defend the anthropocentric view that human beings are more intrinsically valuable than animals, without ending up with the arguably similar but Nazi-like view that some people are more intrinsically valuable than some other people (e.g. people who are less intelligent, less self-aware, less freely willed, or less morally conscientious)?

four Living things: ethics for the non-human world

1. Do sentient living things have more intrinsic value (or inherent worth) than living things that are not sentient under Taylor's biocentrism? Why or why not?

2. Do members of a wild species (e.g. wolves) have more intrinsic value (or inherent worth) than members of a domesticated species (e.g. dogs) under Taylor's biocentrism? Why or why not?

3. Do members of an endangered species (e.g. the bowhead [Greenland] whale) have more intrinsic value (or inherent worth) than members of an abundant species (e.g. the red kangaroo) under Taylor's biocentrism? Why or why not?

4. Do members of an indigenous species (e.g. emus in Australia) have more intrinsic value (or inherent worth) than members of a foreign species (e.g. foxes in Australia) under Taylor's biocentrism? Why or why not?

5. Is killing a plant (or a fly, or a fish, or a snake, or a cat) morally just as evil as killing a human being? Why or why not? In other words, is killing a human being morally no worse than killing a plant.

6. Is a tape worm living in a human being's body just as intrinsically valuable as its human host? Does the human host have a duty not to kill or otherwise get rid of the tape worm?

five Community: how big is our moral world?

1. Is there an absolute moral duty to protect the good of the family that we belong to? Would Callicott's moral holism make more sense as a family ethic, rather than as an environmental ethic?

2. Does sympathy have a role in morality? If so, to how great an extent?
3. Sometimes the most practical way to deal with pest invasions (e.g. plagues of mice) involves causing painful death to animals. Are there any principles that can determine whether and when our duties to animals have priority over our responsibilities to the environment?
4. Some Buddhist and Hindu sects try to live with as little disturbance to nature as possible. Would such a form of life be desirable for everyone? If so, why? If not, then why not?
5. Could the notion of "communicating with nature" ever be more than a metaphor? If so, in what way would this be real communication?

six Natural things: the puzzle of what "natural" means, and whether humans belong to nature

1. Find a piece of writing about nature in a blog, article or newspaper and see if you can identify a number of different senses in which the author uses the word "natural". Are there any senses you can find different from the four meanings identified in the chapter?
2. Is it more plausible to think that values in nature – if they exist – are spread equally over natural things? Or is it more plausible to think they are present to a higher degree in some natural things than they are in others?
3. Why would human intervention with something natural reduce the value of that thing? Try to give two convincing arguments for why gardens are less valuable than wild meadows. Then try to give two arguments for why gardens and wild meadows have the same value. Which of your arguments is (or are) the most convincing?
4. John Passmore once remarked that wilderness would be far better if there were no flies. Would there be a case for arguing that some restored environments are better than the original environments they replace?
5. Edward Abbey in *Desert Solitaire* described how, while working as a park ranger, he took great care to avoid killing snakes and other poisonous creatures that he found around his caravan. Was this just irrational behaviour? Do poisonous creatures have just as much right to the land as humans have?

seven Foundations: can there be a secular basis for the ideas of human dignity and intrinsic value in nature?

1. Rolston claims that the phenomenon of life evokes a religious response. Is this true? Should environmentalists be against human abortion? And should they also be against culling of overabundant species?
2. Are all human beings equal in importance and dignity? Is a serial killer just as entitled to respect as the Pope? If not, then under what conditions do people lose their intrinsic value?
3. Would it be irrational to value some human beings above others? Would it

be irrational to value some irrational people more highly than some rational people?

4. Nietzsche compared living as a human being to creating a work of art. What is the difference between an ethical response and an aesthetic one? Is there a sense in which being ethical is also being aesthetic (or the other way round)?

eight Origins: political, religious and cultural diagnoses of environmental problems

1. According to Genesis, God asks humans to be fruitful and multiply. Is that still good advice today? Can you come up with any better ways to protect the environment than through reducing the number of children people have?

2. Is deep ecology's notion of an extended, ecological self a useful idea? Why did feminist writers think that the extended self idea would lead to less rather than more care for the environment?

3. Why should matters of fact be relevant to philosophical theses? Is feminism an interesting position to study, even if patriarchy does not lead to anthropocentrism?

4. If feminists are right, is there a connection between Christianity and patriarchy?

nine Beyond individual responsibility: governance and the affluenzic society

1. Is it acceptable for people to have as many children as they want? If so, why? If not, what ethical grounds are there for interfering with people's desires to have children?

2. At present human demands on the planet exceed the earth's carrying capacity by around 50 per cent. How can we restructure our lives, societies and communities to bring our demands down to levels that the planet can realistically sustain?

3. Could corporations set an agenda for sustainability that would have more chance of success than government and international attempts at doing so? What do you think such an agenda would be like?

4. If corporations are not the biggest environmental problem, then what is? If they are, then what other means can be used to limit their damage, apart from the suggestions made in this book?

Further reading

one Introduction: the place of environmental philosophy and its basic concepts

Readings on central topics in environmental philosophy are collected in a number of widely available books, including: C. Pierce & D. Vandeveer, *People, Penguins and Plastic Trees: Basic Issues in Environmental Ethics* (Belmont, CA: Wadsworth, 1994); M. F. Zimmerman *et al.* (eds), *Environmental Philosophy: From Animal Rights to Radical Ecology*, 2nd edn (Englewood Cliffs, NJ: Prentice Hall, 1997); R. Elliot (ed.), *Environmental Ethics* (Oxford: Oxford University Press, 1995); D. Schmidtz & E. Willott, *Environmental Ethics: What Really Matters, What Really Works* (Oxford: Oxford University Press, 2002); A. Light & H. Rolston, *Environmental Ethics, An Anthology* (Oxford: Blackwell, 2003); and L. Pojman & P. Pojman, *Environmental Ethics: Readings in Theory and Application* (New York: Barnes & Noble, 2007). For in-depth background reading on most aspects of environmental philosophy, including its history, see D. Jamieson (ed.), *A Companion to Environmental Philosophy* (Oxford: Blackwell, 2003).

The basic approach to doing philosophy that we introduce in this chapter is not covered in any single work, but two readable books will introduce our approach. First, to understand how to uncover the bare bones of arguments in order to analyse their logical structure see R. Munson, *The Elements of Reasoning*, 5th edn (Belmont, CA: Thomson, 2007). Second, to find out the basic ideas in ethics you can read S. Blackburn, *Being Good* (Oxford: Oxford University Press, 2001).

The background to philosophical interest in environmental values was established by a number of popular works written by scientists such as R. Carson, *Silent Spring* (London: Hamish Hamilton, 1969), D. H. Meadows *et al.*, *The Limits to Growth* (New York: New American Library, 1972). For a general overview of environmental philosophy see Clare Palmer's "Overview", in Light & Rolston, *Environmental Ethics*.

On the topic of endangered species, see Holmes Rolston's "Duties to Endangered Species", in Elliot, *Environmental Ethics*.

two Future generations: what considerations do we owe them?

For a general introduction to utilitarianism, see T. Mulgan, *Understanding Utilitarianism* (Stocksfield: Acumen, 2007), the final chapter of which also has a brief introduction to utilitarian arguments about future generations, including the disappearing beneficiaries argument. See also Garrett Hardin's "Who Cares for Posterity" and Derek Parfit's "Energy Policy and the Further Future", both in Pojman & Pojman, *Environmental Ethics*.

A. Carter, "Can We Harm Future People?", *Environmental Values* **10**(4) (2001), 429–54, examines several perspectives on the question whether it is possible for us to harm distant future generations by failing to adopt long-range welfare policies that would conserve resources or limit pollution.

Our version of the younger generation argument is based on Avner de Shalit's claim, in A. de Shalit, *Why Does Posterity Matter?* (London: Routledge, 1994), that we live in a transgenerational community.

The last people argument was originally put forward by Richard Routley and Val Routley (later Richard Sylvan and Val Plumwood). The argument is given in Richard Sylvan's "Is there a Need for a New, an Environmental Ethic?", reprinted in Light & Rolston, *Environmental Ethics*, and see also R. Routley & V. Routley, "Against the Inevitability of Human Chauvinism", in Elliot, *Environmental Ethics*.

A. Carter, "Moral Theory and Global Population", *Proceedings of the Aristotelian Society* **99**(3) (1999), 289–313, uses multidimensional indifference-curves to provide an argument for a significant reduction in human numbers.

three Animals: are they as morally valuable as human beings?

Most of the standard collections have useful readings on animals, including articles by Peter Singer and Tom Regan in Pojman & Pojman, *Environmental Ethics*, and Light & Rolston, *Environmental Ethics*.

Mary Ann Warren's "Critique of Regan's Rights Theory" is in Pojman & Pojman, *Environmental Ethics*, while S. R. L. Clark, *The Moral Status of Animals* (Oxford: Oxford University Press, 1977) was one of the earliest books on animal liberation to suggest extending moral consideration to other natural things too.

D. Jamieson, "Rights, Justice, and Duties to Provide Assistance: A Critique of Regan's Theory of Rights", *Ethics: An International Journal of Social, Political, and Legal Philosophy* **100**(1) (1990), 349–62, provides a critical discussion of Tom Regan's theory of animal rights. It argues that the theory founders on its account of duties of assistance, and on its prescription for how to resolve conflicts of rights, and that plausible responses to these difficulties would begin to close the gap between Regan's theory and its utilitarian rivals.

D. Jamieson, "Against Zoos", in *In Defense of Animals: The Second Wave*, P. Singer (ed.), 132–43 (Oxford: Blackwell, 2006) argues that both humans and other animals will be better off when zoos are abolished.

C. Palmer, "Harm to Species? Species, Ethics, and Climate Change: The Case of the Polar Bear", *Notre Dame Journal of Law, Ethics and Public Policy* 23 (2009), 587–603, critically examines whether species loss is an intrinsically bad thing or merely instrumentally bad for humans.

Tensions between animal liberation and environmental ethics were outlined in J. B. Callicott's "Animal Liberation: a Triangular Affair", reprinted in his *In Defense of the Land Ethic: Essays in Environmental Philosophy* (Albany, NY: SUNY Press, 1989) and Elliot, *Environmental Ethics*, and further discussed in M. Sagoff, "Animal Liberation and Environmental Ethics: Bad Marriage, Quick Divorce", *Osgoode Hall Law Journal* 22(2) (1984), 297–307, as well as in Eric Katz's "Is There a Place for Animals in the Moral Consideration of Nature?" and Gary Varner's "Can Animal Rights Activists Be Environmentalists?", both reprinted in Light & Rolston, *Environmental Ethics*. Scientific racism is helpfully reviewed in K. Malik, *The Meaning of Race: Race, History and Culture in Western Society* (New York: New York University Press, 1996).

four Living things: ethics for the non-human world

Taylor's work on respect for nature has not been the subject of detailed discussion in the literature, in part because it is so highly developed and sophisticated, and was developed with an eye to consistency. An attack on it (and on various other kinds of environmental ethical theory) in J. Thompson, "A Refutation of Environmental Ethics", *Environmental Ethics* 12(2) (1990), 147–60, was answered in M. P. Nelson, "A Defense of Environmental Ethics: A Reply to Janna Thompson", *Environmental Ethics* 15(3) (1993), 245–57, and R. Attfield, *Environmental Ethics: An Overview for the Twenty-First Century* (Cambridge: Polity, 2003).

G. E. Varner, *In Nature's Interests? Interests, Animal Rights, and Environmental Ethics* (Oxford: Oxford University Press, 1994) defends a sentientist principle giving priority to the lives of organisms with conscious desires and an anthropocentric principle giving priority to certain very inclusive interests which only humans have. It argues that these principles provide significant support for environmental goals.

five Community: how big is our moral world?

Key passages from Aldo Leopold can be found in many of the main anthologies, but his *A Sand County Almanac* (Oxford: Oxford University Press, 1949) itself is easy and engaging reading. The historical background to Leopold's work is given in R. F. Nash, *The Rights of Nature: A History of Environmental Ethics* (Madison, WI: University of Wisconsin Press, 1989) and R. F. Nash (ed.), *American Environmentalism: Readings in Conservation History* (New York: McGraw-Hill, 1990).

Callicott's version of the land ethic is discussed in detail, and critiqued, in Y. S. Lo, "The Land Ethic and Callicott's Ethical System (1980–2001): An Overview and Critique", *Inquiry* **44** (2001), 331–58.

The new animism is described in G. Harvey, *Animism: Respecting the Living World* (New York: Columbia University Press, 2005), and a panpsychist metaphysics of nature is ventured in F. Mathews, *Reinhabiting Reality: Towards a Recovery of Culture* (Sydney: UNSW Press, 2005).

All or parts of A. Naess, "The Shallow and the Deep, Long-Range Ecology Movement", *Inquiry* **16**(1) (1973), 95–100, reprinted in G. Sessions (ed.), *Deep Ecology for the 21st Century* (Boston, MA: Shambhala, 1995), 151–5, are printed in many of the main collections, and a statement of the mature deep ecology position is given in A. Naess, *Ecology, Community, Lifestyle*, D. Rothenberg (ed. & trans.) (Cambridge: Cambridge University Press, 1989). The philosophy and metaphysics of deep ecology is scrutinized in Sessions, *Deep Ecology for the 21st Century*, and in N. Witoszek & A. Brennan (eds), *Philosophical Dialogues: Arne Naess and the Progress of Eco-Philosophy* (Lanham, MD: Rowman & Littlefield, 1999).

six Natural things: the puzzle of what "natural" means, and whether humans belong to nature

Wilderness ethics and Rolston's philosophy of nature are discussed by contributions in the main anthologies and in H. Rolston, "Can the East Help the West to Value Nature?", *Philosophy East and West* **37** (1987), 172–90, and see also E. Katz, "The Call of the Wild", *Environmental Ethics* **14** (1992), 265–73. Arguments for and against the value of wilderness are summarized in Michael P. Nelson's "The Great New Wilderness Debate," in Pojman & Pojman, *Environmental Ethics*.

The notion that naturalness is a value-adding property is defended in E. Katz, "The Big Lie: Human Restoration of Nature", *Research in Philosophy and Technology* **12** (1992), 231–41, and R. Elliot, *Faking Nature* (London: Routledge, 1997), extracts from which can be found in Light & Rolston, *Environmental Ethics*.

Implications for environmental restoration projects arising from the work of Katz and Elliot are discussed in Y. S. Lo, "Natural and Artifactual: Restored Nature as Subject", *Environmental Ethics* **21** (1999), 247–66.

Other classic articles on the moral considerability (or moral standing) of nature include Kenneth Goodpaster's "On Being Morally Considerable" in Pojman & Pojman, *Environmental Ethics*, and Christopher Stone's "Should Trees Have Standing?", *Southern California Law Review* **45** (1972), 450–501, later published with a descriptive introduction as *Should Trees Have Standing?* (Los Angeles, CA: Kaufmann, 1974; republished Dobbs Ferry, NY: Oceana Publications, 1996), an extract from which is reproduced in Pierce & Vandeveer, *People, Penguins and Plastic Trees* and also in Pojman & Pojman, *Environmental Ethics*.

seven Foundations: can there be a secular basis for the ideas of human dignity and intrinsic value in nature?

Some of the material on human dignity and its religious foundations is based on A. Brennan & Y. S. Lo, "Two Conceptions of Dignity: Honour and Self-determination", in *Perspectives on Human Dignity*, J. Malpas & N. Lickiss (eds), 43–58 (Dordrecht: Springer, 2007).

A clear introduction to the Kantian ethical framework is in J. O'Neill, *Ecology, Policy and Politics* (London: Routledge, 1993). For introductions to the ethical thought of Kant and Hume, see H. Gensler *et al.*, *Ethics: Contemporary Readings* (London: Routledge, 2004). An overview of the Hume and Lewis approach to value is in Y. S. Lo, "Making and Finding Values in Nature: From a Humean Point of View", *Inquiry* **49** (2006), 123–47.

In relation to the goods and services provided by the natural environment, M. Sagoff, "Four Dogmas of Environmental Economics", *Environmental Values* **3**(4) (1994), 285–310, argues against four dogmas that have shaped modern neoclassical economics, and explores the possible consequences in abandoning such dogmas for the study of economics, such as an increased interest in the institutional context of production, or a turn towards empiricism. M. Sagoff, *Price, Principle, and the Environment* (Cambridge: Cambridge University Press, 2004) argues that while economic theory can inform the design of institutions and processes for settling disputes, it cannot measure the value of environmental goods. In particular, it argues that environmental economics fails as a science of valuation because preference satisfaction, its normative basis, has no relation to any value not trivially defined in terms of it.

Granting the convergence hypothesis put forward by Brian G. Norton, *Toward Unity Among Environmentalists* (Oxford: Oxford University Press, 1994) (namely that both anthropocentric and nonanthropocentric ethics will recommend the same environmentally responsible behaviours and policies), K. McShane, "Anthropocentrism vs. Nonanthropocentrism: Why Should We Care?", *Environmental Values* **16**(2) (2007), 169–85, argues that nonanthropocentrism is still to be preferred to anthropocentrism.

Norton's "Beyond Positivist Ecology: Toward an Integrated Ecological Ethics", *Science and Engineering Ethics* **14**(4) (2008), 581–92, argues that neither economic utilitarianism nor intrinsic value theory in environmental ethics provides a foundation for an ecologically sensitive way to evaluate ecological change. It proposes a more self-reflexive approach of ecological modelling, which can open the door to a new way of integrating values into public discourse and to a more comprehensive approach to evaluating ecological change.

The aesthetics of nature is not well represented in the standard anthologies. "Positive aesthetics" is argued strongly for in E. Hargrove, *Foundations of Environmental Ethics* (Denton, TX: Environmental Ethics Books, 1989), and a thorough treatment of environmental aesthetics is in E. Brady, *Aesthetics of the Natural Environment* (Edinburgh: Edinburgh University Press, 2003).

eight Origins: political, religious and cultural diagnoses of environmental problems

Lynn White's "The Historical Roots of Our Ecological Crisis", *Science* **155** (1967), 1203–7, reprinted in *Western Man and Environmental Ethics*, I. Barbour (ed.), (Reading, MA: Addison-Wesley 1973) and in Pojman & Pojman, *Environmental Ethics*, is short and easy to read. His critique of Christianity was queried by J. Passmore, *Man's Responsibility for Nature*, 2nd edn (London: Duckworth, [1974] 1980) and R. Attfield, *The Ethics of Environmental Concern* (Athens, GA: University of Georgia Press, 1991).

There are no easy introductions to critical theory and its approach to the questions of environmental philosophy. S. Vogel, *Against Nature: The Concept of Nature in Critical Theory* (Albany, NY: SUNY Press, 1996), although comprehensive, is difficult.

V. Plumwood, *Feminism and the Mastery of Nature* (London: Routledge, 1993) is a classic of ecological feminist analysis, and there are sections on feminism in several of the main anthologies, especially Schmidtz & Willott, *Environmental Ethics*, and Light & Rolston, *Environmental Ethics*. A. Brennan (ed.), *The Ethics of the Environment* (Aldershot: Dartmouth, 1995) features strongly worded disputes between supporters of deep ecology on the one side and ecological feminism on the other.

Harvey, *Animism*, and D. Abram, *The Spell of the Sensuous* (New York: Vintage, 1997) cover animist and phenomenological approaches to the problem of disenchantment.

nine Beyond individual responsibility: governance and the affluenzic society

One of the influential early writers on environmental philosophy was Murray Bookchin, whose anarchist orientation led him to the view that ecological disaster was a product of social and political malfunctions; see *Toward an Ecological Society* (Montreal: Black Rose Books, 1980). His work was a powerful influence, along with that of Lewis Mumford, on bioregionalism as a socio-environmental movement; see J. Clark, "A Social Ecology", in M. Zimmerman *et al.*, *Environmental Philosophy*.

D. Jamieson, "Global Environmental Justice", *Philosophy: The Journal of the Royal Institute of Philosophy* **36** (Supplement 1994), 199–210, explores several conceptions of global environmental justice, for example, as a condition on the pursuit of justice, or as distributing the benefits and burdens of environmental commodities. It concludes that existing notions of global environmental justice are problematic, and they need to be supplemented by a more inclusive picture of duties and obligations.

Rolston's demand that environmental conservation have priority over poverty reduction has been criticized in A. Brennan, "Poverty, Puritanism and Environmental Conflict", *Environmental Values* 7(3) (1998), 305–31, and R. Attfield, "Saving Nature, Feeding People, and Ethics", *Environmental Values* 7(3) (1998), 291–304.

A. Carter, *A Radical Green Political Theory* (London: Routledge, 1999) examines the relationships between the ever-worsening environmental crises, the nature of prevailing economic structures and the role of the modern state, and concludes that the combination of these factors is driving humanity towards destruction. A. Carter, "Some Theoretical Foundations for Radical Green Politics", *Environmental Values* **13**(3) (2004), 305–28, looks at mechanism driving human destructive behaviour towards the environment, and argues that the most common strategies offered as a response to our environment impact are unlikely to be sufficiently radical to effectively meet our obligations towards future generations.

T. Hayward, *Constitutional Environmental Rights* (Oxford: Oxford University Press, 2005) examines the case for a constitutional right to an adequate environment from the perspective of political, rather than legal, theory. T. Hayward, "Human Rights versus Emissions Rights: Climate Justice and the Equitable Distribution of Ecological Space", *Ethics and International Affairs* **21**(4) (2007), 431–50, argues that while the world's worse-off have a human right to secure access to the means to a decent life, they do not have a human right to pollute the environment. R. Ziegler, "Tracing Global Inequality in Eco-Space: A Comment on Tim Hayward's Proposal", *Journal of Moral Philosophy* **4**(1) (2007), 117–24, provides a critique of Hayward's theory of ecological space.

Marcel Wissenburg, "Global and Ecological Justice: Prioritising Conflicting Demands", *Environmental Values* **15**(4) (2006), 425–39, argues that "global and ecological justice" – a popular catchphrase in policy documents, treaties, publications by think tanks, NGOs and other bodies – actually represents an informal combination of four distinct and sometimes conflicting ideas: global justice, protection of the ecology, sustainability and sustainable growth. V. Shiva, *Stolen Harvest: The Hijacking of the Global Food Supply* (Cambridge, MA: South End Press, 2000) argues that bioregional and small-scale traditional farming is superior to the industrial agribusiness model for a variety of reasons, such as environmental sustainability, social justice and human health. Using the global water trade as a lens, V. Shiva, *Water Wars: Privatization, Pollution, and Profit* (Cambridge, MA: South End Press, 2002) highlights the destruction of the earth and the disenfranchisement of the world's poor as they lose their right to a life-sustaining common good. Through advocating traditional small-scale bioregional farming practice by the poor, which is sustainable, biologically diverse, and more resistant to disease, drought, and flood, V. Shiva, *Soil Not Oil: Environmental Justice in an Age of Climate Crisis* (Cambridge, MA: South End Press, 2008), argues that the solution to climate change and the solution to poverty are one and the same. For an overview of environmental pragmatism, start with the essays collected in A. Light & E. Katz (eds), *Environmental Pragmatism* (London: Routledge, 1995).

Bibliography

Abbey, E. 1968. *Desert Solitaire*. New York: Random House.

Adam, D. 2005. "Oil Firms Fund Climate Change 'Denial'". *Guardian* (27 January), www.guardian.co.uk/world/2005/jan/27/environment.science (accessed July 2010).

Anker, P. 2001. *Imperial Ecology: Environmental Order in the British Empire, 1895–1945*. Cambridge, MA: Harvard University Press.

Anselm 1965. *St Anselm's Proslogion*, M. Charlesworth (ed.). Oxford: Oxford University Press.

Appadurai, A. 1996. *Modernity at Large: Cultural Dimensions of Globalization*. Minneapolis, MN: University of Minnesota Press.

Aristotle 1996. *Politics: Books I and II*, T. Saunders (trans.). Oxford: Oxford University Press.

Arnould, E. J. & L. L. Price 1993. "River Magic: Extraordinary Experience and the Extended Service Encounter". *Journal of Consumer Research* **20**: 24–55.

Bakan, J. 2004. *The Corporation: The Pathological Pursuit of Profit and Power*. London: Constable.

Barkan, E. 1992. *The Retreat of Scientific Racism*. Cambridge: Cambridge University Press.

Benjamin, J. 1988. *The Bonds of Love: Psychoanalysis, Feminism and the Problems of Domination*. New York: Pantheon.

Bentham, J. [1789] 1970. *An Introduction to the Principles of Morals and Legislation*, J. H. Burns & H. L. A. Hart (eds). Oxford: Oxford University Press.

Berleant, A. 2005. *Aesthetics and Environment: Variations on a Theme*. Aldershot: Ashgate.

Biehl, J. 1997. *The Murray Bookchin Reader*. London: Cassell.

Black, R. 2009. "$100bn a Year for Climate Safety". *BBC News Online*. http://news.bbc.co.uk/2/hi/science/nature/8282308.stm (accessed July 2010).

Bookchin, M. (Lewis Herber) [1965] 1978. "Ecology and Revolutionary Thought". Reprinted in *Antipode* **10**: 21–32.

Bookchin, M. 1990. *The Philosophy of Social Ecology*. Montreal: Black Rose Books.

Bookchin, M. [1987] 1999. "Social Ecology Versus Deep Ecology". *Green Perspectives: Newsletter of the Green Program Project*, **4–5** (Summer 1987). Reprinted in Witoszek & Brennan (1999), 281–301.

Brady, E. 2003. *Aesthetics of the Natural Environment*. Edinburgh: Edinburgh University Press.

Brennan, A. 1984. "The Moral Standing of Natural Objects". *Environmental Ethics* **6**: 35–56.

Brennan, A. 1988. *Thinking About Nature*. London: Routledge.

Brennan, A. 1992. "Moral Pluralism and the Environment". *Environmental Values* **1**: 5–33.

Brennan, A. (ed.) 1995. *The Ethics of the Environment*. Aldershot: Dartmouth.

Brennan, A. 1998. "Bioregionalism – A Misplaced Project?" *Worldviews* **2**(3): 215–37.

Brennan, A. 2004. "Biodiversity and Agricultural Landscapes: Can the Wicked Policy Problems Be Solved?" *Pacific Conservation Biology* **10**(2): 124–43.

Callicott, J. B. 1989. *In Defense of the Land Ethic: Essays in Environmental Philosophy*. Albany, NY: SUNY Press.

Callicott, J. B. 1990. "The Case Against Moral Pluralism". *Environmental Ethics* **12**: 99–124.

Callicott, J. B. 1994. *Earth's Insights*. Berkeley, CA: University of California Press.

Callicott, J. B. 1999. *Beyond the Land Ethic: More Essays in Environmental Philosophy*. Albany, NY: SUNY Press.

Carlson, A. 2008. "Environmental Aesthetics". In *The Stanford Encyclopedia of Philosophy* (Winter 2008 edn), E. N. Zalta (ed.), http://plato.stanford.edu/archives/win2008/entries/environmental-aesthetics/ (accessed July 2010).

Carson, R. 1969. *Silent Spring*. London: Hamish Hamilton.

Cohen, M. P. 1984. *The Pathless Way: John Muir and American Wilderness*. Madison, WI: University of Wisconsin Press.

Crombie, A. G. 1994. *Styles of Scientific Thinking in the European Tradition: The History of Argument and Explanation Especially in the Mathematical and Biomedical Sciences and Arts*, 3 vols. London: Duckworth.

de Shalit, A. 1994. *Why Does Posterity Matter?* London: Routledge.

Darwin, C. [1871] 1989. *The Descent of Man*. New York: NYU Press.

Davis, D. L. 2003. *When Smoke Ran Like Water: Tales of Environmental Deception and the Battle Against Pollution*. New York: Basic Books.

De Graaf, J., D. Wann & T. Naylor 2005. *Affluenza: The All-Consuming Epidemic*, 2nd edn. San Francisco: Berrett-Koehler.

Dillon, R. S. 2008. "Respect". *The Stanford Encyclopedia of Philosophy* (Fall 2008 edn), E. N. Zalta (ed.), http://plato.stanford.edu/archives/fall2008/entries/respect/ (accessed July 2010).

Dunlap, R., K. Van Liere, A. Mertig & R. E. Jones 2000. "Measuring Enforcement of the New Ecological Paradigm: A Revised NEP Scale". *Journal of Social Issues* **56**: 425–42.

Durham, W. 1995. "Political Ecology and Environmental Destruction in Latin America". In M. Painter & W. Durham, *The Social Causes of Environmental Destruction in Latin America*, 249–64. Ann Arbor, MI: University of Michigan Press.

Eckersley, R. 1992. *Environmentalism and Political Theory*. London: UCL Press.

Elliot, R. (ed.) 1995. *Environmental Ethics*. Oxford: Oxford University Press.

Elliot, R. 1997. *Faking Nature*. London: Routledge.

Emerson, R. W. [1844] 1981. "The Young American". In *Collected Works of Ralph Waldo Emerson, Volume I: Nature, Addresses, and Lectures*, Robert E. Spiller (intro. and notes), Alfred R. Ferguson (ed.). Cambridge, MA: Belknap Press.

Fromm, E. 1973. *The Anatomy of Human Destructiveness*. New York: Holt, Rinehart & Winston.

Girard, R. 1977. *Violence and the Sacred*. Baltimore, MD: Johns Hopkins University Press.

Glendinning, C. 1995. "Technology, Trauma and the Wild". In *Ecopsychology: Restoring the Earth, Healing the Mind*, T. Roszak, M. Gomes & A. Kanner (eds). New York: Sierra Club Books.

Goodall, J. 1993. "Chimpanzees – Bridging the Gap". In *The Great Ape Project*, P. Cavalieri & P. Singer (eds), 10–18. New York: St Martin's Press.

Goodin, R. E. 1992. *Green Political Theory*. Cambridge: Polity.

Gray, John 1994. *Enlightenment's Wake: Politics and Culture at the Close of the Enlightenment Age*. London: Routledge.

Gray, J. 2002. "When the Forests Go, Shall we be Alone?" *New Statesman* (22 July), www.newstatesman.com/200207220017 (accessed September 2010).

Gray, J. 2003. *Al Qaeda and What it Means to be Modern*. London: Faber.

Gray, J. 2007. *Black Mass*. London: Allen Lane.

Grove, R. H. 1995. *Green Imperialism: Colonial Expansion, Tropical Island Edens and the Origins of Environmentalism, 1600–1860*. Cambridge: Cambridge University Press.

Gruen, L. & D. Jamieson (eds) 1994. *Reflecting on Nature*. New York: Oxford University Press.

Guha, R. 1989. "Radical American Environmentalism and Wilderness Preservation: A Third World Critique". *Environmental Ethics* **11**: 71–83.

Guha, R. 1999. *Radical American Environmentalism Revisited*. See Witoszek & Brennan (1999), 473–9.

Guha, R. & J. Martínez-Alier (eds) 1997. *Varieties of Environmentalism: Essays North and South*. London: Earthscan.

Hamilton, C. 2009. "Is it too Late to Prevent Catastrophic Climate Change?" www.clivehamilton.net.au/cms/media/documents/articles/rsa_lecture.pdf (accessed July 2010).

Hansen, J., M. Sato, R. Ruedy, L. Nazarenko, A. Lacis, K. Lo, G. A. Schmidt *et al.* 2007. "Dangerous Human-Made Interference with Climate: A GISS Model EStudy". *Atmospheric Chemistry and Physics* 7(9): 2287–312.

Hardin, G. 1972. *Exploring New Ethics for Survival*. New York: Viking.

Hardin, G. 1974. "Lifeboat Ethics: The Case Against Helping the Poor". *Psychology Today* **8** (September): 38–43. Reprinted in *Contemporary Moral Issues: Diversity and Consensus*, 3rd edn, L. Hinman (ed.), 335–42 (Upper Saddle River, NJ: Prentice Hall, 2006).

Harding, S. 1992. "What is Deep Ecology?" *Resurgence* **185** (1997): 14–17.

Hargrove, E. 1989. *Foundations of Environmental Ethics*. Denton, TX: Environmental Ethics Books.

Hartmann, T. 2004. *Unequal Protection: The Rise of Corporate Dominance and the Theft of Human Rights*. Emmaus, PA: Rodale.

Harvey, G. 2005. *Animism: Respecting the Living World*. New York: Columbia University Press.

Heidegger, M. 1975. *Poetry, Language, Thought*, W. Hofstadter (trans.). New York: Harper & Row.

Herber, L. [Murray Bookchin] 1952. "The Problems of Chemicals in Food". *Contemporary Issues* 3: 240.

Hettinger, Ned. 2005. "Allen Carlson's Environmental Aesthetics and the Protection of the Environment". *Environmental Ethics* 27: 57–76.

Hobsbawm, E. 1990. *Nations and Nationalism Since 1780: Programme, Myth, Reality*. Cambridge: Cambridge University Press.

Hogan, J. & R. Littlemore 2009. *Climate Cover-Up: The Crusade to Deny Global Warming*. Vancouver: Greystone Books.

Horkheiner, M. & T. Adorno [1969] 1972. *Dialectic of Enlightenment*, J. Cumming (trans.). New York: Seabury Press.

Hume, D. [1748] 1999. *An Enquiry Concerning Human Understanding*, T. Beauchamp (ed.). Oxford: Oxford University Press.

Hume, D. [1739–40] 2001. *A Treatise of Human Nature*, D. F. & M. J. Norton (eds). Oxford: Oxford University Press.

Huxley, T. H. [1893] 1947. "Evolution and Ethics". In J. S. Huxley & T. H. Huxley, *Evolution and Ethics*, 82. London: Pilot Press.

Jackall, R. 1988. *Moral Mazes: The World of Corporate Managers*. New York: Oxford University Press.

James, O. 2007. *Affluenza*. London: Vermilion.

Jamieson, D. 2002. *Morality's Progress: Essays on Humans, Other Animals, and the Rest of Nature*. Oxford: Clarendon Press.

Jamieson, D. (ed.) 2003. *A Companion to Environmental Philosophy*. Oxford: Blackwell.

Kant, I. [1797] 1996. *Practical Philosophy*, M. Gregor (trans.). Cambridge: Cambridge University Press.

Karliner, J. 1997. *The Corporate Planet*. San Francisco: Sierra Club Books.

Katz, E. 1991. "Restoration and Redesign: The Ethical Significance of Human Intervention in Nature". *Restoration and Management Notes* 9(2): 90–96.

Katz, E. 1992. "The Big Lie: Human Restoration of Nature". *Research in Philosophy and Technology* 12: 231–41.

Katz, E. 1997. *Nature as Subject*. Lanham, MD: Rowman & Littlefield.

Korten, D. 2001. *When Corporations Rule the World*. West Hartford, CT: Kumarian Press.

Korsgaard, C. 1996. *The Sources of Normativity*. Cambridge: Cambridge University Press.

Legge, J. 1972. *The Chinese Classics, vol. 1*. Oxford: Clarendon Press.

Leiss, W. 1994. *Under Technology's Thumb*. Montreal: McGill-Queen's University Press.

Lenton, T. M., H. Held, E. Kriegler, J. W. Hall, W. Lucht, S. Rahmstorff & H. J. Schellnhuber 2008. "Tipping Elements in the Earth's Climate System". *Proceedings of the National Academy of Sciences* 105(6): 1786–93.

Leopold, A. 1949. *A Sand County Almanac*. Oxford: Oxford University Press.

Lewis, D. 1989. "Dispositional Theories of Value". *Proceedings of the Aristotelian Society* 63 (Supplement): 113–37.

Light, A. & E. Katz (eds) 1995. *Environmental Pragmatism*. London: Routledge.

List, P. C. 1993. *Radical Environmentalism*. Belmont, CA: Wadsworth.

Lo, Y. S. 1999. "Natural and Artifactual: Restored Nature as Subject". *Environmental Ethics* **21**: 247–66.

Lo, Y. S. 2001. "The Land Ethic and Callicott's Ethical System (1980–2001): An Overview and Critique". *Inquiry* **44**: 331–58.

Lo, Y. S. 2006. "Making and Finding Values in Nature: from a Humean Point of View". *Inquiry* **49**: 123–47.

Lo, Y. S. 2009. "Is Hume Inconsistent? – Motivation and Morals". In *Hume on Motivation and Virtue*, C. Pigden (ed.), 57–79. Basingstoke: Palgrave Macmillan.

Locke, J. [1690] 2004. *The Second Treatise of Government*. New York: Barnes & Noble.

Lovelock, J. E. 1979. *Gaia: A New Look at Life on Earth*. Oxford: Oxford University Press.

Lovelock, J. E. 1988. *The Ages of Gaia: A Biography of our Living Earth*. Oxford: Oxford University Press.

Mackie, J. L. 1983. *Ethics: Inventing Right and Wrong*. Harmondsworth: Penguin.

Malik, K. 1996. *The Meaning of Race: Race, History and Culture in Western Society*. New York: New York University Press.

Mann, W. 1972. "The Ontological Presuppositions of the Ontological Argument". *Review of Metaphysics* **26**: 260–77.

Mathews, F. 1991. *The Ecological Self*. London: Routledge.

Mathews, F. 2003. "Deep Ecology". In *A Companion to Environmental Philosophy*, D. Jamieson (ed.), 218–32. Oxford: Blackwell.

Mathews, F. 2005. *Reinhabiting Reality: Towards a Recovery of Culture*. Sydney: UNSW Press.

Maturana, H. & F. Varela 1980. *Autopoiesis and Cognition*. Dordrecht: Reidel.

McGinnis, M. (ed.) 1999. *Bioregionalism*. London: Routledge.

McKibben, W. 1989. *The End of Nature*. New York: Random House.

Meadows, D. H., D. L. Meadows, J. Randers & W. W. Behrens 1972. *The Limits to Growth*. New York: New American Library.

Melville, H. 1856. *The Piazza Tales*. New York: Dix & Edwards.

Mill, J. S. 1874. "Nature". In *Three Essays on Religion*. London: Longmans, Green, Reader & Dyer.

Montagu, A. 1950. *Statement on Race*. Paris: UNESCO.

Montaigne, M. de 1991. *The Complete Essays*, M. A. Screech (trans.). Harmondsworth: Penguin.

Morris, D. 1967. *The Naked Ape*. London: Jonathan Cape.

Morris, D. 1994. *The Human Animal*. London: Crown Publishers.

Muir, J. [1911] 1998. *My First Summer in the Sierra*. New York: Houghton Mifflin.

Mulgan, T. 2007. *Understanding Utilitarianism*. Stocksfield: Acumen.

Mumford, L. 1962. *Herman Melville: A Study of his Life and Vision*. New York: Harcourt, Brace & World.

Mumford, L. 1961. *The City in History*. New York: Harcourt, Brace and World.

Murdoch, I. 1970. *The Sovereignty of Good*. London: Routledge & Kegan Paul.

Naess, A. 1973. "The Shallow and the Deep, Long-Range Ecology Movement". *Inquiry* **16**(1): 95–100. Reprinted in *Deep Ecology for the 21st Century*, G. Sessions (ed.), 151–5 (Boston, MA: Shambhala, 1995).

Naess, A. 1986. "Self-Realization: An Ecological Approach to Being in the World". In *Deep Ecology for the 21st Century*, G. Sessions (ed.), 225–39. Boston, MA: Shambhala.

Naess, A. 1999. "Comments on Guha's 'Radical American Environmentalism and Wilderness Preservation: A Third-World Critique'". In *Philosophical Dialogues: Arne Naess and the Progress of Eco-Philosophy*, N. Witoszek & A. Brennan (eds), 325–33. Lanham, MD: Rowman & Littlefield.

Nicolson, M. H. 1959. *Mountain Gloom and Mountain Glory: The Development of the Aesthetics of the Infinite*. Ithaca, NY: Cornell University Press.

Norton, B. 1991. *Toward Unity Among Environmentalists*. New York: Oxford University Press.

Norton, B. G. 2005. *Sustainability: A Philosophy of Adaptive Ecosystem Management*. Chicago, IL: University of Chicago Press.

Norton, B., M. Hutchins, E. Stevens & T. L. Maple (eds) 1995. *Ethics on the Ark*. Washington, DC: Smithsonian Institution Press.

O'Neill, O. 1991. "Kantian Ethics". In *A Companion to Ethics*, P. Singer (ed.), 175–85. Oxford: Blackwell.

O'Neill, J. 1992. "The Varieties of Intrinsic Value". *Monist* 75: 119–37.

Oppy, G. 2009. "Ontological Arguments". In *The Stanford Encyclopedia of Philosophy* (Fall 2009 edn), E. N. Zalta (ed.), http://plato.stanford.edu/archives/fall2009/entries/ontological-arguments/ (accessed July 2010).

Otto, R. 1927. *The Idea of the Holy*. Oxford: Oxford University Press.

Packard, V. 1978. *The Waste Makers*. New York: Simon & Schuster.

Palmer, C. 2001. "Taming the Wild Profusion of Existing Things? A Study of Foucault, Power and Human/Animal Relationships". *Environmental Ethics* 23: 339–58.

Palmer, C. 2009. "Harm to Species? Species, Ethics, and Climate Change: The Case of the Polar Bear". *Notre Dame Journal of Law, Ethics and Public Policy* 23: 587–603.

Parfit, D. 1984. *Reasons and Persons*. Oxford: Clarendon Press.

Passmore, J. [1974] 1980. *Man's Responsibility for Nature*, 2nd edn. London: Duckworth, 1980.

Pfohl, S. 1990. "Welcome to the Parasite Café: Postmodernity as a Social Problem". *Social Problems* 37: 421–42.

Pigden, C. R. 1991. "Naturalism". In *A Companion to Ethics*, P. Singer (ed.), 421–31. Oxford: Blackwell.

Plumwood, V. 1993. *Feminism and the Mastery of Nature*. London: Routledge.

Plumwood, V. 2000. "Being Prey". In *The Ultimate Journey: Inspiring Stories of Living and Dying*, J. O'Reilly, S. O'Reilly & R. Sterling (eds), 128–47. Berkeley, CA: Travelers' Tales. Reprinted as "Prey to a Crocodile", *Aisling Magazine* 30. www.aislingmagazine.com/aislingmagazine/articles/TAM30/ValPlumwood.html (accessed September 2010).

Plumwood, V. 2002. *Environmental Culture*. London: Routledge.

Porter, G. & J. Welsh Brown 1991. *Global Environmental Politics*. Boulder, CO: Westview.

Regan, T. 1983a. *The Case for Animal Rights*. London: Routledge & Kegan Paul.

Regan, T. 1983b. "Animal Rights, Human Wrongs". In *Ethics and Animals*, H. Miller & H. Williams (eds), 19–44. Clifton, NJ: Humana Press.

Revkin, A. 2009. "Industry Ignored Its Scientists on Climate". *New York Times* (23 April): www.nytimes.com/2009/04/24/science/earth/24deny.html?_r=1 (accessed July 2010).

Rohman, C. 2009. *Stalking the Subject: Modernism and the Animal.* New York: Columbia University Press.

Rolston, H. 1979. "Can and Ought We to Follow Nature?" *Environmental Ethics* 1: 7–30.

Rolston, H. 1981. "Values in Nature". *Environmental Ethics* 3: 113–28.

Rolston, H. 1987. "Can the East help the West to Value Nature?" *Philosophy East and West* 37:172–90.

Rolston, H. 1988. *Environmental Ethics: Duties to and Values in the Natural World.* Philadelphia, PA: Temple University Press.

Rolston, H. 1989. *Philosophy Gone Wild.* New York: Prometheus.

Rolston, H. 1996. "Feeding People versus Saving Nature?" In *World Hunger and Morality*, 2nd edn, W. Aiken & H. LaFollette (eds), 248–67. Englewood Cliffs, NJ: Prentice Hall.

Rolston, H. 1998. "Saving Nature, Feeding People and the Foundations of Ethics". *Environmental Values* 7(3): 349–57.

Rolston, H. 1999. *Genes, Genesis and God.* Cambridge: Cambridge University Press.

Rousseau, J.-J. [1782] 1979. *Reveries of the Solitary Walker*, P. France (trans.). Harmondsworth: Penguin.

Rousseau, J.-J. 1998. *Discourse on Inequality*, G. D. H. Cole (trans.). New York: Kessinger Reprints.

Routley, R. & V. Routley 1980. "Human Chauvinism and Environmental Ethics". *Environmental Philosophy*, D. Mannison, M. A. McRobbie & R. Routley (eds), 96–189. Canberra: Australian National University, Research School of Social Sciences.

Russell, C. 2002. *Grizzly Heart: Living Without Fear Among the Brown Bears of Kamchatka.* Toronto: Random House.

Sagoff, M. 1988. *The Economy of the Earth.* Cambridge: Cambridge University Press.

Sagoff, M. 2004. *Price, Principle, and the Environment.* Cambridge: Cambridge University Press.

Sale, K. 1985. *Dwellers in the Land.* San Francisco, CA: Sierra Club Books.

Sartre, J.-P. [1943] 2000. "The Look". In *Being and Nothingness*, H. E. Barnes (trans.), 252–302. London: Routledge.

Savile, A. 1969. "The Place of Intention in the Concept of Art". *Proceedings of the Aristotelian Society, New Series* 69: 101–24.

Sessions, G. (ed.) 1995. *Deep Ecology for the 21st Century: Readings on the Philosophy and Practice of the New Environmentalism.* Boston, MA: Shambhala.

Shah, A. 2002. "The Rise of Corporations", www.globalissues.org/article/234/the-rise-of-corporations (accessed July 2010).

Short, J. R. 1991. *Imagined Country: Society, Culture and Environment.* London: Routledge.

Singer, P. 1975. *Animal Liberation.* New York: Random House.

Singer, P. 1993. *Practical Ethics*, 2nd edn. Cambridge: Cambridge University Press.

Stern, N. 2007. *The Economics of Climate Change.* Cambridge: Cambridge University Press.

Stone, A. 2006. "Adorno and the Disenchantment of Nature". *Philosophy and Social Criticism* 32: 231–53.

Stone, C. 1987. *Earth and Other Ethics.* New York: Harper & Row.

Stretton, H. 1976. *Capitalism, Socialism and the Environment.* Cambridge: Cambridge University Press.

Taylor, P. 1981. "The Ethics of Respect for Nature". *Environmental Ethics* **3**: 197–218.

Taylor, P. 1986. *Respect for Nature*. Princeton, NJ: Princeton University Press.

Taylor, B. & M. Zimmerman 2005. "Deep Ecology". In *The Encyclopedia of Religion and Nature*, B. Taylor (ed.), 456–9. London: Continuum.

Thompson, P. B. 1994. *The Spirit of the Soil*. London: Routledge.

Thoreau, H. D. [1854] 2006. *Walden*, J. S. Cramer (ed.). New Haven, CT: Yale University Press.

Turmeda, A. [1417] 1997. "Disputation of the Donkey, Selections", N. Kenny (trans.). In *Cambridge Translations of Renaissance Philosophical Texts, vol. 1*, J. Kraye (ed.), 3–16. Cambridge: Cambridge University Press.

Varela, F. J., H. R. Maturana & R. Uribe 1974. "Autopoiesis: The Organization of Living Systems, its Characterization and a Model". *Biosystems* **5**(4): 187–96.

Varner, G. 1991. "No Holism without Pluralism". *Environmental Ethics* **13**: 175–9.

Warren, K. J. (ed.) 1994. *Ecological Feminism*. London: Routledge.

Warren, K. 1996. "The Power and the Promise of Ecofeminism". In *Ecological Feminist Philosophies*, K. Warren (ed.), 19–41. Bloomington, IN: Indiana University Press.

Weber, M. [1920] 2001. *The Protestant Ethic and the Spirit of Capitalism*, S. Kalberg (trans.). London: Roxbury.

Weston, A. 1985. "Beyond Intrinsic Value: Pragmatism in Environmental Ethics". *Environmental Ethics* **7**: 321–39.

Weston, A. 1992. *Toward Better Problems: New Perspectives on Abortion, Animal Rights, the Environment, and Justice*. Philadelphia, PA: Temple University Press.

White, L. 1967. "The Historical Roots of Our Ecological Crisis". *Science* **55** (10 March 1967): 1203–7. Reprinted in *Western Man and Environmental Ethics*, I. Barbour (ed.), 19–30 (Reading, MA: Addison-Wesley 1973) and in *Environmental Ethics: Readings in Theory and Application*, Louis P. Pojman & Paul Pojman (eds). Belmont, CA: Wadsworth, 2008.

Whorf, B. L. 1956. *Language, Thought and Reality: Selected Writings of Benjamin Lee Whorf*. New York: John Wiley.

Williams, B. 1985. *Ethics and the Limits of Philosophy*. London: Fontana.

Witoszek, N. & A. Brennan (eds) 1999. *Philosophical Dialogues: Arne Naess and the Progress of Eco-Philosophy*. Lanham, MD: Rowman & Littlefield.

Wolfe, C. 2003. *Animal Rites: American Culture, the Discourse of Species and Posthumanist Theory*. Chicago, IL: University of Chicago Press.

World Bank 2008. *2008: World Development Indicators*. Washington, DC: International Bank for Reconstruction and Development/The World Bank.

World Bank 2009. *The Global Report of the Economics of Adaptation to Climate Change Study*. Consultation draft report for UN climate talks in Bangkok. http://siteresources.worldbank.org/INTCC/Resources/EACCReport0928Final.pdf (accessed July 2010).

Zangwill, N. 2005. "Moral Epistemology and the Because Constraint". In *Contemporary Debates in Moral Theory*, J. Dreier (ed.). Oxford: Blackwell.

Zimmerman, M. F. 1983. "Toward a Heideggerean Ethos for Radical Environmentalism". *Environmental Ethics* **5**: 99–131.

Zimmerman, M. F. 1994. *Contesting Earth's Future*. Berkeley, CA: University of California Press.

Index

Page numbers in italics refer to figures.